Japan's Politics and Economy

For some time Japan has been under fire for adjusting too slowly to new realities. While this criticism may be valid on some levels, Japan has been transforming in tandem with both regional and global forces. However, these changes have been largely overshadowed by the immense changes in Asia, including the rise of China, the 1997 Southeast Asian financial crisis and North Korea's development of nuclear weapons. Has Japan, the world's second largest economy, only been muddling through?

In this volume the contributors show that although the challenges faced are great, Japan is changing in areas ranging from political leadership, education policy, official development assistance, peace building and security, to defence production, business associations and innovation policy. The book analyses *processes of change*, focusing on the dynamics of change – rather than structural change or institutional change per se – from four levels: the individual, domestic, regional and global. Forces from outside Japan, such as a changing world order and changes in power relationships in Asia, have driven change along with pressures emerging within Japan, such as the increasing power of public opinion and competitiveness within markets.

This book will be of interest to scholars and students of Japanese and Asian Studies, Politics, International Relations, Globalization, Business and Economics.

Marie Söderberg is Associate Professor at the European Institute of Japanese Studies at Stockholm School of Economics, Sweden. **Patricia A. Nelson** is Visiting Professor, Faculty of Economics, Seijo University, Japan, and author of numerous articles on the political economy and business of Japan.

European Institute of Japanese Studies East Asian Economics and Business series

Edited by Marie Söderberg

Stockholm School of Economics, Sweden

This series presents cutting edge research on recent developments in business and economics in East Asia. National, regional and international perspectives are employed to examine this dynamic and fast-moving area.

1 **The Business of Japanese Foreign Aid**
Five case studies from Asia
Edited by Marie Söderberg

2 **Chinese Legal Reform**
The case of foreign investment law
Yan Wang

3 **Chinese–Japanese Relations in the Twenty First Century**
Complementarity and conflict
Edited by Marie Söderberg

4 **Competition Law Reform in Britain and Japan**
Comparative analysis of policy network
Kenji Suzuki

5 **Financial Liberalization and the Economic Crisis in Asia**
Edited by Chung H. Lee

6 **Institutional Change in South East Asia**
Edited by Fredrik Sjöholm and Jose Tongzon

7 **Japan's China Policy**
A relational power analysis
Linus Hagström

8 **Institutional Change in Japan**
Edited by Magnus Blomström and Sumner La Croix

9 **North Korea Policy**
Japan and the great powers
Edited by Linus Hagström and Marie Söderberg

10 **Japan's Politics and Economy**
Perspectives on change
Edited by Marie Söderberg and Patricia A. Nelson

Japan's Politics and Economy

Perspectives on change

Edited by Marie Söderberg and Patricia A. Nelson

LONDON AND NEW YORK

First published 2010
by Routledge
2 Park Square, Milton Park, Abingdon, Oxon OX14 4RN

Simultaneously published in the USA and Canada
by Routledge
711 Third Avenue, New York, NY 10017

Routledge is an imprint of the Taylor & Francis Group, an informa business

First published in paperback 2011

Typeset in Times by Wearset Ltd, Boldon, Tyne and Wear

British Library Cataloguing in Publication Data
A catalogue record for this book is available from the British Library

Library of Congress Cataloging in Publication Data
Japan's politics and economy: perspectives on change/edited by Marie Söderberg and Patricia A. Nelson.
p. cm. – (European Institute of Japanese Studies, East Asian Economics and Business series)

1. Japan – Politics and government. 2. Japan – Economic policy. 3. Japan – Foreign relations. 4. Japan – Foreign economic relations. I. Söderberg, Marie. II. Nelson, Patricia A.

JQ1631.J365 2009
320.952-dc22

2009026982

ISBN13: 978-0-415-69012-6 (pbk)
ISBN13: 978-0-415-54752-9 (hbk)
ISBN13: 978-0-203-86187-5 (ebk)

Contents

Figures

Tables

Contributors

Verena Blechinger-Talcott is Chair of Japanese Politics and Political Economy at the Institute of East Asian Affairs, Berlin Free University. She has held appointments as Assistant Professor of government at Hamilton College, Clinton, NY (2003–04) and as Advanced Research Fellow in the Program on US–Japan Relations, Harvard University (2002–03). Her current research project focuses on corporate social responsibility and social business in Japan.

Christopher W. Hughes is Professor of International Politics and Japanese Studies in PAIS, Warwick University, UK. He is co-editor of *The Pacific Review*. He has been a Research Associate at Hiroshima University, and the *Asahi Shimbun* Visting Professor of Mass Media and Politics at the Faculty of Law, University of Tokyo. In 2009–10 he is the Edwin O. Reischauer Visiting Professor of Japanese Studies at the Department of Government, Harvard University.

Paul Midford is Associate Professor of Political Science at the Norwegian University of Science and Technology (NTNU), directs the NTNU Japan Programme, and is Associate Editor of foreign policy and domestic politics at *Japan Forum*. Midford is co-editor of *Japanese Public and the War on Terrorism* (2008).

Patricia A. Nelson is Visiting Professor at the Faculty of Economics, Seijo University, Tokyo, and Associate Partner at S4K Research AB. She received a Ph.D. in international political economy from Warwick University, and was awarded postdoctoral research fellowships at Harvard University's Program on US–Japan Relations and at Hitotsubashi University.

Akihiro Ogawa is Assistant Professor in the Department of Japanese Studies at Stockholm University, Sweden. He received a Ph.D. in anthropology from Cornell University and from 2004 to 2006 conducted postdoctoral work at Harvard University. He is currently developing a comparative project on lifelong learning policies and practices in Japan and Nordic countries.

Norbert Palanovics is Honorary Associate Professor at the Faculty of Business and Economics, University of Pécs, Hungary. He received a Ph.D. from Nagoya University for his work on Japan's development assistance policies.

Besides working as a foreign correspondent for the Hungarian newspaper *Népszabadság* in Tokyo he lectures at the Graduate School of International Development, Nagoya University.

Marie Söderberg is the Director of the European Institute of Japanese Studies at Stockholm School of Economics as well as a Professor of Japanese Studies at Stockholm University. She is the chairman of the Board of the Centre for East and South East Asian Studies at Lund University and head of the executive committee of the European Japan Advanced Research Network (EJARN).

Cornelia Storz holds the Chair of Japanese Economy in the Faculty of Economics and Business Administration at Johann Wolfgang Goethe University, Frankfurt, and is affiliated with the Interdisciplinary Centre for East Asian Studies (IZO). She has been a guest researcher at the Institute of Social Science, University of Tokyo, at the Japan Institute or Labour Policy and Training, at the Kansai University and at RIETI at METI.

John Swenson-Wright is Senior Lecturer in Modern Japanese Studies (Politics and International Relations) at the Faculty of Asian and Middle Eastern Studies, University of Cambridge, and fellow of Darwin College; he is also Associate Fellow of Chatham House (the Royal Institute of International Affairs). He received his Ph.D. in International Relations at St Antony's College, University of Oxford.

Preface

The need to strengthen the European–Japanese link is urgent. While the EU as well as the European countries mostly have been focusing their attention upon China's rapid rise during recent years, Japan is – and will continue to be – both a great power in East Asia and an important player in world politics. Japan matters because of its sheer economic scale. After fifteen years of post-bubble economy with low growth and several recessions, it is still one of the top global economies and is likely to remain so for decades. Japan is also an advanced technological power, and as a mature democracy faces similar challenges as Europe in terms of demography, energy, security and environmental protection.

Both Japan and Europe (in particular the European Union) equally aspire to play a greater role on the international stage than they did during the Cold War. In the age of increasing globalization both have become actively involved in regional issues outside their immediate neighbourhoods. Both are aware of the fact that there is much to gain from cooperation and recently there has been talk of a 'strategic partnership' between the EU and Japan conceived of as a bilateral relationship that goes beyond economic considerations so as to develop an agenda more comprehensive in scope and based on common interest and values.

Still what we see in Europe is something quite different. The strong focus on China has blinded Europeans, who seem to have difficulty in concentrating on more than one country at a time in Asia. As a consequence, Japan has become more and more invisible. Few new initiatives are taken in European–Japanese relations and the debate about Japan is fading away. Although Japan is still the world's second largest economy and shares with Europe an interest in many of the same economic, political and social issues, there is surprisingly little policy coordination and actual cooperation. This is the case although cooperation with Japan is sometimes a necessity for Europe to achieve its own aims in the field of trade, environment or development issues. Japan is simply too important to be left out and needs to be brought to the front of the European agenda again.

Looking at the relationship from a historic perspective, the 1970s and 1980s were dominated by economic issues where trade frictions came to play a dominant part. Although some frictions still persist, these are nowadays dealt with via the Regulatory Reform Dialogue between Japan and EU. Due to structural changes on both sides, tensions have to a large extent dissipated. There is, however, still more to be done in, for example, the field of foreign direct investment (FDI). An attempt to deepen the relationship and venture into other areas was made in the 1991 Hague declaration, which was later followed up in 2001 by the ten-year 'Action Plan for EU–Japan Cooperation' labelled 'Shaping our Common Future: EU–Japan Agenda for Cooperation'. This action plan is the main steering document in the EU–Japan relationship. In it both parties committed themselves to tackle jointly problems and issues related to international security, peace building, fighting terrorism, the economy and trade, environmental protection, development aid, coping with global and social changes as well as cooperation in research and education.

However, the reality of EU–Japan cooperation looks quite different. Results from the action plan are actually rather disappointing to date, leaving many envisaged areas untouched or dealt with only in a superficial and internationally irrelevant way. While the EU is using most of its Asia-dedicated financial and diplomatic resources on expanding relations with China, Japan has failed to reduce its dependence on the US foreign and economic security policy and increase its cooperation with Europe. To be sure, there has been cooperation, for example in the war-torn Balkans in the 1990s, but it did not lead to any substantial expansion of EU–Japan 'soft power' to any other hot spots on the globe. Trade and business ties are solid and expanding but could be much more dynamic and significant, given Japan's and the EU's share of the global GDP. The Action Plan is an all-encompassing document with wide suggestions for cooperation in many areas but it lacks specific focus on important issues, detail on how to make the concepts reality. As a result, it is not likely to have achieved much by the time it expires in 2011. Plans and discussion on what to do next will start in a short time, but as long as the Japanese–EU relationship is not given higher priority the results are likely to be meagre.

In an effort to improve the situation in the academic field, as well as providing some intellectual input into the debate on the EU–Japan relationship, the European Institute of Japanese Studies at Stockholm School of Economics arranged a two-day workshop on Japan's Political Economy on 13–14 June 2008. A number of key high-level European scholars (all Japanese-speakers) were invited to this workshop with the purpose of sharing research on recent events taking place in Japan's politics, security, development aid, education, business and economy.

As scholars – all with a long experience of working on and with Japan – everyone felt they had the capacity, and perhaps even a responsibility, to do something to reinvigorate research on Japan. There are not many scholars undertaking research on Japan in Europe, and they are scattered across a large number of countries (both within and outside the EU). It is not that we do not know each other, but, due to the geography of Europe and the relatively small size of many European countries, we understand that, to make our voices heard and to generate greater impact, we as scholars need to cooperate in a much more systematic fashion than we have to date. This can be achieved through closer networking, which would effectively enrich our research on Japan in general.

At the Stockholm meeting a decision was taken to create the European–Japan Advanced Research Network (EJARN). The main purpose of the network is: to create and apply for funding for joint research projects concerning Japan on a European level; to provide policy-relevant research concerning Japan to the EU, national governments, regional or other organizations as well as to private business; and to establish a hub for Japan-related research in Europe (preferably a 'centre of excellence') where the network members, in addition to intellectual input, would be able to assist each other with various types of information and useful contacts. Stockholm will be the centre of this hub at least in the initial stage.

A second purpose of the workshop was to discuss the changes that are taking place in Japanese politics and economics, seen from a European perspective. The power balance has changed in Asia with an economically stronger and more outward-oriented China. This has of course affected Japan, although if reckoned in terms of GDP Japan still has a far larger economy than China.

Japan is undertaking a number of new measures, in the field of economics and politics as well as in society in general, to adjust to this new power situation in Asia. A constitutional revision is being prepared, the Japanese Defense Agency has been upgraded to the status of a ministry and thorough changes are being undertaken within the defence forces. Concerning foreign aid, the two main implementing agencies the Japan Bank of International Cooperation (JBIC) as well as Japan International Co-operation Agency (JICA) were merged in to the 'New JICA', implying closer cooperation and a changed institutional setting for Official Development Assistance (ODA). In the field of economics, a number of new free-trade agreements that will have significant effects have been signed and at the company level we see more mergers and acquisitions between Japanese firms and foreign firms, a trend which is likely to accelerate as cash-rich Japanese firms look to see how they can grow in the midst of a weak world economy. Japan, affected by the Asian pollution problems as well as by global warming, is participating in a number of initiatives and leading global environmental action such as the Kyoto protocol. Globalization is affecting society in a number of ways and we see a more open Japan that is working to deepen its relations with the outside world.

Japan and Europe share common interests and face many of the same problems. They are both large donors of Official Development Assistance, they are strong supporters of the UN and a number of other multilateral organizations, they are technically advanced and they both have elected governments that have to take domestic public opinion into account. Still, due to their alliance arrangements, their different economic structures, their geopolitical situations as well as their different cultural backgrounds, they do not always act and think alike. When Japan is compared with other industrialized countries, it is most often the United States that is taken as the norm for what is considered a 'normal' country, despite the fact that Japan and the United States are in many aspects farther apart than Japan is from many European countries or for that matter the EU itself.

At the Stockholm workshop a number of papers giving European perspectives on various aspects of change in Japan were presented. The comparative angle was particularly encouraged, as were papers from different disciplines dealing with Japan's political economy. By inviting scholars who take a highly multidisciplinary approach, the aspiration was to increase understanding and broaden the perspectives of the participants while achieving cross-fertilization across disciplinary borders.

This book is based on some of the papers from the workshop. They have been rewritten, incorporating comments received from the workshop participants as well as recent developments in Japanese politics and economics. The aim of the book is to broaden our perspectives and deepen our understanding of the relationship between Europe and Japan and – more than anything else – to pay renewed attention to Japan.

Marie Söderberg
Series editor

Note on names and transcriptions

Japanese names are written with the first name followed by the surname, and Korean and Chinese names are written with surname first, as this is the way they are usually referred to in the English press. The exception is authors, who are better known for writing their first name before the surname.

The Hepburn system is used in transcription from Japanese except for the names of persons, companies or places where the long vowel is not marked.

Abbreviations

APS	Advanced Photo System
ARF	ASEAN Regional Forum
ASDF	air self defence forces
ASEAN	Association of Southeast Asian Nations
ASEM	Asia–Europe meeting
ASW	anti-submarine warfare
BMD	ballistic missile defence
CESA	Computer Entertainment Suppliers Association
CIPA	Camera and Imaging Products Association
CSCAP	Council on Security Cooperation in the Asia-Pacific
DAC	Development Assistance Committee
DDR	disarmament, demobilization and reintegration
DFAA	Defense Facilities Administration Agency
DPJ	Democratic Party Japan
DPRK	Democratic People's Republic of Korea
EAC	East Asian Community
ERA	Engineering Research Association
GSDF	ground self-defence forces
HRM	human resource management
ICRA	International Conference on Reconstruction Assistance
IGDA	International Game Developers' Association
IMF	International Monetary Fund
IOG	International Observer Group
IPE	international political economy
IR	international relations
ISAF	International Security Assistance Force (in Afghanistan)
JCIA	Japan Camera Industry Association
JCII	Japan Camera Inspection and Testing Institute
JDA	Japan's Defense Agency
JETRO	Japan External Trade Organization
JICA	Japan International Co-operation Agency
JMAS	Japan Mine Action Service
JSDF	Japan Self Defense Force

LDP	Liberal Democratic Party
LTTE	Liberation Tigers of Tamil Eelam
MOD	Ministry of Defense
MSDF	Maritime Self Defense Force
NATO	North Atlantic Treaty Organization
NCLL	National Council for Lifelong Learning
NEACD	North East Asian Cooperative Security Dialogue
NGO	non-governmental organization
NPO	non-profit organization
NSRG	National Security Research Group
ODA	official development assistance
OECD	Organisation for Economic Co-operation and Development
OEF	Operation Enduring Freedom
PKO	peacekeeping operation
PLA	People's Liberation Army
PRT	provincial reconstruction team
PSI	Proliferation Security Initiative
R&D	research and development
RCA	relative comparative advantage
ROE	rules of engagement
ROK	Republic of Korea
SCE	Sony Computer Entertainment
SCO	Shanghai Cooperation Organization
SDF	self-defence forces
SME	small and medium enterprises
SSR	security system reform
UN	United Nations
UNDP	United Nations Development Programme
UNSC	United Nations Security Council
UNTAC	United Nations Transitional Authority Mission in Cambodia
VSLI	very large-scale integration
WMD	weapons of mass destruction

1 Introduction

Dynamics of change

Patricia A. Nelson and Marie Söderberg

Japan has been under fire for some time for bringing about changes too slowly, in particular relative to the United States, which tends to move rapidly in response to changing economic and political conditions. We argue in this book that while the criticism may be valid on some levels, Japan has been in transformation. What has happened in Japan has been overshadowed by what has happened elsewhere in Asia, where there have been immense changes both economically and politically. The rise of China, the financial crisis in South East Asia in 1997 and North Korea's development of nuclear weapons are just a few examples of these dramatic changes. But has Japan, the world's second largest economy, only been muddling through?

History tells us that Japan has been most capable of making radical changes in desperate times, for this occurred both during the Meiji Restoration as well as after World War II. The argument of this book is that Japan has been changing in tandem with regional and global forces. Some thought the bursting of the real-estate bubble in Japan in the early 1990s had awoken the government and business leaders to the realities of a post-developmental state and globalized economy.[1] Others interpreted the lack of action as an end to the Japanese model (or models) of export-led economic growth.[2] We maintain that Japan has been in transformation due to pressures both internally and externally.

On the domestic level, Japan's former governing party, the Liberal Democratic Party (LDP), was in trouble after losing its majority in the Upper House, which caused it numerous difficulties in passing legislation through the Diet. However, the former government did take some concrete steps forward. Prime Minister Taro Aso announced a number of stimulus packages, including one with record-breaking actual spending of JPY 15.4 trillion, or approximately 3 per cent of Japan's GDP, to stimulate domestic demand and improve the overall economic picture.[3]

On an external level change has been under way for some time. At the time of this writing the global economy had fallen into its deepest recession in over a half-century, with the OECD predicting that economic growth in developed countries would decline in 2009.[4] The Japanese economy is forecast to have the largest contraction of all, at 6.6 per cent, followed by the United States and the euro area countries, all of which are predicted to contract by an estimated 4 per cent.[5] The ramifications of the economic situation are helping fuel speculation about the collapse of the old Japanese model of export-led economic growth, which in turn is expected to force export-led companies into a much anticipated phase of restructuring.[6] Linked with this is advice from the Asian Development Bank (ADB) to other Asian nations to balance and bolster domestic demand.[7] The upshot is likely to be Japan's further integration with the economies of Asia.

In this book we draw attention to change through a number of case studies. The challenges are great but there have been changes and these are our focus. This chapter begins with a discussion of the processes of change. Next we address change in Japan's modern history, moving on to an analysis of the recent diffusion of the drivers of change. Thereafter follows a discussion of the layout of the book, including a short presentation of the cases.

Processes of change

This book identifies the driving forces behind processes of change. We consider these at four levels: the individual, domestic, regional and global. On the individual level we assert that individual leadership matters. At the domestic level, public opinion is clearly important but so are such issues as demographics, employment and immigration, among many others. Changing political and security relations in Asia are factors driving change at a regional level. Global factors include Japan's role in the international community and the degree of Japan's economic integration into the world economy.

All of the authors who contributed to this book studied *processes of change* in their specialist fields ranging from political leadership, education policy, official development assistance, peace building and security to defence production, business associations and innovation policy. While this is far from a complete list of the processes of change taking place in Japan now, we would like to stress that we focus on the dynamics of change – rather than structural or institutional change per se – as they have been unfolding in recent decades. Changes have been driven by various factors at the four levels described above as well as from pressures outside Japan (such as a changing world order and changes in power relationships in Asia) and pressures within Japan (such as the increasing power of public opinion on politicians and our increasingly competitive domestic and global markets). We will return to this matrix of change in our conclusion.

As noted above, the changes that we have seen in Japan so far might represent the tip of an iceberg of radical change, for the current economic and financial crises could easily produce new drivers and thus stimulate further processes of change. There is good reason to believe that today we might be observing a major transformative period in history. Such periods occur when the old status quo dissolves making way for rapid change, or what Stephen Krasner called 'punctuated equilibrium'. Thereafter a new status quo emerges in which gradual change, not radical change, becomes the norm. Kathleen Thelen and Sven Steinmo argued convincingly that Krasner's model of punctuated equilibrium takes institutions as the independent variable in periods of status quo but then they become the dependent variable in periods of flux. Thus, they noted, institutions 'explain everything until they explain nothing'.[8] Dynamic analysis is preferable to 'punctuated equilibrium' when studying change, for according to Steinmo and Thelen there are opportunities to bring about radical change under conditions which they call 'institutional dynamism'.[9]

We follow this approach for its emphasis on dynamism and dynamic change, using a broadened conceptualization – broader than the focus on institutions alone – that processes of change are vibrant, with both rapid and gradual steps, sometimes alternating, sometimes simultaneous. The changes that are taking place in Japan are multi-faceted and we take the view that dynamism is fundamental to research on processes of change. We take a multidisciplinary approach and aim to achieve cross-fertilization of ideas and research agendas with the overarching objective of attaining a deeper understanding of the processes of change than single-author, single-discipline or single-theory approaches can offer. We believe that processes of change occurring in, for example, the field of economics and business should be put into a broader perspective of politics, security, international aid and training if we are to perceive them fully and vice versa. By focusing on the processes that lead to change, the authors in this volume offer interpretations of specific cases of change many of which are occurring behind the scenes and yet at the same moment right under our noses.

We recognize that there is no single theoretical method or approach that could be applied to all of the issues addressed in the chapters of this book, for none could give a comprehensive perspective on processes of change presented in the book. Collectively, our objective was to analyse change as it happened on the ground, with an eye to questioning whether or not change was taking place at all. As a consequence, we settled on a case study approach, which provides enough flexibility to allow each author some leeway in examining the processes of change from various angles and in applying theory as appropriate to his/her individual discipline. The merits and demerits of the case study method have been debated among academics for some time, as there is always the risk of failing to distinguish between what is unique in a case and what applies in general. One way of getting round this is through comparative studies, and in several of our cases comparisons are drawn, either between Japanese policy and the policy of other countries or comparisons between Japanese approaches and those of other countries. The cases in this book are based on interpretations of a great deal of empirical material and as such are inductive.

We argue that case studies are particularly enlightening when it comes to studies of Japan, because they help underscore the point that change may not occur rapidly in highly coordinated political economies due to the nature of deeply interlinked groups within society.[10] Highly coordinated political economies tend to have multiple interlinkages among actors at all levels of society. These ties are important elements in making the particular political economy function, but they also mean that radical changes do not happen quickly nor without a great deal of preparation and discussion. In the case of Japan, some have criticized this characteristic as a significant disadvantage because faster-moving economies, such as the

United States and the United Kingdom, have been able to react comparatively rapidly to change, for example due to innovation in the financial services industry.[11] Advantage or disadvantage in the capitalist system, the critical analytical point is that change, however fast, is afoot, and in Japan it is afoot in many areas that have not attracted much public attention. This book is an attempt to remedy this shortcoming.

The most common perspective in the English-language literature on Japan is, for better or worse, the American one, due to the sheer volume of the work produced there.[12] Here we offer an alternative perspective, namely analyses from European perspectives. This volume connects the work of academics that are based in or have a long history in Europe. By taking a view on the process of change in Japan from the experiences in European countries, we offer an alternative to the most common perspective, the Anglo-Saxon one, which dominates the English literature on Japan. American scholars tend to take US–Japan comparisons as their frame of reference, due to the dominance of the Anglo-Saxon model of development that has been so successful, especially in recent years.[13]

Two-country comparisons often have the undesirable effect of limiting the perceptions of Japan and thereby restricting our opportunities to appreciate processes of change. In particular, countless developments in Japan in recent years have made it imperative for scholars to take a multi-country approach. Recently this has led scholars to employ European cases that function as reality checks rather than relying predominantly on a US–Japan perspective.[14] If Japan is perceived as similar to Europe rather than very dissimilar to the United States, we suggest that Japan's own self-image might be altered in a positive way and this would be desirable from our perspective. For example, when viewed in comparison with the United States, Japan looks 'unique' in that it is a small country with few natural resources. In reality, however, Japan's natural resource supply is rather normal when compared with most European countries' natural resource supplies.[15]

We note that it is remarkable that many of the cases included in this book have gone largely unnoticed. One reason may be the expectation that 'the more things change the more they stay the same'.[16] While this did characterize Japan during a period of relative stability after the oil shocks of the 1970s, we argue that since about the late 1990s this has simply no longer been true.

Change in Japan's modern history

At certain points in history Japan has shown a remarkable ability to adapt. Perhaps the first and most famous era of dynamic change in Japan's modern period was the so-called Meiji Restoration. Following a coup at the imperial palace in Kyoto in 1868, the Tokugawa shogunate, a military dictatorship, fell after more than 260 years of rule and a new regime grasped power. The young Meiji emperor was formally 'restored' to power, returning the imperial family to its rightful place at the centre of power. At that time, the emperor was only fourteen years old and power was to be managed through a group of leaders surrounding him.

Importantly, the Meiji Restoration and the new Japanese leaders heralded the rise of a nascent market economy. Because of a long period of peace under the Tokugawa, the old hierarchy which rested on a military ethos lost its relevance. Merchants – ranked beneath the military elite, who controlled the rice-based agricultural system established by the shogunate – came to control the money-based economy, which the new Meiji leaders understood would hold the future of Japan.[17] As contact with the outside world has been severely limited, it was inevitable that the closed, isolated system of the Tokugawa would collapse. The first Portuguese ship arrived in Hirado (in the north of Nagasaki prefecture) in 1550, but in 1641 trade and contact were limited to the Dutch, who were granted access to the island of Dejima (in the south of Nagasaki prefecture). 'Dutch learning' had made the Tokugawa aware that Japan lagged behind in science and technology, but they attempted to control its arrival into Japan through strict supervision.

In the new world of exploration, in which territorial conquest had become the hallmark of world power, it had become increasingly clear to the new Meiji leaders that Japan could not survive without opening to the outside world. They needed to modernize or else they would be overrun by foreigners who had superior technology, ships and weapons, something China had already learned to its detriment. Under the new Meiji regime, Japan set out to catch up rapidly with leading European countries and the United States through the modernization of society via state-guided industrialization followed by the establishment of political institutions.

The transformation of society that occurred during the late nineteenth century has most often been presented in historical accounts as an unmitigated success.[18] In reality, the changes that took place during the Meiji era were complex and the processes of change was difficult. Things rarely went smoothly; outcomes were unpredictable and success was uncertain. As is typical during periods of flux, there were periods of trial and error, translating into several decades during which the process of change played out. The extent of information and knowledge available to those involved was limited and decision making at all levels was undertaken on a very pragmatic day-to-day basis.[19] Only the vantage point of history gives an impression of coordination and cohesion.

Still, there were great changes taking place and the drivers of these processes were many. One mentioned above was the unrelenting pressure from the outside (*gaiatsu*) to force Japan to open up to international trade or be taken over. Commodore Perry's Black Ships arrived in Shimoda in 1853, signalling with resolute determination their intention to gain control – in some sense – of Japan. Being colonized as China had been was thought to lead to undesirable and uncomfortable outcomes, including conflict and/or internal strife. As the merchant class rose in power from fourth-class to nearly the top, the internal crisis in Japan's society stirred resentment among the faithful samurai and their warlord leaders. This played out in a number of internal struggles for power as the samurai attempted to regain control by force and return themselves to the top of the class hierarchy. Internal strife and the lack of adequate methods for managing the newcomers to

Japan led to the imposition of unequal treaties by the great powers. A major stimulus to change therefore was the need to adapt to the shifting conditions of the times while recognizing the threat to Japan's autonomy that the great powers could impose.

A force in the direction of change was the prospect of the immediate as well as long-term gains that could be achieved through the transformation of society, the economy and political systems. To the national government the imperative was clear: there would be no revision of the unequal treaties, which gave foreign powers extensive rights in Japan, unless Japanese institutions were established along lines that would instil confidence in Japan among the dominant world powers.[20] Forward-thinking samurai of the revolutionary – and peripheral – regions of Satsuma, Choshu and Tosa, who, among other things, embraced the new money economy for the opportunity that it promised while forgoing their previous status, became the new elite. They set up various new institutions, e.g. the imperial university system and its elite bureaucrat training system, the modern military and police force, nationwide communications systems such as the postal and railway systems, while paving the way for new technologies such as electricity to spread throughout the country.[21]

The new Meiji leaders also recognized that the great powers of Europe and the United States were far ahead of Japan in military strength and degree of relative world power, defined in that era by the holding of colonies. The goal of catching up with them provided a rationale to dispatch a number of delegations abroad, notably the Iwakura mission. Those who went abroad on these missions would be future leaders who would help Japan embark on and continue along the path of modernization and change.[22] The objective of these fact-gathering delegations was to look for models to follow in modernizing various aspects of the Japanese economy, politics and society.[23] As a signal of openness, foreign experts were invited to Japan to assist with training and development through the introduction of skills from manufacturing to administration. Military knowledge and know-how were priority areas at the end of the nineteenth century, and Japan's ambition to catch up quickly through rapid industrialization as befitted a world power was epitomized by the phrase *fukoku kyōhei*, 'rich nation, strong army'.[24]

The reform of the financial system is an example of change that came about gradually after 1868. As early as 1872 the government encouraged the development of currency-issuing national banks modelled after those in the United States, but the whole process of achieving a coordinated nationwide banking system took three decades to put in place and required cooperation and coordination between the public and private sectors. Most notable perhaps was the Meiji government's reliance on the financial strength and experience of the House of Mitsui to help establish a modern economy. During the Tokugawa era the Mitsui businesses expanded from textile trading (the precursor of the Mitsukoshi department store) into the exchange business, which proved more lucrative during the Meiji era than textiles. Leading figures in the house of Mitsui developed close relations with government leaders, including handling most of the government's accounts. In 1876 the Mitsui Bank was established, followed quickly by other emergent group banks, including Dai-Ichi and Yasuda. The Bank of Japan, modelled upon the Belgian central bank, was established in 1882, when the government's accounts were transferred to it.[25]

By the time of Emperor Meiji's death in 1912 Japan had defeated both Russia and China in separate wars.[26] Japan was expanding through international trade, and society benefited from a modern, functioning infrastructure, including the dissemination of electricity and the construction of a national railway system, post offices, banks as well as the expansion of local and regional trade, the early growth of the export market through ceramics and later textiles, as well as the creation of an excellent education system. A national government based on the parliamentary system was in a nascent stage and political parties began to form and become highly active in the subsequent era, the so-called Taisho Democracy of the 1920s. Ambition and vision had moved the industrialization process along rapidly, much as had happened in other late developers in Europe, specifically Italy, Germany and Sweden.[27] Japan had become a power to rival the major European nations and the United States. Japan understood territorial expansion and the requisite military force as symbols of a nation to be reckoned with in the world.

Perhaps better known than the Meiji Restoration is the major period of change that occurred in Japan right after World War II that was largely imposed during the post-war Allied occupation. General Douglas MacArthur, Supreme Commander of the Allied Powers (SCAP), arrived in Japan with directives in hand; Japan was to be demilitarized, deconcentrated and democratized. Never again would Japan be allowed to carry out such aggression as in World War II. Further, as a precautionary measure, the economy would be allowed to return to the pre-war level of 1939 to help ensure that there would be no opportunity for Japan to rearm for world war. Drivers of change this time came in new forms quite different from the Meiji era.

To secure the peace between Japan and the Allies, Japan signed the peace treaty in 1951 and then immediately signed a Mutual Security Assistance Pact with the United States. Despite a public outcry and popular protest, the latter was replaced in 1960 by the Treaty of Mutual Cooperation and Security between the United States and Japan. On the domestic side, a National Police Reserve Force was established in 1950 to uphold law and order. Its mission was gradually expanded to protect Japan against attacks from the outside, and over time these forces evolved into the National Safety Forces, and by 1954 into the present Self Defense Forces.

The *zaibatsu*, or large family-centred business groups that were key to the success of the industrialization process after the Meiji Restoration, helped – to greater and lesser degrees – support the war effort with both the financing and production needed for war. Dissolution of concentrations of power in business became one of the cores of the post-war anti-trust policy developed by American New Dealers. They sought to make holding companies and thereby the *zaibatsu* illegal and unethical and forced the removal of the family from the centre of the groups (e.g. Mitsui, Mitsubishi and Sumitomo).[28] Given the suspicion of collusion between business leaders and the military, and the initial policy of preventing Japan from ever becoming a nation able to wage war again, this seemed wise at first blush. However, such turned out not to be the case.

When Mao Zedong founded the People's Republic of China (PRC) in 1949 the security realities of China as a major communist power in Asia and Japan as an economic burden on the US taxpayer became clearer.[29] The 1947–48 'reverse course' allowed Japan not only to recover to pre-war economic levels, but also to re-establish a functioning economy befitting a typical industrial nation. As a counterweight to the emerging encroachment of communism in Asia (namely the Soviet Union and China), a consensus was built around the idea of Japan as the democratic workshop of Asia, a bulwark against communism. The practicalities of recreating a functioning economy after the reverse course necessitated the restoration of economic organizational structures such as industry associations and business groups. At the same time, new and different drivers of change were triggered in line with the reverse course. The new idea of Japan as a workshop meant not only the revival of Japan's economy and politics beyond pre-war levels[30] but also the consolidation of the post-war political parties.

When Japanese politicians and experts who laboured under the Occupation forces could not come up with a new constitution of their own, a group of American scholars gathered and wrote one for them.[31] As Japan was the submissive loser, it is not surprising that many changes were imposed top-down. A new parliamentary system was imposed, with equal voting rights for all, regardless of status or sex. Equal rights for women and men, the freedom of religion and the freedom to speak and write about anything people desired were also included. Education was made free and available to all. Change also occurred in the agricultural sector, where land was redistributed and farmers were given the right to own their own plots.

Throughout the early post-war years there was a process of building a vision of what a peaceful, democratic Japan could become. That process led to the creation of post-war institutions, systems, norms and practices as a result of changes that occurred over the first decade after the war. There was a certain solidification of the system by the mid-1950s with the emergence of a post-Occupation political and economic system.[32] The main tenets of the immediate post-war system included the right to vote for all, the realignment and re-establishment of political parties, a system of mandarinization of the bureaucracy (through the renamed elite university system), long-term stable employment at large firms with their in-house labour unions to help assure a cooperative and reliable work force, seniority wage systems, the initial dislocation and then reconstitution of business groups and networks, and the like. Through the importation of and adaptation of new technologies and know-how there were spurts of change in some areas while there were setbacks in others, resulting in a certain unevenness along the path of change.

In summary, the process of agreeing upon standards, norms and practices was evolutionary.[33] It took time to settle upon what worked best in a particular environment across the board, from the financial system to the labour market.[34] Even when new institutions were put in place, they were not immediately welcomed and needed time to become firmly established. The military security relationship with the United States is one example of a highly political issue still quite visible today in popular demonstrations, shifting factional alliances and party politics. Although it took a great deal of time and effort, Japan eventually was perceived as having unique strength and cunning, this time in the business arena, not on the battlefield, and particularly in efficient and effective manufacturing capabilities.

Recent diffusion of drivers

Today we find ourselves in the midst of yet another wave of change. It is singularly different because in the two periods discussed above change was ushered in through momentous events that directly affected Japan: pressure from the outside to end the Tokugawa seclusionist policy and unconditional surrender after military defeat. Identifying the drivers of change in recent years is tough because today the drivers of change are more diffuse than the two periods discussed above. Japan's experience of change is, as of this writing, unfinished. The most commonly identified driver in the process of change today is the increased level of interconnectedness – and as a consequence interdependence – with other leading world economies and governments. The most frequently identified event to usher in this era was the fall of the Berlin Wall and the subsequent collapse of the Soviet Union followed after a few years by the bursting of Japan's real estate bubble.

Even before that time, Japan was under intensifying pressure – especially during the 1980s – to adjust to the growing level of globalization of the world economy. In particular, pressure mounted on leading world economies to converge to the 'winning' US free-market model.[35] Pressure escalated further after the Japanese real-estate bubble burst, all at once replacing hubris with a crisis mentality, while the US economy pursued the information superhighway and grew through a proliferation of IT start-ups, the so-called 'dot-coms'. This led to a general feeling that the Japanese model had failed and that the US system was in comparison vibrant, flexible and entrepreneurial. Japan reacted by deregulating a number of economic – particularly financial – areas that effectively opened up a rather closed economic, political and social system, although some argue that there is still much to be done.[36] While deepening Japan's level of interdependence with other economies, it also helped eliminate the myth of the 'uniqueness' of Japan.

In an era of globalization a new division of labour links Japanese and other Asian workers and thereby the world economy. The integration of Japan's economy with East Asia through foreign direct investment (FDI) via overseas manufacturing plants for the production of export-oriented goods and more recently the role of financial markets were complemented by gains in manufacturing productivity. The result was integration in production and trade in Japan with other developed economies on the one hand and the expanding economies of Asia on the other. The resulting reliance on profits from goods manufactured in a coordinated fashion across several countries looks today like a somewhat shortsighted strategy. Local demand in Asia (and elsewhere) may be critical for the continued development of Japanese manufacturers. At present, the current financial and economic crisis is threatening to bring back isolationist ideas, which in turn may dampen international trade, and demand for Japan's export-oriented goods may fade over the longer term.[37]

On the political side, Japan has also been experiencing an era of adjustment. In 1994 the election system for the Lower House was changed completely in a way that marked the end of the post-war political system that favoured rural districts. Adjustments to political districts meant that they became more representative of the population and were no longer heavily dominated by the interests of the countryside, where, for better or worse, few people live today. Further, as the large population born during the so-called post-war 'baby boom' era are beginning to retire, Japan is undergoing significant demographic changes. Birth rates are among the world's lowest (well below the replacement rate) at the same time as the population is aging. An aging society means young Japanese will carry the burden of the pension system on their shoulders as fewer workers must provide for more people. These dual challenges, a low birth rate and a rapidly rising number of pensioners, are shared with many European countries.

With the rise of globalization and Japan's realization that its own wealth and prosperity are increasingly dependent on the world beyond its borders, pressure has been escalating to find 'Japanese' ways independent of outside pressures to contribute to international society. Change in Japan's foreign policy, for example, has ranged from Prime Minister Aso's moves to warm up relations with China and the Better Market Initiative (a plan to create a favourable environment for a vibrant financial market in Tokyo) to foreign aid in which peace building has played an important part and environment policy which holds the promise of future economic growth.[38] In these and other areas that are addressed in the chapters of this book Japan appears to be taking a more active approach than in the past.

Layout of the book

We present this book in two parts. The first serves to set the stage for the book, offering a background for the general reader of Japan's greater political, security, economic and business environment. Part II presents seven case studies highlighting specific instances of change in Japan. The cases assume an understanding of the larger environment, and delve deeper into the specifics involved in each case. The seven cases address the following topics: political leadership; lifelong learning; peace building; aid and its link with national security; the military's role in industry; organizational change in the business community; and innovation in future-oriented sectors. These cases are notable because they examine aspects of change in Japan that have not been covered to any degree elsewhere.

This volume's contribution to the existing literature is the depth and range of sophisticated analyses on change in Japan on several levels and from the vantage point of a variety of academic fields. A number of books take up the theme of change in Japan from various perspectives such as institutional change,[39] the transformational effects of globalization,[40] as well as those that deal with change from specific disciplines such as security,[41] foreign policy[42] or economics.[43] However, no single volume offers such a range of cross-disciplinary perspectives on the processes of change in Japan as collected here.

The first stage-setting chapter is 'Contending with regional uncertainty: Japan's response to contemporary East Asian security challenges', by John Swenson-Wright. Giving an overview of change in the Asian region, Swenson-Wright makes two major points. First, he identifies the principal sources of tension, regional rivalry and regional instability in the area. Swenson-Wright notes how certain former flashpoints, such as Taiwan, no longer act as destabilizing factors in the same sense as before. Further, he teases out the competition between major powers such as the United States and China and how they – while in pursuit of regional dominance – enhance their security, economic and/or political influence. Second, he analyses possible mechanisms – bilateral or multilateral – by which the Japanese government might alleviate regional tensions in a manner consistent both with national interests and the interests of the current major and rising powers in the region. Beginning with a consideration of the change in the normative context of security options in Japan, Swenson-Wright comments that Japan has become less constrained by the pacifist legacy of World War II. Swenson-Wright's analysis takes into account specific bilateral relationships a broader range of multilateral options that may add to or detract from Japan's policy flexibility, and then he assesses the performance of past and present Japanese administrations in meeting various challenges. While his purpose is to assess the degree to which the Japanese government is prepared and able to adopt a focused and strategic response to the main political challenges of the Asian region, he argues that the impact of shifting power relations is notoriously difficult to predict.

In the second stage-setting chapter, 'Japan: balancing between a hegemon and a would-be hegemon', Paul Midford explores the processes of change from the Yoshida Doctrine to the Koizumi Doctrine. Reflecting on ambitions for an expanded military role for Japan, Midford argues that the modest nature of what Koizumi eventually achieved revealed the unexpected strength of the political opposition. Midford shifts our attention to Japan's domestic political situation and the role of public opinion. He analyses the domestic situation to understand Japan's international engagements. Specifically, Midford examines the rising influence of public opinion in shaping the decision paths available to Japan's elected officials. Public opinion is one method through which ideas can be transmitted to people in power, and, as Midford shows, it can effectively lead to a shift in power. The role of public opinion would appear to be growing in Japan's politics as people understand what effect their views can have on Japan's leadership and the choices it makes. Constitutional reform and an expansion of

Japanese overseas security are two issues that make his point clear. Midford sees Defensive Realism as the dominating paradigm in Japan's grand strategy. The rapid lifting of the ban on using space for military purposes as well as general public support for missile defence can be seen as signs of a recession of anti-military distrust and of a growing interest in homeland defence. He sees in Japan a lack of perception of Chinese malevolence and at the same time a desire to reassure its Asian neighbours that Japan itself will not change its defence position. Since the Iraq War there has been a fear of becoming entrapped in American overseas conflicts, something that would not be in Japan's national interest. According to Midford, we are likely to see Japan retreat from international activism as it instead turns inwards to manage its struggle to address an aging society through reforms of the pension and health-care systems.

Starting off the case study section in Chapter 4, 'Shifting incentives for political leadership', Verena Blechinger-Talcott continues the theme of domestic politics by analysing aspects of the training and career development of Japanese politicians, especially in the LDP. She explains how leaders have emerged within the party and the effect the process of becoming a party leader has had on leadership style in domestic politics. While the old system favoured political leaders who were highly skilled as mediators between conflicting interests, the new electoral system for the Lower House provided politicians with different incentives for career building. In the future we will see more politicians who strive to appeal directly to a broader, more urban voter base and to the media. A majority of the new generation of politicians are second-generation Diet members or graduates of political training academies, all of which translates into an increased level of professionalization among politicians. These politicians have a competitive advantage over others as they are better prepared for political office, have more international experience and are better skilled in handling the media than their predecessors. Blechinger-Talcott states that the core legacy of former Prime Minister Koizumi's regime was that he managed to destroy the established decision-making structure within the LDP, which led to a number of new patterns of behaviour, including a rise in the number of cross-party working groups staffed by young Diet members interested in fundamental change. Innovations such as these are likely to invigorate the role of the Diet in the future.

Akihiro Ogawa in Chapter 5, 'The construction of citizenship through volunteering: the case of lifelong learning', delves into how lifelong learning initiatives at the grass-roots level enrich the public sphere. The Japanese government has added the term 'lifelong learning' (*shōgai gakushū*) to the national education charter. Lifelong learning has quickly become one of the top priorities on the national policy agenda as Japan seeks to create a more dynamic, knowledge-based society. While the Japanese concept of lifelong learning traditionally was a cultural construct aimed at self-actualization through the liberal arts and enjoyment of hobbies and sports primarily in the context of an aging society, the current discussion on the topic goes beyond this scope. Lifelong learning is now an individual's contribution to the public sphere. A New Public (*atarashii kōkyō*) is a concept through which good citizens should be enabled to promote a better society. It is defined as increased civic engagement, which would create a more dynamic society but at the same time also act as a cost-cutting policy for the public administration. By locating grass-roots learning as a reformulation of the conventional rigid relationship between the state and society, lifelong learning participants realize learning as a step towards achieving active 'citizenship'. Ogawa focuses in particular on the cultural volunteers (*bunka borantia*) that are at the forefront of a change in contemporary Japan. They are key players in local public facilities as they have the ability to galvanize local neighbourhoods from the grass-roots level.

The two chapters that follow focus on Japanese official development assistance (ODA), which is becoming more and more entangled with issues of peace and security not only in Japan but among donor countries in general. A number of policy documents both within the UN system and from other donor organizations have worked to establish the importance of this link. Marie Söderberg in Chapter 6, 'Foreign aid as a tool for peace building: is the goal security or poverty reduction?', examines what has happened with Japan's policy of peace building through ODA at the implementation level. When tracing the Japanese policy of peace building, Söderberg also touches on its non-ODA element and assesses the difficulties that arise due to Article 9, the peace clause in the Constitution that forbids Japan from making military contributions in the pursuit of solving overseas conflicts. Afghanistan is taken as a case study to show how Japanese policy works on the ground. To make clear what peace-building measures are being used by other nations that do not have an Article 9-like peace clause, a comparison is made with Swedish actions in Afghanistan. Japanese ODA has to fulfil many missions in peace building, and it is obvious that everything cannot be done via foreign aid alone. This means that there are limits on the role that Japan can play, compared with other nations. Söderberg's aim is to identify and describe the link between security and development in the implementation phase and then to draw some conclusions concerning the goals of Japanese ODA.

In Chapter 7, 'Peace diplomacy by ODA: rhetoric and reality', Norbert Palanovics illustrates how Japan conducts its ODA-based peace diplomacy. The chapter focuses on Japan's rhetoric regarding foreign policy – particularly on development assistance and peace building – and examines the link between rhetoric and action. Palanovics carries out his analysis by exploring Japan's participation in the peace process in Sri Lanka, and comparing it with Japan's earlier participation in the Cambodian case. The chapter begins by introducing the whole-of-government approach to peace building in which political, defence, diplomatic and economic instruments of national power are used in parallel to make and keep peace and to restore and develop economies, social structures and institutions in unstable or conflict-torn regions around the world. Palanovics then discusses to what degree Japanese policy is changing through the adoption of the whole-of-government approach by analysing the relationship between ODA and peace building on the one hand and between human security and peace building on the other. Taking Sri Lanka and Cambodia as case studies of Japanese peace diplomacy, Palanovics offers some recommendations as to how Japanese peace diplomacy could improve.

From peace diplomacy we venture into processes of change in security from quite another angle, namely the military-industrial complex. Christopher W. Hughes in his chapter, 'The changing political economy of defence production: the rise of a military-industrial complex?', introduces the militarization framework to examine the trajectory and implications of Japan's security policy. Although this discourse is not mainstream, Hughes argues convincingly that it has much to offer. The militarization framework helps us understand the key drivers of change, it illuminates the debate on the continuities and discontinuities of Japan's security stance and it provides critical analyses to question the dominant orthodoxies and discourses of the policy mainstream. Hughes uses Japan's defence production and the question of an emerging military industrial complex to test the militarization framework. The degree of autonomy in Japanese defence production has been seen as an indicator of Japanese strategic autonomy vis-à-vis the United States. Hughes concludes that there are indeed signs of an emerging Japanese military-industrial complex embedded in the domestic political economy. More crucially, however, there is also an emerging transnational complex, driven in particular by the US–Japan alliance. This spells entrapment for Japan in US global strategy and poses important questions for the discourse of 'normalization' in Japan's security policy.

The next two chapters are directly related to the Japanese economy. Patricia A. Nelson argues that *zaidan hōjin*, specifically industry associations, are a particular feature of coordinated economies such as Japan and they are the subject of Chapter 9, 'Stability and the status quo: changing power structures in the optics industry'. Noting that the purpose and structure of organizations change over time, Nelson stresses that it is important to understand what they do, how they change and why. Nelson notes that inter-organizational business institutions (in this case *zaidan hōjin*) are often assumed to be cartels when analysed in the context of neoclassical economics. In general, there is a fundamental expectation of evil intent whenever business people meet and talk about issues that affect their business activities. Nelson suggests that, to the contrary, in highly coordinated economies *zaidan hōjin* such as industry associations become activated in the search for solutions to shared problems, not simply pursuing the goal of collusion to cheat the unknowing customer. Taking the optics industry as a case study of change in *zaidan hōjin*, she uses a historical analysis to demonstrate that Japanese optics (and camera) manufacturers were prepared for the so-called 'disruptive innovation' brought about by the rise of digital imaging and increasing levels of globalization. Nelson shows how leading firms reorganized the *zaidan hōjin* over time in response to changing business conditions. In order to manage change rather than be overtaken by it, visionary leaders skilfully propelled the industry forward through its business associations to meet the changing conditions head-on. Nelson's chapter draws from and contributes to the growing work on the roles of inter-organizational institutions in coordinated economies.

In the final case study, 'Sources and processes of change: the case of the game software', Cornelia Storz analyses the process of new industry formation within Japan's national innovation system. The Japanese software industry is for the most part absent from the world market. This is most often attributed to a mismatch between the Japanese innovation system and the needs of new industries. The system is said to offer incentives to 'catching up' with world leaders rather than to the creation of new industries. In sharp contrast is a subsector of the software industry, namely Japan's video game software industry, with companies including Sony, Nintendo and Sega producing world-leading products. Recognizing the role of path dependence – a key concept in institutional economics which explains why a desirable institutional change does not take place even if it would bring positive results – Storz assesses how novelty emerges in path-dependent systems. She identifies plasticity as one of the key concepts to analyse the success of the game software industry. The research is exploratory, qualitative and built on a number of interviews with various game software firms. With this study Storz contributes to recent efforts to document how the resources for change and the emergence of new forms are contained within the systems themselves.

Finally, in the conclusion, 'Perspectives on change', Marie Söderberg and Patricia Nelson, the editors, draw together the implications from the chapters collected in this volume. What we found is that, while processes of change have been ongoing for some time, the results have not always attracted much notice. Given the variety of disciplines and subjects explored throughout this volume, it is simply not possible to settle on a shortlist of specific drivers of change. Such drivers are on global, regional, local and individual levels but the forces as such and the extent of change vary considerably with the issues researched as well as the methods used. Nonetheless, we know from history that Japan is most capable of change. As with other countries, there have been significant periods of trial and error, sometimes taking several decades before real change took root. Often decision making was undertaken in a very pragmatic way. This does not seem too far from the present situation, where we see a number of concrete changes that apparently have occurred under the radar and generally gone unnoticed. It is to offer visibility and perspective on the changes that are occurring in Japan's politics and economy that this book has been written.

Notes

1 Books in this vein include R. B. Katz, *Japanese Phoenix: The Long Road to Economic Revival*, Armonk, NY: M. E. Sharpe, 2003; and K. B. Pyle, *Japan Rising: The Resurgence of Japanese Power and Purpose*, New York: Public Affairs Books, 2007.
2 K. McCormick, 'Whatever happened to "the Japanese model"?', *Asian Business and Management* 3 (4), December 2004, pp. 371–93 (23).
3 T. Fukuda, 'Aso unveils record stimulus: latest package brings total cost to JPY 57 trillion', *Japan Times*, 11 April 2009, http://search.japantimes.co.jp/cgi-bin/nb20090411a1.html (accessed 11 April 2009).
4 The OECD Interim Economic Outlook, March 2009, www.oecd.org/document/59/0,3343,en_2649_33733_42234619_1_1_1_1,00.html (accessed 19 April 2009).
5 Ibid.
6 Richard Katz has stressed that during the 1990s Japan went through far less real structural reform than reported, making the post-2002 growth vulnerable to an economic

downturn and dip in demand for exports. However, Katz also argues that, if Japan had not resolved its bad debt problems, it would not have been able to gain from global demand for its exports. See R. B. Katz, 'Comparing crises: Katz replies', *Foreign Affairs* 88 (3), May–June 2009, www.foreignaffairs.com/articles/64917/robert-madsen-richard-katz/comparing-crises (accessed 5 May 2009).

7 Asian Development Bank, *Asian Development Outlook, 2009*. www.adb.org/Documents/Books/ADO/2009/default.asp (accessed 11 April 2009).

8 K. Thelen and S. Steinmo, 'Historical institutionalism in comparative perspective' in S. Steinmo, K. Thelen and F. Longstreth (eds) *Structuring Politics: Historical Institutionalism in Comparative Analysis*, Cambridge Studies in Comparative Politics, Cambridge: Cambridge University Press, 1992, p. 17. On punctuated equilibrium and its link with the work of evolutionary biologist S. J. Gould see S. Krasner, 'Approaches to the state: alternative conceptions and historical dynamics', *Comparative Politics* 16 (2), 1984, 223–46.

9 See Thelen and Steinmo, 'Historical Institutionalism in comparative perspective', pp. 1–32.

10 See, for example, M. Witt, *Changing Japanese Capitalism: Societal Coordination and Institutional Adjustment*, Cambridge: Cambridge University Press, 2006.

11 J. Rogers Hollingsworth and Robert Boyer point to the importance of differences in capitalist systems and the benefits to the global system of a variety of systems. See J. R. Hollingsworth and R. Boyer (eds) *Contemporary Capitalisms: The Embeddedness of Institutions*, Cambridge: Cambridge University Press, 1997. For a firm-centred approach see P. A. Hall and D. Soskice (eds) *Varieties of Capitalism: The Institutional Foundations of Comparative Advantage*, Oxford: Oxford University Press, 2001.

12 Similar books written largely from an American perspective include D. Arase (ed.) *The Challenge of Change: East Asia in the New Millennium*, Research Papers and Policy Studies 44, Berkeley, CA: Institute of East Asian Studies, University of California at Berkeley, 2003; E. S. Krauss and T. J. Pempel (eds) *Beyond Bilateralism: U.S.–Japan Relations in the New Asia-Pacific*, Stanford, CA: Stanford University Press, 2004; S. K. Vogel (ed.) *U.S.–Japan Relations in a Changing World*, Washington, DC: Brookings Institution, 2002.

13 See, for example, M. Albert, *Capitalism against Capitalism: How America's Obsession with Individual Achievement and Short-term Profit has led it to the Brink of Collapse*, New York: Four Walls Eight Windows, 1993; Hall and Soskice, *Varieties of Capitalism*; Hollingsworth and Boyer, *Contemporary Capitalisms*; and S. Berger and R. P. Dore (eds) *National Diversity and Global Capitalism*, Ithaca, NY: Cornell University Press, 1996.

14 It should be noted that rather few American scholars of Japan are also scholars of Europe, for it is no simple task to compare the major advanced industrialized nations, the European Union, Japan and the United States. In this sense, Europeans have an advantage in that if they know something of their own countries (and the European Union) and if they have read the massive literature on Japan analysed from an American perspective, then they have an opportunity to synthesize all three when writing about Japan from a European perspective. Notable European and American comparisons in studies of Japan include S. K. Vogel, *Freer Markets, More Rules: Regulatory Reform in Advanced Industrial Countries*, Ithaca, NY: Cornell University Press, 1996; R. P. Dore, *Stock Market Capitalism, Welfare Capitalism: Japan and Germany versus the Anglo-Saxons*, Oxford: Oxford University Press, 2000; and S. K. Vogel, *Japan Remodeled: How Government and Industry are Reforming Japanese Capitalism*, Ithaca, NY: Cornell University Press, 2006.

15 R. J. Samuels, *Machiavelli's Children: Leaders and their Legacies in Italy and Japan*, Ithaca, NY: Cornell University Press; and S. R. Reed, *Making Common Sense of Japan*, Pittsburgh, PA: University of Pittsburgh Press, 2006.

16 The phrase is 'plus ça change, plus c'est la même chose'. See, for example, J. Haffner, T. Casas i Klett and J. P. Lehmann, *Japan's Open Future: An Agenda for Global Citizenship*, London: Anthem Press, 2008, p. 153.
17 T. C. Smith, *Native Sources of Japanese Industrialization, 1750–1920*, Berkeley, CA: University of California Press, 1988; and J. Hirschmeier and T. Yui, *The Development of Japanese Business, 1600–1980*, 2nd edn, London: Allen & Unwin, 1981.
18 E. O. Reischauer and A. M. Craig, *Japan: Tradition and Transformation*, rev. edn, Sydney: Allen & Unwin, 1989.
19 J. Hunter, 'Institutional change in Meiji Japan' in M. Blomström and S. La Croix (eds) *Institutional Change in Japan*, London and New York: Routledge, 2006, pp. 45–79.
20 The great powers active in Asia at the time included Great Britain, France, Spain, Portugal, the Netherlands, Russia and later the United States.
21 D. Eleanor Westney's seminal work on the transfer of the organizational patterns of the post office, police and the newspaper from Europe and the United States to Japan during the Meiji era illustrates the scale of the challenges that faced leaders in both business and government at that time. See D. E. Westney, *Imitation and Innovation: The Transfer of Western Organizational Patterns in Meiji Japan*, Cambridge, MA: Harvard University Press, 1987.
22 I. Nish, *The Iwakura Mission to America and Europe: A New Assessment*, London and New York: RoutledgeCurzon, 1997; and K. Kume, C. Tsuzuki and R. J. Young (eds) *Japan Rising: The Iwakura Embassy to the USA and Europe, 1871–1873*, Cambridge: Cambridge University Press, 2009.
23 Nish, *The Iwakura Mission.*
24 See, among others, R. J. Samuels, '*Rich Nation, Strong Army': National Security and the Technological Transformation of Japan*, Ithaca, NY: Cornell University Press, 1996.
25 Hirschmeier and Yui, *The Development of Japanese Business*, pp. 136–8, 193–6.
26 These were the Sino-Japanese War of 1894–95 and the Russo-Japanese War of 1904–05.
27 On 'take-off', see R. Minami, *Economic Development of Japan: A Quantitative Study*, 2nd edn, Basingstoke: Macmillan, 1994; on the developmental state, see C. Johnson, *MITI and the Japanese Miracle*, Stanford: Stanford University Press, 1982.
28 E. M. Hadley, *Antitrust in Japan*, Princeton, NJ: Princeton University Press, 1970; J. B. Cohen, *Japan's Economy in War and Reconstruction*, Minneapolis, MN: University of Minnesota Press, 1949.
29 Cohen, *Japan's Economy in War and Reconstruction.*
30 Ibid. and T. Nakamura, *Japan's Postwar Economy: Its Development and Structure*, Tokyo: University of Tokyo Press, 1981.
31 Today this constitution is nicknamed *ōchitsuke kempo*, or the constitution pushed upon the Japanese people.
32 In recent years this has been labelled the '1955 system' in recognition of the consolidation of many aspects of Japan's politics, society and economy that occurred at about that time. See, for example, R. J. Samuels, 'Kishi and Corruption: An Anatomy of the 1955 System', Japan Policy Research Institute Working Paper 83, December 2001, www.jpri.org/publications/workingpapers/wp83.html (accessed 15 May 2009).
33 See, for example, Thelen and Steinmo, 'Historical institutionalism in comparative perspective'.
34 It thus goes without saying that, as new eras emerge, norms and practices shift with what is viewed as acceptable by the wider public. Thelen and Steinmo, 'Historical institutionalism in comparative perspective'.
35 The upshot was a proliferation of studies of varieties of capitalist systems exploring whether or not they could converge on to one 'best' system. Some representative studies are: Hall and Soskice, *Varieties of Capitalism*; Hollingsworth and Boyer, *Contemporary Capitalisms*; and Berger and Dore, *National Diversity and Global Capitalism.*

36 Vogel, for example, argued that Japan pursued not so much deregulation but re-regulation (see Vogel, *Freer Markets, More Rules*). The contributors to the volume edited by Schaede and Grimes argued that Japan pursued 'permeable insulation', that is, despite pressure to open up and deregulate, Japan still maintained a distance from the rest of the world economy while simultaneously interacting with other countries mainly through trade and foreign direct investment (see U. Schaede and W. Grimes, *Japan's Managed Globalization: Adapting to theTwenty-first Century*, Armonk, NY: M. E. Sharpe, 2003).

37 As of this writing, Japan's exporters are being severely hurt by the turn-down in the world economy. Major exporters from Toyota to Sony announced poor results for the last quarter of 2008 and the first quarter of 2009 and many shed staff in order to manage the cut in profits over the short term. See, for example, 'Electronics firms see major overhauls as ticket back to black', *The Nikkei* (morning edition), 16 May 2009, www.nni.nikkei.co.jp/e/fr/tnks/Nni20090515D15JFA17.htm (accessed 16 May 2009).

38 'President Hu meets Japan's Aso, calling for cherishing achievements in bilateral ties', *Xinhua*, 30 April 2009, see http://news.xinhuanet.com/english/2009-04/30/content_11290307.htm (accessed 2 May 2009); Financial Services Authority, 'Progress of Better Market Initiative (Plan for Strengthening the Competitiveness of Japan's Financial and Capital Markets)', 27 June 2008, see www.fsa.go.jp/en/news/2008/20080627.html (accessed 21 April 2009).

39 M. Blomström and S. J. La Croix (eds), *Institutional Change in Japan*, London: Routledge, 2006.

40 Schaede and Grimes, *Japan's Managed Globalization.*

41 K. B. Pyle, *Japan Rising: The Resurgence of Japanese Power and Purpose*, New York: Public Affairs, 2007, and R. J. Samuels, *Securing Japan: Tokyo's Grand Strategy and the Future of East Asia*, Ithaca, NY: Cornell University Press, 2007.

42 T. U. Berger, M. Mochizuki and J. Tsuchiyama (eds) *Japan in International Politics: The Foreign Policies of an Adaptive State*, Boulder, CO: Lynne Rienner, 2007.

43 D. Bailey, D. Coffey and P. Tomlinson (eds) *Crisis or Recovery in Japan: State and Industrial Economy*, Cheltenham: Edward Elgar, 2007; J. Hunter and C. Storz (eds) *Institutional and Technological Change in Japan's Economy, Past and Present*, London: Routledge, 2005.

Part I

Setting the stage

2 Contending with regional uncertainty

Japan's response to contemporary East Asian security challenges

John Swenson-Wright

Today's Asia-Pacific is a region where, despite the potential for significant instability and tension, there are important emerging signs of enhanced bilateral and multilateral cooperation. Compared with other parts of the globe – either the Middle East (where the war in Iraq, the challenge of Al Qaeda, the proliferation challenge posed by Iran, and the long-standing Arab–Israeli standoff are all sources of instability), or Central Asia (where the US-led coalition remains embroiled in the Afghan conflict), the Asia Pacific presents a more variegated picture, in which interstate tension and new security challenges are offset by new opportunities for cooperation, challenging past patterns of rivalry. Traditional tensions over North Korea's nuclear ambitions and weapons of mass destruction (WMD) programme, or over the status and independence of Taiwan remain important, but arguably no longer act as destabilizing flashpoints or trip wires for immediate conflict in the way they did during the Cold War.

Nonetheless, in a more fluid post-Cold War environment, there are real tensions based on competition between the region's major powers, most notably traditional large states such as the United States and China, to enhance their regional influence economically, politically and militarily in pursuit of regional dominance or hegemony. These states are joined by rising 'middle powers'[1] with aspirations either to acquire new influence or reclaim part or all of their former regional status, creating in the process added uncertainty. A still powerful Japan, despite facing economic difficulties at home, is promoting a more assertive set of foreign and security policies as part of its transformation into a more 'normal' power;[2] India, given its rapid economic growth and its demographic heft (with a population of more than one billion), is pursuing a 'hedging' strategy of new pragmatic relations with China and the United States;[3] while Russia, since March 2008 under the new dyarchy of President Medvedev and Prime Minister Putin, embraces a recidivist foreign policy in which energy and resource diplomacy have served (at least until the recent decline in oil prices) as key weapons for enhancing and expanding its regional influence and status, in the process bringing it into an increasingly fractious relationship with the United States.[4]

The impact of these shifting power relations, freed from the traditional Cold War ideological moorings of the past, is difficult to predict, but the analysis in this chapter attempts to make sense of these changes by identifying the following two points: first, the principles sources of tension, regional rivalry and regional instability in the Asia-Pacific; second, the possible mechanisms – bilateral and multilateral – by which the Japanese government might alleviate such tensions in a manner consistent with its national interests as well as with the aspirations and ambitions of the current major and rising powers in the region. The purpose is to assess the degree to which the Japanese government is prepared and able to adopt a focused and strategic response to the main political challenges of the Asian region.

The chapter begins by identifying, in the next section, some of the core sources of regional instability before considering the responses and capabilities of recent Japanese administrations in meeting these contingencies. The intention is not to itemize systematically the specific policy options faced by Tokyo in every instance, but rather, by surveying today's threats, to better appreciate the magnitude and range of the challenges faced not only by Japan, but by all the major powers involved in Asia.

The following section shifts from this broad perspective to a more concentrated discussion of past and present Japanese policy decisions. It begins with a consideration of the change in the normative context for security options in Japan, particularly the emergence of what some have referred to as a more 'normal' Japan, less constrained by the pacifist legacy of World War II. From here, it considers specific bilateral relationships that may add to or detract from Japan's policy flexibility, looking specifically at US–Japan ties, Sino-Japan, Korea–Japan, and finally Russo-Japan relations. The chapter then examines the broader range of multilateral options for Japan, whether via new regional security and political frameworks, larger supra-regional bodies such as the United Nations (UN), or new initiatives to confront climate change and regional trade. The concluding section assesses the performance of past and present Japanese administrations in meeting regional security and political challenges, noting in the process the constraining impact of domestic political issues, the current global economic crisis, and some of the suggested remedies for developing a more calibrated and successful set of responses consistent with Japan's national interest.

Principal sources of tension, rivalry and regional instability

Identifying the principal challenges to regional stability in the Asia-Pacific is, in some respects, a contentious, some might argue artificial, process. Inevitably, the significance of a particular challenge will depend on the perspective of the individual state or constituency affected and proximity may often encourage some actors to assign more or less weight to a particular issue. However, a comprehensive survey of the region might arguably single out the following four key sources of tension: a nuclear North Korea; territorial disputes; competition over access to energy resources; and non-traditional security threats associated with the rise of separatist movements.

A nuclear Democratic People's Republic of Korea

The risks from a nuclear North Korea are multi-faceted. Since October 2006, when the Democratic People's Republic of Korea (DPRK) apparently test-detonated a crude nuclear device, there have been fears that this may prompt a destabilizing regional arms race. For neighbours such as Japan (potentially susceptible to nuclear blackmail given its proximity to the Korean peninsula and exposed to the threat of the DPRK's considerable ballistic missile capabilities) this is a particularly powerful concern. Recent Japanese academic, policy and media debate has increasingly focused on the merits of ending or qualifying the country's three 'non-nuclear principles' – the post-1967 prohibition against the production or possession of nuclear weapons or their transportation through Japanese territory. While a sudden reversal of Japan's non-nuclear status is very unlikely, given the reassurance provided by America's extended deterrence umbrella and Japanese popular aversion to nuclear weapons, a public debate over the merits of nuclearization is highly unusual and signifies an important shift in Japanese public attitudes.[5]

The threat from the DPRK is not purely the existential challenge of nuclear weapons (in addition to the North's already considerable armoury of conventional, chemical and biological weapons), but also the risk of proliferation. Pyongyang has long made clear that it has no intention of exporting its fissile material or selling its weaponry to other powers, but US intelligence reports of a covert arrangement by the North to supply Syria with nuclear technology have raised fears worldwide that the DPRK may have overstepped one of the United States' critical 'red lines' against proliferation.[6] The emergence of this issue risked strengthening the hand of hard-liners in the Bush administration sceptical of the merits of the Six Party Talks with the DPRK, potentially derailing in turn the February 2007 agreement for the permanent disabling of North Korea's nuclear capabilities and undermining any hope of a diplomatic solution to the nuclear crisis. For the new Democratic administration of President Barack Obama the proliferation issue remains a core concern, alongside growing fears that the DPRK is dragging its feet on key verification aspects of the 2007 nuclear deal. While the current Secretary of State, Hillary Clinton, has hinted at a willingness to open a broader dialogue with the leadership in Pyongyang and there is talk of appointing a new special envoy to the DPRK, the Obama administration has also made it clear that it is willing to adopt a hard line towards the DPRK, including the imposition of new political and economic sanctions, if there is no progress on the key verification question.[7]

Territorial disputes

There are a number of high-profile unresolved territorial disputes in the Asia-Pacific region, many of them the legacy of either the Cold War or the colonial experience of the late nineteenth and twenties centuries. Chief among these is the persistent question of Taiwan's international status, which China views as an unresolved legacy of the 1927–49 nationalist–communist civil war. Reuniting the territory with the mainland (whether by force or more realistically through a gradual process of economic convergence and political and social integration)[8] will, in Beijing's judgement, allow China to reassert its sovereignty and territorial integrity and is critically important for a communist leadership that increasingly needs to underscore its political legitimacy by accommodating a more assertive and vocal nationalistic public opinion at home.

Taiwan is one, albeit the most high-profile, of such regional tensions. Others include (but are not limited to) Japan's efforts to reclaim the four 'northern territories' to the north of Hokkaido, occupied by the Soviet Union (now Russia) since 1945; rival sovereignty claims between Japan, China and Taiwan, over the Senkakus (or Daiyoutai Islands) in the East China Sea; the longer standing Takeshima–Tokto dispute between South Korea and Japan; rival Chinese and Korean claims over Koguryo (Gaoguli in Chinese), the ancient seventh-century kingdom that straddles the northern part of the Korean peninsula, encompassing parts of contemporary North Korea, southern Manchuria and the southern Russian maritime province; contested claims over the Spratly Islands in the South China Sea between most of the states of South East Asia; border disputes between India and China dating from the war of 1962, most notably China's claim over the Indian state of Aranachal Pradesh; and the long-standing and periodically explosive Kashmir dispute between India and Pakistan.[9]

For Japan, the Senkakus, Takeshima and the Northern Territories have the most immediate significance, but some of the others are relevant to Tokyo because they involve disputes over access to scarce oil and natural gas reserves (such as the Spratlys), or raise important sovereignty issues or questions relating to maritime navigation and access rights across some of the key transportation routes in the region. More speculatively, resolution of such disputes is one area where Japanese administration might have a constructive role to play. In the past, for example in the Konfrontasi crisis between Indonesia and Malaysia in the early 1960s or the Cambodian conflict of the 1990s, Japanese politicians and government officials sought to play a mediating role, capitalizing on Japan's perceived role as a disinterested go-between, culturally and politically equidistant between East and West. It is debatable whether Japan can continue to play such a role today, but acknowledging its past activity and these current tensions highlights the opportunities that a proactive Japanese leadership, intent on enhancing its political involvement in the region, might embrace in the future.

Competition over access to energy resources

Rapid economic growth means that for energy-hungry states such as China and India, with rapidly expanding populations, as well as for states such as Japan (critically short of fossil fuels) obtaining vital supplies of oil and natural gas and maintaining secure land and maritime fuel supply routes is essential. Conversely, for oil and natural gas rich countries such as Kazakhstan and Russia, control over these scarce resources has enhanced their political profile and leverage, allowing Moscow in particular to place an increasingly pivotal role in today's analogue to the nineteenth-century 'Great Game' for strategic influence in Asia and Central Asia by parlaying access to oil and natural gas (i.e. pipeline access and extraction rights) for substantial financial returns from national governments (most notably China and Japan) and from private firms. Since 2004, and especially after August 2006, when then Prime Minister Junichiro Koizumi visited the Central Asian republics of Kazakhstan and Uzbekistan, Japan has been raising its profile in the region, bolstering its diplomatic ties with local states, in part by promoting educational reform and regional economic development.[10] Japan also finds itself in a competitive race with the People's Republic of China (PRC) to secure preferential oil and natural gas pipeline deals with Russia. This process continues to lumber on unresolved, but it is one which has particular sensitivity for Japan given its energy-hungry economy and its high dependence on foreign supplies of fossil fuels, particularly from the Middle East.

Non-traditional security challenges

Separatist movements and the risk of secession and/or state fragmentation remain a critical issue for many of the states of the Asia-Pacific. China struggles periodically with separatist movements in Xinjiang, and most recently in Tibet, following the demonstrations there of March 2008; Russia continues to contend with the Chechnya resistance in its north Caucasus; Burma and Thailand are vulnerable to domestic political protest in opposition to military rule; radical Islamic fundamentalist groups such as Jemaah Islamiyah threaten the stability of a number of states in South East Asia, including the Philippines, Indonesia, Malaysia, Singapore and Brunei; India and Pakistan are caught in a tug-of-war involving rival separatist groups in Kashmir; and India also confronts Maoist 'Naxalites' groups in West Bengal and Bihar and separatist groups in India's north-east variously and periodically supported by Bangladesh, Burma, Nepal and Bhutan.[11] In addition to these threats to the integrity of individual states, the region is vulnerable to international terrorism; international piracy; environmental challenges, most notably global climate change; the rise of trade protectionism and the growth of trade-inhibiting rival economic blocs.

The diversity of such challenges demonstrates vividly the policy-making dilemma faced by any government concerned to promote regional stability. For Japan (as for other governments), the challenge is twofold, namely, first, how best to measure and assess the relative importance of each of these different threats in terms of its national interests, and, second, how to apply in a coordinated fashion its substantial, but nonetheless limited diplomatic, economic and security resources to best advance its national goals.

Japan's response to regional security challenges: Japan's normalization agenda

Viewed broadly, Japan's armoury of foreign and security instruments for dealing with East Asian security challenges had grown considerably since the late 1990s and has been reinforced by increased willingness on the part of the country's leaders, both politicians and government officials, to confront these challenges directly. New policy-making flexibility has also been bolstered by evidence that Japanese public opinion is increasingly less fettered by the normative constraints that discouraged past administrations from responding proactively to security risks. (On the influence of domestic issues and public opinion see also Chapter 3 by Paul Midford in this volume.) The clearest expression of this is the continuing debate over constitutional reform and the suggestion that public opinion, across the political spectrum, is willing to see a relaxation or at the very least a redefinition of Article 9, the peace clause of the Constitution.[12] The impetus behind both this change in attitudes and in actual policies has arguably not been limited to the emergence of new, or more pronounced regional threats to Japan (whether a nuclear North Korea or the emergence of a more regional assertive China); it has also been grounded – at least at the elite level – in a strong desire to provide a corrective to the legacy of the first Gulf War of 1990–91, a psychologically bruising experience when the Japanese establishment, despite providing considerable amounts of financial support to the Allied campaign (some USD 13 billion in total), was widely criticized internationally for being a half-hearted and dilatory supporter of the war.[13]

Japan's forthright support for the post-9/11 global response to international terrorism – and particularly for the American-led invasion of Iraq – stands in marked contrast to the first Gulf War and has materially enhanced the speed of Japan's security policy normalization. The first signs of this came in October 2001 with the passage of Japan's Anti-Terrorism Special Measures Law, followed in November 2001 by the despatch of Japan Self Defense Forces (SDF) to the Indian Ocean to provide logistical support for Operation Enduring Freedom (OEF) in Afghanistan, and reinforced in 2002 by the sending of some 500 Ground SDF (GSDF) to Iraq in support of reconstruction efforts in the region – the first time in the post-1945 period that Japan's peacekeeping forces have been deployed to an active combat zone.[14] Significantly, although Japanese public opinion was initially ambivalent about the merits of such action, over time this ambivalence appears to have been replaced by general, albeit cautious, support for this more active role for Japan. Illustrative of this shift in attitudes was the election to the Japanese Diet in 2007 of Colonel Masahisa Sato, the commander of the first GSDF deployment to Iraq, an unexpected outcome, given the country's long-standing sceptical attitude towards the uniformed military in positions of political power.[15]

Part of the success in pushing this more active role for Japan's SDF and for the rapid passage of enabling legislation can be laid at the door of former Prime Minister Junichiro Koizumi. Echoing the approach in the 1980s of Prime Minister Yasuhiro Nakasone, another similarly proactive Japanese premier committed to strong alliance relations with the United States, Koizumi moved swiftly and boldly early on in his tenure to underline symbolically and substantively Japanese support for the United States. At the time, such action was not without significant political risk, but it appears, with hindsight, to have been, at the very least, consistent with a new, more flexible public attitude and may also have played a role in persuading public opinion more generally of the merits of adopting a more proactive posture.[16]

Change in Japanese security policy should not be couched only in personal terms or exclusively in terms of the situation in the Middle East. Alongside the importance of individual leadership has been the steady institutional evolution of Japanese security policy, beginning with the passage of the National Defense Programme Guidelines of 2004, representing a major overhaul of Japan's security doctrine and a focused effort to harmonize Japanese security policy with America's Global Force Posture Review.[17] The distinctive elements of this new doctrine have been the stress on the more flexible use of an increasingly more mobile Japanese military, a reduced focus on the risk of a direct attack on Japanese territory, and greater emphasis on measures to deal with regional and particularly global security challenges.

The clearest expression of the enhanced security partnership with the United States has been the May 2006 United States–Japan Roadmap for Realignment Implementation. As part of this and related initiatives, plans have been set in train for the redeployment of some 8,000 US Marines from Okinawa to Guam, the promotion of enhanced command and control facilities between the American and Japanese militaries, the development of a joint operations doctrine, the creation of a Japanese integrated Joint Staff Office, and the passage of vital domestic legislation enhancing the Japanese Prime Minister's crisis management capabilities. In addition, there has also been a gradual easing of the long-standing restrictions limiting Japan's ability to participate in collective security initiatives. Although the prohibition on Japanese involvement in collective security activities is an interpretative norm (dating from a decision by the government's Cabinet Legislation Office in the late 1950s) rather than a formal, codified constitutional constraint, the restriction has long been a central feature of Japan's cautious approach to security policy. Its partial relaxation, as exemplified by Japanese support for and involvement in activities such as the Proliferation Security Initiative (PSI)[18] – the multilateral effort to limit North Korean access to WMD technology, or Japan's substantially expanded joint development and testing of missile defence technology with the United States and the related easing of restrictions on the overseas export of dual-use weapons technology – signals a more pragmatic and less doctrinaire approach to security policy by the Japanese government.[19]

Emblematic of the desire by Japan's leaders to broaden their foreign and security policy-making options has been the agreement with Australia in March 2007 to establish a new bilateral security partnership and the upgrading of Japan's Defense Agency to a fully fledged ministry in December 2007. This was the culmination of a series of reforms signalling powerfully and unmistakably the movement of security issues to the centre-stage of policy making in contemporary Japan.

These important institutional and attitudinal changes in Japan have had a number of important policy implications. In terms of the general deployment and use of its military forces, Japan gradually became better placed to adopt a more high-profile role as part of the Bush administration's efforts to develop regional and global 'coalitions of the willing', with Japan's Self Defense Forces bolstering the defensive component of the alliance's 'sword and shield' strategy in East Asia.[20] Japan is also arguably now an enhanced, and more valuable, partner in the worldwide 'War on Terror', providing to a globally stretched United States increasing economically valuable host-nation support, as well as logistical and technical assistance. While the rhetorical branding of the United States' global security stance will change under the Obama administration, embracing a less Manichaean, dualistic, all-or-nothing, 'with us or against us' approach, the United States will, if anything, place greater reliance on its Alliance partnerships in the future, and Japan's importance is certain to be undiminished following the shift of political power from the Republicans to the Democrats in Washington.

In general peacekeeping initiatives, an area where the SDF has in the past concentrated much of its energies, Japan's military is also undergoing important changes. The experience of deployment to Iraq is arguably quite different from earlier UN-supporting activities, such as those in Cambodia, Kosovo or Rwanda, where Japan's Self Defense Forces have been involved in the past. (For details on earlier UN-supporting activities see Chapter 7 by Norbert Palanovics.) In Iraq, for the first time, Japanese troops were allowed to carry heavy weapons, and gained valuable experience from their training and coordination with the Dutch, Australian and British forces deployed in southern Iraq.[21] The Iraq experience has also required more sophisticated and imaginative coordination between different branches of the Japanese bureaucracy, with the Japanese Foreign Ministry managing the provision of financial assistance that enabled the Japanese deployment to the region and Japan's GSDF taking charge over the distribution of vital humanitarian aid and logistical support. Successful efforts to liaise with local communities (in part the result of effective Arabic-language training for Japanese forces) has helped to demonstrate to Japanese public opinion back home the value added by Japanese forces. This, together with the absence of any major Japanese casualties in Iraq, and comparable peacekeeping successes for Japan's forces in dealing with ethnic unrest in East Timor in 2002, or in coping with the post-Tsunami humanitarian tragedy in South East Asia, have helped to reinforce the impression that Japan's military can and should play a more active and regularized role in addressing a broad range of security challenges overseas. It is this growing realization which arguably explains reports in 2008 that the GSDF were considering the establishment of a 700 member rapid response regiment for deployment to deal with similar missions in the future.[22] The difficulty in realizing such a plan is that, for now at least, Japan lacks a permanent law that enables the SDF to be deployed overseas, other than under the umbrella of existing UN missions. (For more on these legal issues see Chapter 6 by Marie Söderberg.)

Since May of 2008, Prime Minister Fukuda talked publicly of the importance of drafting such legislation, but was unable to push through such initiatives in his brief one year tenure as premier. It remained unclear whether the governing

Liberal Democratic Party (LDP) had enough political strength at home to introduce and pass such important provisions. Fukuda's successor, Prime Minister Aso, was able on 12 December 2008 to enact a one-year extension of the SDF's refuelling mission in the Indian Ocean. With the Democratic Party of Japan (DPJ) now in power after a landslide victory in August 2009, it is unclear if the new Prime Minister and his government will prolong the one-year extension and continue the refuelling mission.[23] Similarly, the Aso government issued instructions in late January 2009 authorizing the despatch of two Maritime Self Defense Force (MSDF) destroyers to assist in an anti-piracy mission off the coast of Somalia. However, the basis for this action remains highly qualified, allowing the MSDF ships, under the terms of the Self Defense Forces Law, to use their weapons only in self-defence when fired upon and exclusively for the protection of Japanese or Japanese-related ships. The legislation is ad hoc, rather than permanent, and there are significant ambiguities surrounding the operational role of Japan's forces in confronting Somali pirates attempting to board commercial vessels.[24] Absent new, clear permanent legislation, the issue is sure to be a point of major political disagreement between the LDP and its DPJ opposition rival, highlighting in the process the difficulties faced by the government in meeting this increasingly important challenge to its commercial and security interests.

Bilateral options for addressing regional security challenges

An enhanced US–Japan security partnership

In many respects the old adage, popularized by former Senator Mike Mansfield, that the US–Japan relationship is 'America's most important relationship bar none' still holds true. To policy makers on both sides of the Pacific, the alliance is central to the respective foreign policies of the two countries. Japanese public opinion remains broadly supportive of the partnership with the United States, a position that has remained essentially unchanged for over half a century now. With some 53,000 US troops stationed in Japan, the United States remains the lynchpin of Japan's regional security strategy.[25] The 2006 Roadmap has laid out the direction for the enhancement of the military partnership, while Fukuda's November 2007 visit to Washington, DC (the Prime Minister's first overseas trip) was, by all accounts, a success.[26] President Bush provided rhetorical support for Japan's campaign to secure from the DPRK an account of the fate and whereabouts of its abducted citizens; the United States and Japan both agreed on the importance of enhancing deterrence via the US–Japan security partnership; and Prime Minister Fukuda stressed the importance of expanding bilateral student exchanges.[27] More recently, Prime Minister Aso was the first foreign leader to meet with President Obama on 24 February 2009 in Washington. Obama went out of his way to thank the Japanese premier for Japanese contributions in Afghanistan, while avoiding any suggestion that the United States was attempting to pressure or cajole Japan to make additional contributions to US security interests. Similarly, Secretary of State Hillary Clinton in her visit to Japan in February 2009 went out of her way to underscore the importance of the US–Japan alliance as the 'cornerstone' of US security policy in the region, reinforcing unambiguously the US commitment to a strong and mutually beneficial Alliance partnership.

In general the two countries have steadily enhanced their bilateral security cooperation in a range of areas, including missile defence (not only in terms of joint development, but also more recently in the testing of new technology), and via Tokyo's hosting in October 2007 of the Pacific Shield exercises, a multinational initiative that forms part of the PSI's maritime interdiction efforts, involving Australia, France, New Zealand, Singapore, the United Kingdom and the United States, and of course Japan.[28] Even areas where there would once have been potentially considerable scope for bilateral friction, most notably over trade, are now remarkably trouble free and both countries participate in a regular US–Japan sub-Cabinet Economic Dialogue distinctly free of tension. Some of this can be attributed to the relative easing of friction between the two in bilateral trade and foreign direct investment. Japan was fourth in size (behind Canada, Mexico and China) as a merchandise export market for the United States, as well as the fourth largest source of US merchandise imports.[29] Increasingly, the US Congress has focused on the economic challenge from China, while reliance on the World Trade Organization (WTO) process as a means of resolving trade disputes has helped to depoliticize many bilateral trade tensions between Tokyo and Washington.[30] This is not to say that occasional issues are not important, for example over US beef exports to Japan, but it is clear that security issues have taken precedence over economic concerns in defining the tenor and character of the bilateral relationship.

Despite these important elements of cooperation, it would be wrong to assume that the relationship is uncomplicated or not prone to periodic stresses and strains. Senior Japanese Foreign Ministry officials directly involved in negotiating with the DPRK worry that the United States may have recently been backpedalling on its support for the Japanese position on abductions. In its eagerness to sustain the momentum of the Six Party Talks and North Korea's denuclearization, Washington in October 2008 dramatically lifted its designation of the DPRK as a state sponsor of terror. Such a shift is necessary if the North is to qualify for international financial assistance – one of a number of critical incentives to ensure compliance by the North with the terms of the February 2007 denuclearization agreement. Removing the terror label has, invariably, weakened Japan's negotiating position with the DPRK in seeking resolution of the abductee issue, and public statements by the US ambassador to South Korea in 2008 suggested, troublingly for Japan, that Washington no longer views a solution of the abductee question as essential for a removal of the state sponsor designation.[31] There is little doubt that senior Japanese officials, including both the Foreign Minister, Hirofumi Nakasone, and Prime Minister Taro Aso himself were sharply opposed to the US decision and it is likely to have irritated many in Tokyo.[32] Aso reportedly was informed of the US decision to delist the DPRK as a state sponsor of terror a mere thirty minutes before the decision took effect, prima facie evidence of a worrying lack of prior consultation between these two key allies.[33]

There are other aspects to the bilateral relationship where the potential for future conflict should not be overlooked. The Okinawa-to-Guam redeployment plan for 8,000 marines and their dependants is likely to prove very costly, some USD 26 billion altogether to cover the four-year period from 2008 to 2012. When set alongside Japan's annual defence budget of some USD 45 billion, it is easy to see why this major economic burden is raising concerns on the part of Japanese defence planners about a possible hollowing out of the SDF's military effectiveness and fears that the Japanese military's ability to perform its newly expanded role and missions function may end up being fatally compromised.[34]

Bilateral security collaboration with the United States remains a core element of the alliance, but one which is sometimes cast into relief most vividly when it is qualified or undermined rather than when it is maintained and enhanced. A number of developments have revealed some of the limits to this collaboration: Washington's failure to approve the export of F-22 Raptor fighter planes to Japan in 2007[35] rankled with a Japanese defence community that saw the decision as reflecting the limits of trust in the bilateral relationship; enhancement of operational coordination in the field of missile defence was undermined in late 2007 following damaging revelations of the leak by a Japanese MSDF official of classified secret data on the US Aegis missile defence system;[36] and in March 2008 the suspected rape of a fourteen-year-old Japanese girl in Okinawa by a US Marine once again exposed the perennial tensions associated with the large US military personnel presence in Japan.[37] On top of this are the domestic political tensions associated with the reallocation as part of the new 2006 Roadmap of base facilities within the four principal islands of Japan, particularly the establishment of new facilities at Iwakuni, in Yamaguchi prefecture, a decision that has sparked strong resistance from the local populace.

Diplomatically, Japanese officials have arguably good reason to question the willingness of the United States to expend all of its political capital in supporting Japan's initiatives. While the Bush administration remained, for example, publicly supportive of Tokyo's desire to secure a permanent seat on the UN Security Council, American support has been restricted to the notion of Japanese representation and has not been extended to the more ambitious G4 initiative backed by Tokyo to see Japan, Germany, India and Brazil simultaneously added to the Security Council. More generally, Japanese decision makers, inclined to view Republican administrations in the United States as instinctively more sympathetic to Japan than their Democrat rivals, worry (perhaps unduly) about the consequences of a Democrat Obama administration and the risk that this will lead to a resurgence in protectionist sentiment in Washington harmful to Japan's economic interests. None of the above factors constitutes fundamental a weakness in the bilateral relationship, but they do expose significant strains in the relationship and highlight the obstacles that the two countries face in working together to address present and future security challenges in the East Asian region.

Reinvigorating Japanese–South Korean cooperation

The election in 2007–08 of two new leaders – Fukuda in Japan, and Lee Myung-bak in South Korea – opened the door to a significant improvement in bilateral ties between Seoul and Tokyo and has provided a much needed corrective (continued under Aso) to the tension that undermined relations during the period from 2002 to late 2006. Seen at face value, it is curious that past administrations in Japan and the Republic of Korea (ROK) have found it so difficult to cooperate. After all, given the shared alliance relationship that both countries enjoy with the United States, and the common threat posed by the DPRK, it would be rationally in the interests of both governments to cooperate closely on regional security matters. However, rationality is not always the most powerful of factors in shaping international behaviour and in the case of the Japan–Korea relationship, historical tensions, the long shadow cast by the colonial and wartime period and a deep sense of grievance and resentment on the part of many Koreans towards Japan have limited the scope for effective cooperation.[38]

During the tenure of Lee's predecessor, President Roh Moo-hyun, relations with Japan were especially fraught, shaped in part by Roh's apparent personal dislike of Koizumi, the fallout from the Prime Minister's visits to the Yasukuni shrine and periodic tension over the status of Takeshima/Tokto, fuelled on the Japanese side not so much by national decision makers but rather by local politicians in Japan's western Shimane prefecture. Roh's election as President in 2002 also represented an important generational break from the past and the rise to prominence of younger politicians, who became known in the 1990s as the so-called 386 constituency: individuals in their thirties, educated at university in the 1980s and born in the 1960s. New to government, this group included many former radicalized, progressive politicians, predisposed to be hostile to Japan. The departure from the South Korean political scene of individuals with long-held and closely cultivated ties with senior figures in Japanese politics signalled an important break from the past and helps to explain the difficulty that both governments faced in managing the bilateral relationship. Roh's difficulties with Japan were also an indirect consequence of the President's attempt to promote a more open style of government in the ROK, an initiative that has prompted the declassification of a number of ROK archival records, some of it relating to controversial and critical events in the post-war relationship between the two countries. These included the normalization of diplomatic ties between the two countries in 1965, the abduction from Tokyo in 1973 of the then opposition politician Kim Dae-jung by the Korean Central Intelligence Agency (KCIA) and the attempted assassination of President Park Chung-hee by a Japanese-resident Korean national in 1974.[39]

Under Fukuda there was a welcome and concerted effort to improve ties between the two countries. The Prime Minister was one of the first foreign leaders to meet with Lee, following the President's official inauguration on 25 February, and the Japanese side took the unusual step of inviting the ROK to participate as an observer in the G8 Summit meeting in Hokkaido in July 2008.

Lee, for his part, has struck a notably pragmatic tone, stressing the importance of a 'future-oriented relationship' and deliberately downplaying past historical controversies. In this, Lee is helped by his personal ties with Japan (he was born in Osaka in 1941) and by the restoration of some of the personal 'pipes' that in the past kept the decision-making elites in both countries closely connected with one another. For example, the ROK Foreign Minister, Yu Myung-hwan, was, until very recently, ambassador to Japan.

The new, more positive mood in the bilateral relationship has already begun to produce important early signs of progress. Talks – stalled since 2004 – have reopened on a possible Economic Partnership Agreement or Free Trade Agreement (FTA) between the two countries; there are plans in the security sphere to reactivate the Trilateral Coordination and Oversight Group (TCOG), bringing together mid-level defence officials from Japan, South Korea and the United States; and there is even ambitious discussion in some quarters of the possibility of building a new 200 km underwater tunnel to link the countries together.[40]

One should not minimize the potential hurdles that the relationship may encounter. Japan is the ROK's second largest trading partner after China, and enjoys a USD 21 billion trade surplus with South Korea.[41] Although business interests in both countries are strongly supportive of a bilateral FTA, South Korean agricultural interests are far more sceptical and worry that they will be the net losers in any future agreement, given the strong resistance to agricultural trade liberalization in Japan.

Moreover, President Lee, a former business executive, is likely to be an aggressive, results-oriented negotiator with Japan at least in the trade context. Given his early ambitious '747 pledge' to promote 7 per cent growth in the ROK economy, to raise the country's per capita income to USD 40,000 within the decade, and a commitment to boost South Korea to the No. 7 slot in the global economy, the President will doubtless be little inclined to give much, if any ground, in trade talks with Japan.[42] In the security context, officials in both Tokyo and Seoul will have to take pains to ensure that their strengthening relationship and their enhanced trilateral coordination with Washington will not be perceived by the Chinese government as an indirect effort to realign against Beijing or to foster a 'containment-lite' form of minilateralism to constrain Chinese influence in the region. This will be a particularly sensitive issue if the ROK chooses, as has been suggested, to promote its own missile defence programme as a way of offsetting the ballistic missile challenge from North Korea or if it chooses to join the PSI. Managing regional expectations and perceptions will, therefore, be a critically important part of any enhanced Japan–ROK security dialogue.

The Aso government has moved a significant way to diffusing fears of a new regional attempt to constrain China. On 13 December, Japan played host to the Chinese, South Korean and Japanese premiers meeting for a historic trilateral summit in Dazaifu, Fukuoka. Such trilateral get togethers are not unprecedented and have typically taken place on the margins of the regular annual ASEAN summit. This one-day gathering was significant since it took place outside the

ASEAN context, suggesting the beginning of a new self-sufficient and potentially more ambitious agenda. While it would be a mistake to exaggerate the significance of this meeting, the willingness of the Japanese and Chinese leaders to approve currency credits for South Korea, talk of a potential new set of regional currency swap agreements, a possible long-term trilateral free-trade agreement, and the issuing of an 'Action Plan for Promoting Trilateral Cooperation' in a broad range of areas, including environmental protection and human exchanges, all bode well for the future.[43]

Sino-Japanese elite-level pragmatism

High on the list of regional security anxieties for Japan's defence planners is the growing Chinese military presence in East Asia. Steady increases in China's official defence budget, averaging approximately 17 per cent growth per annum, China's sizable missile force of some 806 strategic intercontinental, intermediate and short-range ballistic missiles[44] and repeat incursions by Chinese submarines and surface vessels into Japanese territorial waters on spurious 'research visits' all add up to a real and present potential threat to Japanese security interests. Relations since the late 1990s have been complicated by volatile public opinion in both countries, but especially among a Chinese public – most notably among young Chinese in their twenties and thirties – exercised by Japanese revisionist historical accounts which reinforce the impression that Japan has not fully apologized for the excesses of the 1930s.[45] For their part, the Japanese media frequently contribute to and reinforce the emotionalism that threatens to destabilize the bilateral relationship, depicting China's economic growth trajectory in inevitable zero-sum terms and arguing (in a manner reminiscent of the alarmist accounts that dominated US–Japan economic relations in the 1980s) that China will eventually and ineluctably overtake Japan as the leading economic power in the region.

Since the stresses and strains of the Koizumi years the bilateral relationship has improved, especially at the elite level. Politicians from both the LDP and the now governing DPJ have visited Beijing on a number of occasions. Prime Minister Wen Jiabao's visit to Tokyo in the spring of 2007 was notably uncontroversial and laid the foundation for an equally successful and positive visit by Prime Minister Fukuda to China in December 2007. Fukuda was warmly received by his Chinese hosts and was given the opportunity to make a live televized address at Beijing University, only the second foreign visitor to be afforded such a privilege. (The first was President Bush in 2005.) Strikingly, the Prime Minister used the occasion in part to talk diplomatically and constructively about the past, stressing unusually for a Japanese leader the importance of Japan demonstrating the 'courage and wisdom to repent what we must repent'.[46] The two countries' leaders also used the summit to explore joint initiatives to promote climate change and measures to enhance bilateral ties by promoting student exchanges and by continuing the work of an established joint history textbook commission. Both governments also went out of their way to emphasize their shared Asian cultural heritage. Fukuda visited Confucius's birthplace during his December visit and in May 2008, during President Hu Jintao's visit to Japan, the Chinese leader visited Nara, Japan's eighth-century capital.

Capitalizing on the successes of Fukuda's China diplomacy, on 24 October Prime Minister Aso met with both President Hu and Premier Wen, on the fringes of the Asia–Europe Meeting (ASEM) in Beijing. Aso was at pains to point out the indispensable nature of the Sino-Japanese relationship, Japan's commitment to reflecting on the past, while also building a future-focused relationship.[47] It would be going too far to present such meetings as a grand rapprochement between two former adversaries but it is encouraging, even in this tentative form, to see historical issues addressed from a long-term perspective that looks beyond the more immediate tensions of the early twentieth century.

On security matters, the language and atmospherics between senior Japanese and Chinese officials has been broadly positive. Cui Tiankai, China's ambassador to Japan, has talked encouragingly of a strategic reciprocal relationship between the two countries,[48] and in November 2007 the first port visit to Japan by a People's Liberation Army (PLA) warship took place. China's leadership has spoken positively about the possibility of encouraging trilateral cooperation between China, South Korea and Japan, and with China showing increasing concern at the slow pace of progress in the Six Party Talks with the DPRK,[49] Japan's leaders may increasingly look to Beijing to find support for dealing with North Korea (in the words of former Prime Minister Fukuda) in a 'comprehensive manner'.

President Hu's May visit to Japan was striking in its clear avoidance of contentious historical issues (a far cry from the controversial visit to Tokyo by Jiang Zemin in 1998), for its forward-looking emphasis and for the general progress on a range of issues including food security, climate change, the importance of instituting regular bilateral summits, expanded dialogue on human rights and measures to promote equal access for Japanese and Chinese firms to oil and natural gas reserves close to the Senkaku Islands in the East China Sea. Yet, despite these important markers of progress, the prospects for enhanced Sino-Japanese dialogue and possible cooperation on security matters are still modest and should not obscure some of the fundamental issues that could still derail bilateral relations. While the two countries have inched forward towards a compromise on joint energy exploration rights in the East China Sea, the fundamental sovereignty dispute over the Senkakus remains unresolved.[50] Sightings of Chinese military vessels close to Japanese waters near Aomori prefecture in October 2008, and a more unambiguous incursion into Japanese waters near the Senkakus in December 2008, have raised bilateral tensions. Similarly, suggestions that China will commence plans in 2009 to build two large aircraft carriers by 2015 have intensified Japanese worries that Chinese maritime expansion will inevitably conflict with Japan's regional security interests.[51] Trade and investment relations remain important to the business communities in both countries, but, as the dispute over the import to Japan of insecticide-contaminated Chinese dumplings reveals, bilateral economic relations can easily be blown off course by economic controversies.[52]

Moreover, one should not underestimate the role of unexpected events as a source of instability in the relationship. A controversial essay by the Air Self Defense Forces (ASDF) chief of staff, Toshio Tamogami, in late October 2008, denying that Japan had acted as an aggressor nation in China during the 1930s and suggesting instead that Japan had been ensnared into its involvement both in China and in the Pacific War by foreign powers, prompted official protests from the Chinese government and led to Tamogami's forced resignation.[53] Such frictions have the potential, when set against a climate of public opinion in Japan that is broadly unsympathetic to China (some 66.6 per cent of the Japanese public claimed in a December opinion poll to have no affinity towards China),[54] to derail a volatile and often uncertain bilateral relationship.

Finally, looming unpredictably in the background is the ever present uncertainty associated with Taiwan. Ma Ying-jeo's victory in Taiwan's March 2008 presidential elections has helped to dampen tensions with China, since the new Guomindang President is seen as more pragmatically inclined than his predecessor.[55] However, a future political standoff between the mainland and island, were it to spill over into military action, could easily lead to a wider regional conflict involving the United States and Japan. Since February 2005, when the Japanese and US governments jointly and unusually called formally for a peaceful resolution of cross-straits tensions, China's government viewed with some apprehension the signs of closer coordination between Tokyo and Washington on Taiwanese issues. There have been suggestions, unconfirmed, that the closer strategic partnership between the United States and Japan has involved the drafting of joint contingency plans as well as joint training to address a future conflict over Taiwan. However unlikely such a conflict may be in the immediate future, the possible existence of such plans is evidence that the region's key strategic actors continue to view one another with guarded scepticism.

Seeking a thaw with Russia

Along with the still polarized and antagonistic Japan–North Korea relationship, Russo-Japanese ties remain one of the few unresolved legacies of the Pacific War and the Cold War. Russia, given its involvement in the Six Party Talks, can, in theory, serve as an important interlocuter for the Japanese government, potentially intervening to exert greater indirect leverage on the DPRK to be more forthcoming over the abductions issue. Similarly, Russia's substantial oil and natural gas reserves in eastern Siberia are a potentially rich source of energy to which Japanese officials and businessmen are eager to gain access. For now, however, despite a visit by then Prime Minister Fukuda to Russia in late April 2008, the bilateral relationship remains frustratingly underdeveloped.

While both leaders gave rhetorical support during their April summit to the notion of cooperation to secure progress in the Six Party Talks, it remains unclear how much Moscow is willing or able to extract from Pyongyang. On energy policy, the Japan Oil Gas & Metals National Corporation and Russia's private Irkutsk Oil Company have agreed to a joint natural gas exploration project in eastern Siberia, but a pipeline deal between Japan and Russia remains still unresolved and it remains in Moscow's interest to continue to play China and Japan, its two principal oil pipeline suitors, off against one another.[56] Most critically of all, Tokyo and Moscow remain at loggerheads over the status of the four Northern Territories to the north of Hokkaido, islands that Japan claims as its own but which have remained in Russian hands since the closing stages of the Pacific War in August 1945.

In the absence of a breakthrough on the territorial issue, full normalization of relations with Russia remains at best a distant prospect and the two sides have had to confine themselves to piecemeal modest improvements in their bilateral relationship. Such improvements have included a commitment to increase bilateral student exchanges, a willingness by Japanese banks, such as Bank of Tokyo-Mitsubishi UFJ and Sumitomo Mitsui Banking Corporation, to increase their exposure and presence in Russia, and efforts by some Japanese local governments to explore options for new combined sea and rail-based freight and auto transport arrangements between northern Japan and Russia.[57]

Multilateral initiatives

Interlocking alliances

Working on the assumption that cooperation between allies can deliver an outcome that is more than the sum of its individual parts, Japan might be tempted to look beyond its existing bilateral partnerships and embrace new, more flexible arrangements in addressing contemporary security challenges in East Asia. Already, with the July 2008 agreement to establish a security partnership with Australia, the Japanese government has been moving in such a direction. Similarly, under Prime Minister Abe's leadership, Japan began to give greater weight to its economic and security relationship with India. During the period 2006 to 2008, for example, a succession of Japanese SDF chiefs visited Delhi for discussions with their Indian counterparts, and in December 2006 Prime Minister Manmohan Singh visited Tokyo.[58] In light of the Bush administration's attempts since 2002 to radically redefine its relationship with India, by crafting a 'strategic partnership' that includes a landmark July 2007 peaceful nuclear cooperation agreement (the so-called '123' Accord) effectively endorsing India's status as a nuclear weapons state,[59] it is understandable why Japan should have felt comfortable with a closer partnership with India.[60] It simply reflects a new regional strategic reality, in which India is increasingly courted by a number of key powers as part of a precautionary anti-China hedging strategy. Indeed, during the Abe administration there were suggestions that it might be possible to establish a new quadrilateral security structure in East Asia, embracing the defence capabilities of Japan, India, Australia and the United States.

Yet there are real limits to the pursuit of such an agenda. Former Prime Minister Aso served as Abe's Foreign Minister, and in that capacity talked in November 2006 of the merits of promoting an 'arc of freedom and prosperity' in the region,[61] an approach that resonated with the values-based diplomacy favoured by some neo-conservative advocates in the Bush administration. Such an approach risks creating an open-ended commitment that can easily spill over into an interventionist and confrontational approach to authoritarian states in the region, whether Burma, North Korea or China itself. Indeed, in the latter case, some worry that the values-based approach will accelerate an alignment of states around two competing post-Cold War axes, China, Russia and the Central Asian republics gravitating around the existing structure of the Shanghai Cooperation Organization (SCO) and liberal democratic states such as Japan, South Korea and the United States reacting by fostering the development of a new NATO-like collective security structure in Asia.[62] Although the Six Party Talks may constitute the basis for such a new embryonic regional security forum, East Asia is still some distance away from the solidification of such new structures. Moreover, other key regional players, most notably Australia under the leadership of a new Mandarin-speaking Prime Minister, Kevin Rudd, are anxious to avoid stoking Chinese fears of growing encirclement by the United States and other states.[63] Partly because of this pragmatic Australian caution, the values-based agenda appears to have been shelved for the time being, and Aso's arc of freedom concept was quietly dropped from the Japanese Foreign Ministry's annual foreign policy Blue Book.

Institutionalizing international responses to regional insecurity

A perhaps safer, less problematic approach for Japan in minimizing the threats to its own security is to strive to promote and support existing international bodies. Arguably, the Japanese government has done especially well in this regard, particularly in the context of the United Nations, where Japanese behind-the-scenes activity was instrumental in allowing the passage of two key UN Security Council Resolutions – UN 1695 and UN 1718 – designed to express the international community's opposition (both rhetorically and substantively) to the DPRK's test detonation of a nuclear device in October 2006 and to the launch of its ballistic missiles into the East Sea in July of the same year.[64]

On 1 January 2009 Japan became a non-permanent member of the UN Security Council, a two-year position which it has held nine times in the past. Such a role gave the Aso government once again the opportunity to make the case for permanent membership, a formal status that would be commensurate with its contribution of some 20 per cent of the United Nations' operating budget. Effecting such a proposal will, however, be difficult, given the number of competing national candidates vying for membership, and Tokyo would almost certainly have to demonstrate major forms of international activism in peacekeeping or peace enforcement in order to win the support of some of its key allies (most notably the United States) in such a campaign.

Another promising arena where Japan might be expected to take a leading and active role is via the G8 Summits, which Japan chaired in 2008 under Fukuda's leadership. Fukuda had compelling personal and political reasons to emphasize the G8 approach. His father, Takeo Fukuda, narrowly missed the opportunity to host the 1979 G8 Summit, and Fukuda junior's desire to make the Hokkaido summit a success may in part have reflected his desire to compensate for his father's earlier disappointment. Here the most immediately clear context in which Japan can arguably make a difference is in promoting constructive environmental initiatives to address the threat of climate change – a non-traditional security challenge that affects not only East Asia but the planet as a whole.

From his speech to the Davos World Economic Forum in January 2008 it was clear that Fukuda placed the environmental agenda at the heart of his government's policy-making agenda.[65] Japan appeared and remains eager to broker a compromise between the United States and the European Union in devising a mechanism for a post-Kyoto deal on climate change. While Brussels favours a top-down system of individual country or EU-based unified standards for controlling pollution, together with a market-compliant system of emissions trading, Washington, at least under the Bush presidency, has been reluctant to endorse binding national targets. Tokyo, by contrast, has positioned itself roughly mid-way between these two positions and has attempted to square the difference between the United States and Europe by advocating an industry-specific, bottom-up approach. At the same time, the Japanese government still appears inclined to hold to a position that midterm targets will eventually be needed for individual countries in order to secure a global target of halving emissions by 2050, and in this regard appears to be tilting somewhat in the direction favoured by Europe.[66]

For Japan the key challenge in crafting an effective global environmental strategy is in setting specific targets and a time frame that all countries can agree on. Tokyo appears inclined to adopt 1990 as a base year for measuring emission reduction and has also been reluctant to adopt short-term targets either for itself or for other countries, a position which has been criticized by a number of pro-environmental non-governmental organizations (NGOs).[67] In addition, there are serious doubts about Japan's ability to meet its own Kyoto-sanctioned 6 per cent emissions reduction target by 2013 and the government appears internally divided, with the environment and trade Ministries in the past taking contrasting policy positions, respectively opposing and supporting the notion of binding, national targets.

For now, at least, the government can fall back on its willingness to stump up some of the cash needed to foster sound environmental policies. Japan agreed to provide USD 10 billion over five years to developing countries to reduce emissions. In addition, the government can bolster its position by pointing to the country's particular technological expertise, whether in developing solar and alternative energy sources or in managing better control of water resources. However, it is not enough for Japan to be viewed as simply a financier of worthy international activities. Ultimately the government will need to deliver an effective international agreement and here the political skills and acumen of the Aso government are likely to be strenuously tested. Given the difficulties that the Aso LDP administration has faced at home in securing political consensus and accommodation with its DPJ rival, it is doubtful whether it is well placed to promote agreement overseas.

Japan's G8 activism need not be limited to environmental initiatives. In the traditional security context, Japan can, in offering constructive solutions to current challenges, point to important past agreements, most notably the Global Partnership against the Spread of Weapons of Mass Destruction, first announced at the 2002 G8 Summit in Kananakis, Canada. As part of this initiative, Japan has already played an important role, not only helping to dismantle chemical weapon stockpiles in China but also by working to dismantle Soviet-era nuclear submarines as part of the 'Star of Hope' programme. Such initiatives are not only important in their own right, they are also valuable in broadening the scope of participating countries beyond the G8 itself.[68] This type of technical disarmament experience could be very usefully applied in the North Korean context, not only in drawing down the DPRK's nuclear weapons programme, but also in helping to retrain North Korean nuclear scientists.[69] The appeal of this type of denuclearization initiative is its marrying of Japanese technical expertise with the country's deep-seated aversion to nuclear weapons.

Conclusion

Adopting a pragmatic and ad hoc approach to solving regional security problems, opens up many areas in which Japan can play a constructive role. In late May 2008 Prime Minister Fukuda had suggested that Japan might take the lead in coordinating international disaster management cooperation through establishing a network of regional emergency relief organizations to cope with major disasters, whether natural or man-made. The Prime Minister's plans were preliminary in nature, but strikingly (and in a manner reminiscent of his father's approach) they appeared to envisage cooperation between Japan, China, South Korea and the ten member nations of the Association of South East Asian Nations (ASEAN).[70] The December 2008 trilateral meeting in Fukuoka between Aso, Lee Myung-bak and Wen Jiabao suggests there is real scope for further productive collaboration in such areas. Prime Minister Aso has sought also to bolster Japan's global contributions in a variety of areas – not only announcing in November 2008 a bridging loan of some USD100 billion to the International Monetary Fund (IMF) to combat the effects of the global economic downturn, but also importantly authorizing the despatch of two Maritime Self Defense Force vessels to help combat the challenge of piracy off the coast of Somalia.

Regionalism in East Asia is seemingly alive and well, albeit in an incomplete and underdeveloped format. There exist a number of Track I and Track II fora that might act as proto-institutions for wider and more focused regional cooperation (whether economic or security based) through such bodies as the ASEAN Regional Forum (ARF), the North East Asia Cooperation Dialogue (NEACD), the East Asian Community (EAC) and, most promisingly of all, notwithstanding recent difficulties, the Six Party Talks process associated with the North Korean nuclear issue.[71] Despite the gravity of the challenges facing East Asia, Japan appears well placed to capitalize on these positive opportunities, and its leaders might usefully begin to think of those conflicts or disagreements where it might play a mediating or facilitating role in helping to ameliorate tension.[72] Of course, there are many areas where Japan's experience to date could be improved on; most notably in fostering regional trade integration or in helping to design and promote a region-wide security architecture that might address a range of pressing security challenges. On the trade front, Japanese administrations (partly as a result of internal bureaucratic disagreements over the competing merits of bilateral versus multilateral trade agreements) have often found themselves outmanoeuvred by China.[73] Where grand security structures are concerned, South Korea, particularly in the past under President Roh, has frequently taken the lead, most notably in 2007 in calling for the application of the Helsinki process to the Asian context.[74]

Regrettably, the evidence to date does not suggest that Tokyo has yet to devise a distinctive approach, let alone an explicit strategy, for addressing these multiple security concerns. However, it is debatable whether a grand strategy is necessary or appropriate in addressing East Asia's regional challenges. Japan's foreign policy specialists and its political leadership have often been criticized for lacking vision, or for their failure or reluctance to approach such issues strategically. If strategy is defined as 'a plan of action or policy designed to achieve a major or overall aim', then it is clear from the above analysis that the Aso administration has a variety of plans for addressing a number of pressing security goals. The problem for the current Japanese government (and for some of its predecessors), as the analysis above has shown, is the intervention of domestic politics in a manner that distracts attention away from or in some instances actively undermines foreign policy, most notably in the case of Japan's North Korea policy. Moreover, with public opinion in Japan increasingly expressing disquiet and frustration with their political leadership (both government and opposition party leaders), the ability of figures such as Aso or Yukio Hatoyama, the head of the governing DPJ, to articulate a clear set of foreign policy priorities that are actively supported by the Japanese electorate may be very limited.

Tip O'Neill, the fifty-fifth Speaker of the US House of Representatives, famously said, 'All politics is local.' This adage remains persuasive, demonstrating the difficulty of devising international strategy in a political vacuum, and helping to explain the limitations that Japan faces in advancing its interests in East Asia. The domestic side of Japan's policy making is the focus of the next chapter.

Notes

1 For an authoritative Japanese account of the importance of 'middle powers' see Y. Soeya, *Nihon no midoru pawaa gaikō: sengo Nihon no sentaku to kōsō*, Tokyo: Chikuma Shinsho, 2005.

2 See, for example, T. Inoguchi, 'Japan's ambition for normal statehood' in J. I. Dominguez and B-K. Kim (eds) *Between Compliance and Conflict: East Asia, Latin America and the 'New' Pax Americana*, New York: Routledge, 2005, pp. 135–65. For further discussion in the present volume see the chapters by Midford and Hughes.

3 E. Chanlett-Avery and B. Vaughn, 'Emerging Trends in the Security Architecture in Asia: Bilateral and Multilateral Ties among the United States, Japan, Australia, and India', *CRS Report for Congress*, 7 January 2008, p. 7.

4 For a useful analysis of the new condominium of power between the Russian President and Prime Minister see S. D. Goldman, 'Russia's 2008 Presidential Succession', *CRS Report for Congress*, 26 February 2008, pp. 1–8.

5 For an extended discussion of Japan's recent approach to the nuclearization debate see M. Mochizuki, 'Japan tests the nuclear taboo', *Nonproliferation Review* 14 (2), July 2007; B. Glosserman, 'Japan peers into the abyss', *PacNet* 20, Pacific Forum CSIS, 20 March 2008, 1. Available on line at: www.csis.org/index.php?option=com_csis_pubs&task=view&id=4405 (accessed 23 November 2008).

6 For a sceptical reading of the DPRK–Syria nuclear connection see S. Hersch, 'A strike in the dark: why did Israel bomb Syria?', *New Yorker*, 11 February 2008. Available on line at: www.newyorker.com/reporting/2008/02/11/080211fa_fact_hersh (accessed 29 January 2009).

7 R. Cossa and B. Glosserman, 'From bad to worse', *Comparative Connections* 10 (4), January 2009, 4.

8 D. Lampton, 'A moment of opportunity in the Taiwan Strait?' in Asia Foundation, *America's Role in Asia: Asian and American Views*, San Francisco, CA: Asia Foundation, 2008, p. 197.

9 K. A. Kronstadt, 'India–US Relations', *CRS Report for Congress*, 19 December 2007, p. 51.

10 T. Dadabaev, 'Japan's Central Asian Diplomacy and its Implications', *Analyst*, Central Asia–Caucasus Institute, 9 June 2006. Available online at: www.cacianalyst.org/?q=node/4173 (accessed 1 February 2009).

11 Kronstadt, 'India–US Relations', p. 56.

12 Many writers point to a growing consensus in Japan in favour of constitutional revision and a relaxation of the long-standing prohibition of Japan's armed forces in collective security activities. See, for example, H. Okazaki, 'Time to resolve issue of collective self-defense', *Daily Yomiuri*, 26 January 2009, p. 9.

13 A. L. Oros, *Normalizing Japan: Politics, Identity and the Evolution of Security Practice*, Stanford, CA: Stanford University Press, 2008, pp. 86–7.

14 International Institute for Strategic Studies, *Strategic Survey, 2001/2002*, Oxford: Oxford University Press, 2002, p. 279.

15 M. J. Green, 'The Iraq War and Asia: assessing the legacy', *Washington Quarterly*, spring 2008, 183.

16 J. Swenson-Wright, 'The limits to normality: Japanese–Korean post-Cold War interactions' in D. Welch (ed.) *Japan as a Normal Nation*, Toronto: University of Toronto Press, 2009, p. 11.

17 The Global Posture Review (GPR) dates from 2004 and reflected the Bush administration's efforts to develop a more flexible military structure designed to respond to a variety of security contingencies worldwide. It represents a reconfiguring, rather than a drawing down, of US military assets worldwide, with a particular stress on flexibility and a more active use of America's strategic assets to go beyond the traditional structures associated with the Cold War conflict with the Soviet Union.

18 For more on this topic see M. J. Valencia, *The Proliferation Security Initiative: Making Waves in Asia*, Adelphi Papers 376, London: International Institute for Strategic Studies, 2005.

19 H. Kaneda, K. Kobayashi, H. Tajima and H. Tosaki, *Japan's Missile Defense: Diplomatic and Security Policies in a Changing Strategic Environment*, Tokyo: Japan Institute of International Affairs (JIIA), March 2007, pp. 53–70. Available on line at: www2.jiia.or.jp/en/pdf/polcy_report/pr200703-jmd.pdf (accessed 28 November 2008).

20 G. A. Rubinstein, 'U.S.–Japan Missile Defense Cooperation: Current Status, Future Prospects', 5 September 2007, p. 10. Available online at: www.japanconsidered.com/OccasionalPapers/Rubinstein%20USJA%20BMD%20article%20090507.pdf (accessed 3 December 2008).

21 D. Fouse, 'Japan's Dispatch of the Ground Self-defense Force to Iraq: Lessons Learned', Asia-Pacific Center for Security Studies, July 2007. Available on line at: www.apcss.org/Publications/Japan's%20Dispatch%20of%20the%20GSDF%20 to%20Iraq.Fouse.doc.pdf (accessed 7 June 2008).
22 'Jieitai kaigai haken "Heiwa kyōryoku kokka" o mezasu nara', *Yomiuri shimbun*, 15 April 2008, morning edition, p. 3.
23 M. J. Green and N. Szechenyi, 'Traversing a rough patch', *Comparative Connections* 10 (4), January 2009, 26.
24 'MSDF to receive orders for antipiracy mission', *Daily Yomiuri*, 28 January 2009, p. 1; 'Tough calls await on antipiracy use of weapons,' *Daily Yomiuri*, 30 January 2009, p. 3; 'MSDF set to escort commercial ships through pirate-infested gulf: government applies law meant for Japanese waters, plans to submit anti-piracy Bill to Diet', *Nikkei Weekly*, 2 February 2009, p. 5.
25 E. Chanlett-Avery, M. E. Manyin and W. H. Cooper, 'Japan–U.S. Relations: Issues for Congress', *CRS Report*, 27 September 2007, p. 1.
26 M. J. Green and N. Szechenyi, 'Distracted governments make some positive progress', *Comparative Connections* 9 (4), 2009, 19–20.
27 'Japan–US Summit Meeting (Summary)', 16 November 2007, www.us.emb-japan.go.jp/english/html/japanus/japanusSummit1116.htm (accessed 7 June 2008).
28 Proliferation Security Initiative (PSI) Maritime Interdiction Exercise 'Pacific Shield 07' hosted by Japan. See www.mofa.go.jp/announce/event/2007/9/1175444_856.html (accessed 7 June 2008).
29 E. Chanlett-Avery, W. H. Cooper and M. E. Manyin, 'Japan–U.S. Relations: Issues for Congress,' *CRS Report for Congress*, 30 December 2008, p. 12.
30 Ibid., p. 13.
31 One glimmer of hope for Japan's officials is the suggestion that Kim Hye-gyong – the daughter of one of Japan's most high-profile abductees, Megumi Yokota – may still be alive and might be returned to Japan by the DPRK as a means of resolving the stand-off on the abduction issue. Despite the absence of incontrovertible evidence, many writers, both in Japan and elsewhere, accept now that Yokota is unlikely to be still alive. See *The Nelson Report*, 27 May 2008, Washington, DC: Samuels International Associates.
32 Green and Szechenyi, 'Traversing a rough patch', p. 19.
33 D. Kang and J-Y. Lee, 'In a holding pattern with hope on the horizon', *Comparative Connections* 10 (4), January 2009, 122.
34 For a detailed study of US overseas military bases policy, including extensive consideration of the Japanese case, see K. Calder, *Embattled Garrisons: Comparative Base Politics and American Globalism*, Princeton, NJ: Princeton University Press, 2008.
35 'Potential F22 Raptor Export to Japan', *CRS Report for Congress*, RS22684, 2 July 2007.
36 'Japan finds leak in military security', *UPI Asia Online*, 18 December 2007, www.upiasiaonline.com/Security/2007/12/17/japan_finds_leaks_in_military_security/5198/ (accessed 7 June 2008).
37 'Return to the focus on mutual goals', *Japan Times*, 1 March 2008, p. 1.
38 J. Swenson-Wright, 'Assassination, abduction and normalisation: historical mythologies and misrepresentation in post-war South Korea–Japan relations' in R. Frank, J. Hoare, P. Kollner and S. Pares (eds) *Korea Yearbook*, Vol. II, *Politics, Economy and Society*, Leiden: Brill, 2009, pp. 96–8.
39 Ibid., pp. 98–9.
40 'Is Japan–ROK tunnel feasible?', *Daily Yomiuri*, 22 February 2008, p. 4.
41 D. Kang and J-Y. Lee, 'Lost in the six party talks', *Comparative Connections* 9 (4), 2009, 127.

42 'Japan–S. Korea ties hinge on economy: while Fukuda prioritizes improving relations, several barriers could keep neighbours apart', *Nikkei Weekly*, 3 March 2008, p. 3.
43 D. Kang and J-Y. Lee, 'Lost in the six party talks', p. 125.
44 International Institute for Strategic Studies, *The Military Balance*, London: Routledge, 2008, p. 376.
45 P. Hays Gries, *China's New Nationalism: Pride, Politics and Diplomacy*, Berkeley, CA: University of California Press, 2004, p. 53.
46 'Tai chūgoku, Fukuda gaikō: Shushō, Pekin dai de kōen, kako no sensō 'hansei subeki wa hansei', *Nihon keizai shimbun*, 29 December 2007, morning edition, p. 2.
47 J. J. Przystup, 'Gyoza, beans, and aircraft carriers', *Comparative Connections* 10 (4), January 2009, 113.
48 'Joint statement planned during Hu's visit', *Daily Yomiuri*, 13 March 2008, p. 3.
49 A report from the US Institute of Peace has suggested, for example, that the Chinese government has drafted contingency plans, in the event of the collapse of the North Korean regime, for a possible Chinese-led intervention into the DPRK, either with or without UN support, to restore internal stability and to offset the risks associated with a 'loose nukes' scenario. See B. Glaser, S. Snyder and J. S. Park, 'Keeping an eye on an unruly neighbour: Chinese views of economic reform and stability in North Korea', United States Institute of Peace, working paper, 3 January 2008.
50 K. Dumbaugh, 'China–U.S. Relations: Current Issues and Implications for U.S. Policy', *CRS Report for Congress*, 17 March 2008, p. 21.
51 Przystup, 'Gyoza, beans, and aircraft carriers', pp. 113–14.
52 China is the second largest supplier of food to Japan and accounts for more than 50 per cent of Japan's frozen food imports. 'Avoid hysteria over food', *Japan Times*, 11 February 2008, p. 1.
53 Przystup, 'Gyoza, beans, and aircraft carriers', p. 115.
54 Ibid., p. 111.
55 K. Dumbaugh, 'Taiwan's 2008 Presidential Election', *CRS Report for Congress*, 2 April 2008, p. 1.
56 'Fukuda, Putin agree to accelerate talks on isles', *Daily Yomiuri*, 27 April 2008, p. 1.
57 'Top banks build up in Russia', *Nikkei Weekly*, 17 March 2008, p. 12.
58 E. Chanlett-Avery and B. Vaughn, 'Emerging Trends in the Security Architecture in Asia: Bilateral and Multilateral Ties among the United States, Japan, Australia, and India', *CRS Report for Congress, RL 34312*, 7 January 2008, p. 10.
59 K. A. Kronstadt, 'India–U.S. Relations', *CRS Report for Congress*, 19 December 2007, p. 1.
60 The latest expression of this is the new, landmark Japan–India Joint Declaration on Security Cooperation, signed by Prime Minister Taro Aso and the Indian Premier Manmohan Singh on 22 October 2008. Looser in form and less ambitious than the parallel Japan–Australia Security Declaration, this agreement focuses on shared democratic values and embodies a common pledge to protect vulnerable sea lanes of communication in East Asia. See S. Gupta, 'Japan–India Joint Declaration on Security Cooperation: Groping towards an Asia-wide Security Architecture', *Policy Forum Online 08-085A*, Nautilus Institute, 4 November 2008. Available on line at www.nautilus.org/fora/security/08085Gupta.html.
61 Taro Aso, 'Arc of Freedom and Prosperity: Japan's Expanding Diplomatic Horizons', 30 November 2006, www.mofa.go.jp/announce/fm/aso/speech0611.html (accessed 7 June 2008). Aso a more extended discussion of this concept in Taro Aso, *Jiyū to hanei no ko*, Tokyo: Gentosha, 2007.
62 For two thoughtful analyses that are sceptical of the claim that the SCO will evolve into an anti-Western bloc see A. Iwashita, 'The Shanghai Cooperation Organization and Japan: Moving Together to Reshape the Eurasian Community', and M. N. Katz, 'The Shanghai Cooperation Organization: A View from the U.S.,' both available on line at: http://src-h.slav.hokudai.ac.jp/kaken/iwashita2007/contents-e.html (accessed 7

November 2008). See, also, R. Sutter, 'Durability in China's strategy toward Central Asia', *China and Eurasia Forum Quarterly* 6 (1), February 2008, 29–30.

63 Chanlett-Avery and Vaughn, 'Emerging trends in the security architecture in Asia', p. 16.

64 J. Swenson-Wright, 'The Role of the United Nations', conference presentation, *Fostering International Dialogue on Korean Security*, International Institute for Strategic Studies (IISS), London, 8–9 February 2007.

65 'Fukuda's speech prelude to G8 Summit', *Daily Yomiuri*, 28 January 2008, p. 2.

66 'Tough road ahead to achieve Fukuda's vision', *Daily Yomiuri*, 27 January 2008, p. 4; 'Fukuda to tell Davos of energy plans: "Japan to help boost world efficiency by 30 per cent",' *Daily Yomiuri*, 25 January 2008, p. 1.

67 R. Black, 'Japan vows future emissions cut', BBC News Website, 9 June 2008, http://news.bbc.co.uk/1/hi/sci/tech/7443833.stm (accessed 9 June 2008).

68 *Global Partnership Update* 10, January 2008, www.csis.org/component/option,com_csis_pubs/task,view/id,4331/.

69 Joel Wit of the Brookings Institution has proposed an imaginative set of policies that address this need, modelled in part on the success of the earlier Nunn–Lugar initiative to confront the weapons capabilities of the former Soviet Union. See J. S. Wit, 'Enhancing U.S. engagement with North Korea', *Washington Quarterly*, spring 2007, 53–68.

70 'PM calls for disaster relief network: Fukuda urges Asia-wide system to respond to large-scale emergencies, disease outbreaks', *Nikkei Weekly*, 26 May 2008.

71 S. Lee, 'Realities and Possibilities for a Peace System in Northeast Asia', Washington, DC: Center for Northeast Asian Policy Studies, Brookings Institution, 1 November 2007, pp. 12–14. Available on line at: www.brookings.edu/~/media/Files/rc/papers/2007/1101_northeast_asia_lee/1101_northeast_asia_lee.pdf (accessed 24 November 2008).

72 Japan's role in brokering the International Conference on Reconstruction Assistance to Afghanistan in January 2002 is one example of such a mediating and coordinating role. See 'Afghan rebuilding makes good start: success of Tokyo meeting in terms of cooperation bodes well for task ahead', *Nikkei Weekly*, 4 February 2002, p. 7. Similarly, Japan could also do more to use its overseas development assistance to meet a number of key regional security objectives, including in Afghanistan. 'Since 2001, Japan has offered Afghanistan a total of USD 1.38 billion in aid to help disarm former soldiers and militiamen, provide training and equipment for police officers and construct roads and schools. Japan's assistance is the second largest after that of the United States.' 'What Japan should do to assist Afghanistan', *Daily Yomiuri*, 18 May 2008, p. 4.

73 D. K. Nanto, 'East Asian Regional Architecture: New Economic and Security Arrangements and U.S. Policy', *CRS Report for Congress*, 4 January 2008, pp. 15–16.

74 K-T. Lee, 'Assessing the Roh Moo-Hyun Initiative for economic community building: constraints, opportunities, and prospects' in Jeju Peace Institute and East Asia Foundation, *Peace and Prosperity in Northeast Asia: Exploring the European Experience*, Vol. II, Seogwipo City: JPI Press, 2008, pp. 36–48.

3 Japan

Balancing between a hegemon and a would-be hegemon

Paul Midford

Pundits have often ridiculed Japan for having no strategy.[1] Nonetheless, Japan has long had a clear, if low-profile strategy. Generally dubbed the Yoshida Doctrine, this strategy consisted of containing the state's military potential within Article 9 of Japan's war-renouncing constitution and the US–Japan alliance, depending upon the United States for defence, maintaining a low military profile and reassuring its Asian neighbours that Tokyo would not again emerge as a threat.[2] Japan perceived a more autonomous and proactive security stance as more likely to provoke than deter potential threats. Behind these perceptions lay the devastating experience of the Pacific War that produced strong distrust of the state's ability to control and wisely wield the military, a distrust that in this chapter will henceforth be referred to as anti-militarist distrust of the state, or simply as anti-militarist distrust.[3]

The Yoshida Doctrine came under pressure in the second half of the 1990s as Japan came to perceive an increasing short-term threat from North Korea and a potential longer-term threat from a rising China. The accumulated weight of these growing threat perceptions along with domestic political reform and realignment set the stage for a significant shift in grand strategy by 2001. With Junichiro Koizumi's accession to the premiership Japan adopted a more proactive balancing strategy, a strategy that will be referred to in this chapter as the Koizumi Doctrine. The main characteristics of the Koizumi Doctrine were tighter alliance cooperation and integration with the United States, including overseas deployments in support of global US military operations, proactive responses to missile and small-scale territorial threats, combined with a deemphasizing of reassurance and a greater and more direct political assertion of Japan's national interests vis-à-vis Asian neighbours, and a push for 'normalizing' Japan's security institutions. This last point ultimately entailed reforming Article 9 of Japan's war-renouncing Constitution.

The fundamental outlines of the Koizumi Doctrine continued under his first successor, Shinzo Abe. Nonetheless, an accumulation of domestic and regional political challenges, culminating in the LDP's historic defeat in the July 2007 Upper House elections and Abe's subsequent resignation, has caused important aspects of the Koizumi Doctrine to collapse. Most important, Japan is now moving away from tightening its alliance with the United States, and especially from supporting US military operations overseas. In its wake we have seen a partial return to Yoshida Doctrine policies in some areas and a continuation of Koizumi Doctrine policies in a few areas. In particular, Japan appears to have returned to its previous emphasis on reassuring Asian states, starting with China, about its intentions. On the other hand, Japan continues to forge ahead with missile defence. Aspects of Japan's missile defence policy ironically involve Japan distancing itself further from the United States, such as the decision to permit the acquisition of military-quality spy satellites with missile detection capabilities, a development not welcomed by Washington. This step appears to signal a desire to have greater control over homeland defence and how to respond to threats from North Korea and China.

These changes in grand strategy appear to reflect a calculation that overseas missions in support of American forces risk entrapment in conflicts not in Japan's interest more than they act as insurance against abandonment by the United States. Overseas deployments that smack of involvement in military operations also face significant public opposition and may drain away resources better concentrated on homeland defence. Overall, the strategy emerging since late 2007 can best be described as defensive realist, with an emphasis on strengthening territorial defence and a retreat from overseas commitments. It is also a strategy that more closely resembles the Yoshida Doctrine than the Koizumi Doctrine.

Grand strategy during the Cold War and the post-Cold War decade

As briefly mentioned above, the Yoshida Doctrine is the name given to Japan's distinctive Cold War era strategy. The substantial literature on the Yoshida Doctrine tends to view the doctrine as a free-riding strategy designed to trade military dependence on the United States for gaining the opportunity to concentrate on promoting techno-economic development and power.[4] A second theme observers have emphasized is a desire to avoid entrapment in American overseas conflicts not seen as serving Japan's national interests.[5]

In this chapter I deemphasize the importance of free-riding and economics-first motivations, and agree with the importance of avoiding entrapment. However, I also emphasize another aspect not so prominent in the Yoshida Doctrine literature: the importance of reassuring neighbouring Asian nations of Japan's disposition as a military power, thereby avoiding counterbalancing by these nations, and especially by China. The Yoshida Doctrine consisted of three pillars that served to reassure China and other Asian countries.

First, the Yoshida Doctrine entailed Japan voluntarily accepting self-containment in the US–Japan security alliance (the so-called cap in the bottle), and the US-written 'peace constitution', two self-containment structures that are sometimes referred to in Japanese as a single structure known as 'Kyūjō-Anpo Taisei', or the 'Article 9 Security Treaty System'.[6] These containment structures were designed to prevent Japan's re-emergence as a military power and thus reassure neighbouring countries. The second pillar of the Yoshida Doctrine entailed Japan pursuing a military doctrine of defensive defence, or *senshū bōei*. In practice, this meant eschewing offensive weapons, power projection capabilities and nuclear weapons.

The third and final pillar of the Yoshida Doctrine was the promise to never again become a 'military power'. This pillar was not fully developed until Prime Minister Takeo Fukuda announced this promise in the so-called 'Fukuda Doctrine' of 1977. Essentially the diplomatic enunciation of the defensive defence military doctrine and the Fukuda Doctrine has meant a promise not to play a direct or unilateral military role in regional security, and not to obtain offensive or power projection capabilities.[7] To increase the credibility of this pledge, Japan abstained from virtually any form of direct security contact with its neighbours. Yet the end of the Cold War altered this aspect of the Fukuda Doctrine. While maintaining the Fukuda pledge to never again become a 'military power', Japan in the 1990s became willing for the first time to discuss security openly with its Asian neighbours. This was a major purpose of the 1991 Nakayama initiative, by which Japan proposed a regional multilateral security forum (initially through the ASEAN post-Ministerial Conference) to discuss, among other things, Asian apprehensions about the direction of Japan's security policy.[8] Japan subsequently promoted the ASEAN Regional Forum (ARF), regional Track II security dialogues, such as the Council on Security Cooperation in the Asia-Pacific (CSCAP) and the North East Asian Cooperative Security Dialogue (NEACD). Japan is also now promoting bilateral confidence-building security dialogues with most of its neighbours, including ASEAN, China, South Korea and Russia.[9]

This change to the Fukuda Doctrine was one of several adjustments made during the post-Cold War decade of the 1990s. The Yoshida Doctrine came under stress during this decade due to American pressure, especially intense during the first Gulf War, to provide more than financial burden sharing. After 1992, concern began to increase about China's rising economic and military power and indications that economic development was not producing a more liberal or friendly China.[10] Finally, growing perceptions of a North Korean threat also served to create pressure for changing the Yoshida Doctrine.

One change in the Yoshida Doctrine that resulted from these pressures is what I will call 'expanded self-containment', and involved expanding Japan's military role within the framework of the familiar US–Japan alliance and within a new containment structure: UN peacekeeping operations. The decision to use the United Nations as a new containment framework for channelling Japan's first overseas deployments of its military since the end of World War II complemented the new focus on regional security multilateralism, especially the promotion of the ARF. What is striking about all of the changes made in the 1990s is their extremely modest nature. The enactment of the PKO law in 1992 and the decision to dispatch the SDF to Cambodia, Mozambique and the Golan Heights to participate in UN peacekeeping operations was precedent setting, but extremely modest in terms of substance. Rather than engaging in peacekeeping operations per se, Japanese troops primarily conducted humanitarian relief and reconstruction operations in relatively safe areas far removed from the dangers of combat. Indeed, these missions resembled nothing so much as the domestic disaster relief and reconstruction missions the SDF conducts in Japan, and which are its most popular role domestically. Rules of Engagement (ROEs) were much more restrictive than UN standards and deployed SDF units successfully managed to avoid any entanglement in combat, receiving or inflicting casualties.

The Revised US–Japan Defense Guidelines of 1997 were aimed at US, and to some extent Japanese, perceptions of a growing North Korean threat. China did not figure as a significant concern in Japanese and US policy deliberations about the Revised Guidelines.[11] The substance of the Revised Guidelines, like Japan's new participation in UN peacekeeping operations, was extremely modest. The SDF was not to get involved in combat, but could offer logistic support in international air and waters in areas far removed from combat. Such logistical support could include transporting personnel and material (including weapons and ammunition) to US ships on the high seas, cooperation in noncombatant evacuation, cooperation in surveillance and minesweeping, and search and rescue.[12] Because of the extremely modest nature of these changes, they did not fundamentally alter the Yoshida Doctrine. Nonetheless, the revised guidelines did succeed in antagonizing China, which saw them as signalling the conversion of the US–Japan alliance from a structure containing Japan's reemergence as major military power into a catalyst for promoting just such a development.[13]

China's reaction, which featured a campaign to remind Japan and the United States of Japan's history of aggression, and culminated in Chinese leader Jiang Zemin's disastrous visit to Japan in 1998, served to undermine the consensus in Japan in favour of reassuring Asian neighbours about Japan's benign intentions, especially in the area of historical reassurance.[14] Observers pointed to an emerging 'apology fatigue'. In this respect, the US–Japan Revised Defense Guidelines, although extremely modest in content, by producing an adverse reaction from China helped to undermine the consensus in favour of the Yoshida Doctrine's emphasis on reassurance. This, and rising perceptions of a North Korean threat, a threat that was crystallized for Japanese by the launching of a two-stage Taepodong missile over northern Honshu in late August 1998, and perceptions of a growing long-term potential threat from China, put further pressure on the Yoshida Doctrine.

The emergence of a Koizumi Doctrine

Junichiro Koizumi's rise to the premiership in April 2001 arguably put the most hawkish leader in power since Nobusuke Kishi. The growing strategic pressures of the late 1990s, which were described in the previous section, helped to create a political atmosphere that was conducive to significant change in military doctrine. The new Bush administration's emphasis on building up the alliance with Japan and viewing China more as a potential adversary than a partner also helped to create an opportunity for fundamental change. Finally, of course, the catalyst of 9/11 allowed Koizumi, a leader elected prime minister primarily to promote domestic economic reform, to switch direction and focus on security policy. In short, the Koizumi Doctrine stressed tightening the alliance with the United States, supporting US out-of-area combat missions, avoiding abandonment, promoting constitutional reinterpretation and revision to remove restraints on using force so Japanese troops could fight alongside US forces, deploying missile defence and promoting Japanese patriotism if not nationalism. More than anything, the Koizumi Doctrine reflected Koizumi's large ambitions to expand Japan's military role, and emerge as a normal if not a great military power. Yet the modest nature of what he was eventually able to achieve reflects the unexpected strength of domestic political opposition and also fallout from the Iraq War.

The hallmark of the Koizumi Doctrine was the emphasis on tightening the alliance with the United States and becoming an active partner in supporting US military operations in out-of-area conflicts. Koizumi appeared to support moving Japan toward the goal of making it the 'Britain of Asia', in as much as he showed little reluctance about involving the SDF in potential combat situations.[15] Whereas the Yoshida Doctrine focused more on avoiding entrapment in US wars, the Koizumi Doctrine was more geared, implicitly and at times explicitly, toward avoiding abandonment. This can be seen as a reaction to the perceived growing threat from North Korea and China. Significantly, the 2004 *Taikō*, or National Defense Programme Guidelines, named China as a potential threat for the first time. In February 2005 Japan agreed to join the United States in identifying peace and security in the Taiwan Straits as an area of common concern for both alliance partners.[16]

In the wake of the 9/11 attacks, Koizumi pushed to dispatch the SDF overseas to provide logistical support for US military forces engaged in combating Al-Qaeda. The Special Anti-Terrorism Measures Law that resulted had, as its centrepiece, the dispatch of a SDF flotilla to provide fuel (hence the term 'floating gas station'), water and other supplies to US Navy ships, and later Allied naval vessels operating in the Indian Ocean. It is important to note, however, that Koizumi's ambitions went well beyond this mission. The law included provisions for dispatching GSDF troops to provide medical and other humanitarian relief to refugees in camps in Pakistan, and even Afghanistan once combat had finished, provisions of the law that were never implemented. These missions were deemed to be too risky, despite Koizumi's own insistence that the SDF must be dispatched without regard to the risk of suffering casualties. Responding to criticism about dispatching the SDF to conflict zones, Koizumi claimed 'it will not do to say that we should not allow the SDF to go to dangerous places.'[17]

Initial proposals for the Anti-Terrorism Bill had also included dispatching P-3C and AWACs planes for surveillance and patrol operations. Koizumi's desire to dispatch an Aegis destroyer from the beginning of the MSDF operations in the Indian Ocean was quashed by a combination of internal LDP and Komei Party opposition that was supported by opinion polls showing public opposition. A weakening of the DPJ in late 2002, which in turn weakened Komei's bargaining position and that of internal LDP opponents, allowed

Koizumi to ignore the critics and dispatch an Aegis destroyer to the Indian Ocean, where an Aegis remained on station for eight months before being permanently withdrawn. The MSDF avoided transporting weapons or ammunition for US or Allied forces, again as a result of combined opposition from the Komei Party and internal LDP critics.[18]

Koizumi took an even bolder step to strengthen the bilateral alliance when he decided to publicly endorse the Iraq War, versus just express understanding for it, which had been Japan's stance during the Kosovo War, and then pushed to dispatch the SDF to Iraq after the United States had occupied the entire country. Expressing concerns about the North Korean threat and a potential China threat, Koizumi also emphasized the danger of abandonment by the United States: 'Damaging the confidence in the Japan–US relationship [...] would go against the national interest of Japan.'[19] In mid-April, picking up on the fear-of-abandonment rhetoric then being used by Koizumi and his Cabinet, the *Yomiuri Shimbun* editorialized in favour of dispatching troops: 'Under the US–Japan Security and Cooperation Treaty, the United States has a duty to protect Japan', but not the other way round. Nonetheless, 'even if Japan did not support the US attack on Iraq, it would be incorrect to argue that this would fail to work against the alliance [...] history is full of broken alliances'.[20]

Again, Koizumi had large ambitions, and the Iraq Special Measures Reconstruction Law that he forced through the Diet in summer 2003 reflected a desire to involve the SDF in security and stabilization missions in Iraq, and thereby set a precedent for future missions.[21] Nonetheless, opponents in the LDP and Komei, backed up by public opinion (including Koizumi's lacklustre public approval ratings),[22] as had been the case in fall 2001, again prevailed in scaling back Koizumi's ambitions in four areas. First, they succeeded in limiting deployment to relatively 'safe' regions deemed to be non-combat zones (*sentō kōi ga okawarete orazu*).[23] Second, early plans to have the GSDF provide logistical support for US forces were dropped and the SDF was barred from transporting weapons or ammunition (although it could transport troops carrying personal weapons). Third, early provisions calling for the SDF to engage in policing, or more ambitious anti-terrorism and stabilization missions, were dropped from the bill, as were plans to have the GSDF search for, collect and dispose of weapons of mass destruction (WMD).[24] Although language forbidding these operations was not clearly written into the law, the government pledged that the SDF would not engage in policing or more ambitious anti-terrorism or stabilization missions. This compromise left Koizumi room to expand the mission to include some of these areas if he were able to move public opinion in his favour. Finally, to avoid provoking a large and stable opposing public opinion majority, the Iraq Team of the Cabinet Secretariat decided that SDF rules of engagement (ROEs) would not be liberalized, this despite demands from hawks that ROE liberalization take place.[25]

Nonetheless, strong opposition from public opinion and the DPJ to even this watered down the Iraq Reconstruction Special Measures Bill, coupled with rising violence in post-reconstruction Iraq, forced Koizumi to shelve the dispatch until after the November Lower House election. Although the opposition DPJ expanded their number of seats in this election, the Koizumi administration survived, and in December 2003 Koizumi forged ahead with the dispatch. Nonetheless, the Koizumi Cabinet had to respond to public concerns as voiced by Komei and portions of the LDP to limit the risks of the SDF becoming involved in combat and suffering casualties.[26] Notwithstanding US demands that Japan dispatch the SDF to dangerous regions north of Baghdad, and more generally share risks along with the United States and other allies, the Cabinet decided to deploy the SDF to the relatively peaceful southern town of Samawah. Earlier plans to use the GSDF to provide rear-area logistical support for US forces were also dropped in favour of an exclusive concentration on humanitarian and reconstruction missions.[27]

Koizumi justified the dispatch as necessary for Japan to fulfil its responsibility to help maintain international peace and stability, and to strengthen the US–Japan alliance so as to avoid abandonment by the United States.[28] Public opinion polls subsequently showed overwhelming majorities of the public rejected this explanation. Subsequently the Koizumi Cabinet sought to boost support by de-emphasizing this explanation and instead shifting the focus to providing humanitarian relief and reconstruction assistance to Iraqis, a justification very similar to previous UN peacekeeping missions in Cambodia and elsewhere.[29] (See also M. Söderberg, Chapter 6, and N. Palanovics, Chapter 7.) This strategy was successful to the extent that the public came to evaluate SDF operations in Iraq highly. Nonetheless, every subsequent poll during the course of the GSDF deployment in Iraq found substantial majorities favouring the withdrawal of the GSDF and ASDF from Iraq quickly.[30] In short, the public evaluated SDF accomplishments in Iraq highly but did not support their presence there.

Beyond the Iraq dispatch, Koizumi worked to tighten the US alliance in other ways, most notably by moving forward with joint production and deployment of missile defence and by cooperating with US plans for global realignment of its military forces. Koizumi's support for realigning US forces was by and large successful, except for controversial plans to realign US bases in Okinawa, a problem he inherited and which he did little to resolve. Koizumi's plans for missile defence were well supported by the public, reflecting a difference in the way many elites and the public (made known through opinion polls) viewed the utility of missile defence versus involvement in US military conflicts far from Japan. For example, a Prime Minister's Office poll conducted in 2006 found 56.6 per cent of respondents supported missile defence.[31]

Beyond tightening the alliance with the United States, Koizumi also pushed to 'normalize' Japan's national security institutions. He called for promoting the Defense Agency to Ministry status and proposed ending the ban on the exercise of collective self-defence, a move that would allow the Japanese military to fight overseas alongside US forces. Koizumi was unsuccessful in lifting the ban as were his attempts to loosen it incrementally through his initial proposals for the Anti-Terrorism Special Measures law and the Iraq Reconstruction Special Measures law. Nonetheless, his successor, Shinzo Abe, promoted both of these elements of the Koizumi Doctrine and succeeded in raising the Defense Agency to ministry status in early 2007. At the same time, the Abe Cabinet inserted language into the same ministry-promotion bill that elevated a number of SDF overseas activities from subsidiary to 'main-line duties' (*honrai ninmu*) including international peace cooperation activities, the emergency evacuation of Japanese expatriates overseas, and minesweeping.[32] In most respects, however, this language did little more than ratify the status quo. Abe also formed an advisory panel to make recommendations for revising the ban on collective security and proposed establishing an American-style National Security Council to manage greater overseas deployments in support of US military operations.[33]

Beyond lifting the ban on the exercise of collective defence through constitutional reinterpretation, the Koizumi Doctrine called for a revision of Article 9 of the Constitution to reduce further, if not altogether eliminate, any remaining restraints on Japan's exercise of force. Although supporting constitutional reinterpretation, Koizumi failed to make any progress in this direction. Abe also picked up this part of the Doctrine and vigorously promoted a political debate on constitutional revision. In May 2007, he succeeded in enacting a national referendum law establishing procedures for holding a constitutionally-mandated referendum in order to realize constitutional reform.[34]

Although not explicitly a part of alliance tightening, Koizumi, and especially his immediate successor Shinzo Abe, moved Japanese diplomacy sharply away from the Yoshida Doctrine's developmentalist paradigm, emphasizing the importance of economic development for promoting peace and security and toward a paradigm emphasizing the promotion of democracy and human rights as the key to achieving peace and stability, especially in Asia. (See also M. Söderberg, Chapter 6, and N. Palanovics, Chapter 7.) This new paradigm was much more consistent with US foreign policy in general, and the Bush administration's strategy in particular, and in Asia, focused on promoting an 'arc of freedom'[35] aimed at building cooperation, if not an alliance, among democracies and semi-democratic states in order to contain China. This shift also entailed deemphasizing if not eliminating altogether the previous emphasis on reassuring Asian states, especially China, about Japan's disposition as a military power.[36]

A final characteristic of the Koizumi Doctrine was an emphasis on promoting patriotism, or even nationalism. This took several forms, including moves toward historical revisionism and stronger assertions of Japanese claims over disputed territories and other national interests. Most striking were Koizumi's attempts to break the taboo on prime ministerial visits to Yasukuni Shrine, in place since former Prime Minister Yasuhiro Nakasone's ill-fated visit in 1985 (although Prime Minister Hashimoto visited once in 1996). Visits to Yasukuni were a transparent appeal to nationalist voters in Japan, and especially to the politically influential *Nihon Izokukai*, the Japan Society of Bereaved Families, an organization that promotes visits to Yasukuni. Koizumi dismissed appeals by members of his own party, including his own Cabinet Secretary Yasuo Fukuda, to build a non-religious war memorial as an alternative commemorative site.[37] Beyond trying to build personal political support, it is plausible to hypothesize that Koizumi was trying to build patriotic pride as a prerequisite for building support for a more active security role overseas and more normal security institutions domestically.[38] Certainly Koizumi, who ignored vociferous Chinese and Korean opposition, did not make reassurance, especially historical reassurance, a priority. At worst, Koizumi actually used Chinese and Korean opposition to justify his visits.

Despite his support of visits to Yasukuni in principle, Abe, who was at least as much of a nationalist as Koizumi, did not continue to make visits to Yasukuni. Abe emphasized other areas of the nationalist agenda, such as attempting to reverse the so-called *Kono danwa*, an apology by then Chief Cabinet Secretary Yohei Kono in 1993 in which he apologized for the Japanese use of so-called comfort women, or sexual slaves, until 1945.[39] The Abe Cabinet also worked to remove references in Japanese school textbooks to Imperial Army officers who ordered Okinawans to commit suicide during the battle for Okinawa. Further, Abe personally expressed doubt about whether the fourteen A-class war criminals convicted at the Tokyo Tribunal were really war criminals and whether Japan was legally obligated to regard them as such.[40] Abe made clear his determination to revise or reinterpret the Constitution during his tenure.[41] Finally, Abe successfully enacted an education reform bill that mandated promoting patriotism as a fundamental goal of education.[42]

Koizumi's ambitions to end the ban on collective self-defence, to support US military operations overseas actively, to begin balancing China politically by emphasizing the importance of democracy, to normalize domestic security institutions, and to promote constitutional reform and patriotism domestically were only partially successful during his own term and in Abe's term. The Koizumi Doctrine as used in this chapter thus refers to Koizumi's ambitions and agenda more than his and Abe's accomplishments, as these fell significantly short.

There are at least two other anomalies that should be noted. Despite Koizumi's ambition to play a larger security and political role, during the Koizumi and Abe cabinets military spending stagnated or declined, and ODA spending declined unambiguously,[43] thereby reducing Japan's potential for influencing the international environment. (See also Marie Söderberg, Chapter 6, and Norbert Palanovics, Chapter 7.) During the Koizumi premiership Chinese military spending unambiguously surpassed Japanese military spending.[44] The stagnation/decline in military spending is especially striking given how rapidly Chinese military spending increased during the same period, with annual increases averaging over 10 per cent per year. Major Chinese spending priorities included naval and especially submarine assets, assets that arguably could pose a direct threat to Japan's security, especially the security of its sea lanes.

Although the Chinese build-up is mostly aimed at Taiwan scenarios, it is striking that Japan has allowed its anti-submarine warfare (ASW) capabilities to decline as China's submarine capabilities grow substantially. As part of the New Defense Programme Outline, Japan is cutting its fleet of destroyers from fifty-four down to forty-seven, cuts that reduce its ASW capabilities even as the MSDF adds modernized Aegis class air defence and anti-missile destroyers.[45] One answer to this paradox is that Koizumi sought to do more with less: by reducing restrictions on the SDF and normalizing Japan's national security institutions, he sought to make more effective use of Japan's stagnating and relatively declining defence resources. Nonetheless, to the extent that one views the Koizumi Doctrine as seeking to counterbalance China, the stagnation of defence spending and the decline in the ODA budget stand out as anomalies. A power determined to balance China should not behave that way.

The return of the Yoshida Doctrine

The year 2007 marked an important turning point in Japan's grand strategy as the accumulation of domestic and international political obstacles caused the Koizumi Doctrine agenda to collapse and policy reverted back to the Yoshida Doctrine. The emergence of an Iraq syndrome, or a backlash to participation in the Iraq War, among the public and many elites plus a robust national consensus against using military force overseas conspired to derail the Koizumi Doctrine.

The political obstacles were already becoming clear by mid-2006. Taku Yamasaki, senior LDP leader and erstwhile Koizumi ally, issued a prophetic warning to his party against excessive hawkishness almost exactly one year before the 2007 Upper House election. According to Yamasaki, if a movement developed within 'my party, the Liberal Democratic Party, to pull the country into a warlike direction, Japan is a democracy and my party could be chased out of the government'. Regarding political support within Japan for pre-empting North Korean nuclear facilities, Yamasaki stated, 'There is absolutely no movement in that direction in Japan'. Similarly, in talks with US officials, Yamasaki warned that extending the MSDF refuelling mission, then scheduled to expire in November 2006, would require 'a lot of political energy'.[46]

Yamasaki's prediction was borne out when Abe decided to renew the Anti-Terrorism Special Measures Law, the legal basis for the MSDF providing fuel and water for US and Allied vessels involved in maritime interdiction operations related to the Afghan War, set to expire in November 2006. Despite his desire to expand SDF operations overseas, Abe did not try to take advantage of this opportunity to expand the MSDF mission to include maritime inspection, or to dispatch the SDF to Afghanistan to assist in reconstruction efforts. Most striking of all, Abe did not try to make this law permanent, or to establish a permanent law on SDF overseas dispatch, as many hawks in the LDP had been calling for, including Abe himself, only two months earlier.[47] Indeed, instead of extending this law for another four years, in a decision that would have huge implications one year later, Abe settled for a mere one-year extension.[48]

Despite his often expressed ambitions for Japan to play a larger military role, even in fall 2006, when Abe had approval ratings averaging well over 50 per cent, DPJ and public opposition to continuing – not to mention expanding – overseas SDF deployments connected with US military operations significantly constrained Abe. Abe managed to avoid expending much political capital on this issue primarily because he settled for a very modest extension. In the months that followed, Abe made no attempt to dispatch the SDF to Afghanistan to participate in NATO's provincial reconstruction teams, despite the Abe administration's obvious interest in doing so. At the same time, elite LDP support for the Koizumi Doctrine goal of forging closer alliance ties with the United States showed signs of fraying as Abe's own Defense Minister, Fumio Kyuma, and his Foreign Minister, Taro Aso, broke with the Koizumi–Abe line of unequivocally supporting the Iraq War and publicly criticized the war.[49]

More than Koizumi had before him, Abe made constitutional reform, especially reform of Article 9 to promote a more active security role for Japan, and overseas SDF deployments, campaign issues. This became evident in spring 2007 as Abe began early campaigning for the Upper House election. Given that, only nine months earlier, North Korea had staged its first-ever nuclear test, and engaged in major missile tests only three months before that, there was good reason to expect that security concerns would dominate in the minds of voters as they went to the polls. Yet, like his predecessor, many of Abe's security policies did not enjoy public support. More important, the public had other priorities and this time it, not the Prime Minister, 'changed the channel' to issues they cared about, namely pension reform and growing economic inequality and insecurity. In an *Asahi Shimbun* poll taken in January, a plurality of 48 per cent claimed that it was 'inappropriate' to make constitutional reform the central issue in the upcoming Upper House election, while only 32 per cent considered it appropriate.[50] An annual *Yomiuri Shimbun* poll asking about support for constitutional revision recorded a sharp drop of over 9 per cent between April 2006 and April 2007.

Taking a broader look at these 2003–08 data, we see that support for constitutional reform peaked at 65 per cent in 2004 but declined consistently thereafter, with the decline continuing even after Abe stepped down as prime minister. While Koizumi made progress increasing support for constitutional reform in the beginning of his premiership, this progress eroded in the last two years of his premiership and accelerated during Abe's year as premier. By April 2008 not only did a plurality oppose constitutional reform but the rate of support had fallen back to levels not seen since 1993, when *Yomiuri* began polling annually on constitutional reform and began its own programme for constitutional reform. In other words, supporters of constitutional reform would have to start from scratch to rebuild public support for revision.

Table 3.1 Yomiuri Shimbun polling question 'Do you think the Constitution should be revised?'

Response	*2003*	*2004*	*2005*	*2006*	*2007*	*2008*
Yes	54.3	65.0	60.6	55.5	46.2	42.5
No	29.9	26.6	26.6	32.2	39.1	43.1
DK/other	15.8	12.9	12.9	12.3	14.7	14.4

Source: *Yomiuri Shimbun*, 8 April 2008 (morning edition), p. 12; 6 April 2007 (morning edition), p. 14; 4 April 2006 (morning edition), p. 14; 'Balance of support shifts against top law reform', *Yomiuri Shimbun*, 8 April 2008; 4 April 2006 (morning edition), p. 14; 8 April 2005 (morning edition), p. 12; 2 April 2004 (morning edition), p. 10; 2 April 2003 (morning edition), p. 30.

Moreover, support for reforming Article 9 has been consistently lower than support for constitutional reform, and has never achieved majority status in opinion polls. In an April 2008 *Asahi Shimbun* poll, 66 per cent opposed amending Article 9, versus a mere 23 per cent who thought it should be amended.[51] In 2007 the same *Asahi* poll found 49 per cent opposed amending Article 9 versus 33 per cent who supported amendment. Ratifying the status quo seemed to be the most important motivation behind those supporting change in 2007, with 70 per cent of respondents answering that the Constitution should mention the existence of the SDF. Nonetheless, 70 per cent wanted to maintain the status quo of the SDF, a sentiment shared by even 52 per cent of those favouring an amendment to Article 9. These results suggest that even many of the supporters of amending the Constitution, including Article 9, do not support the proposals of Abe and other hawks to create a 'normal' military that could engage in overseas combat.[52]

Opposition to the Iraq War and a more enduring opposition to the SDF engaging in overseas combat operations appear to be the root causes of this reversal. Another *Yomiuri Shimbun* poll regarding reclaiming the right to collective self-defence is also suggestive. In 2002, before the start of the Iraq War, public support peaked at 35.2 per cent, well short of a majority. However, beginning in 2003, support began to decline. By 2005 support for reclaiming this right stood at 30.5 per cent. (For some unstated reason, after 2005 *Yomiuri Shimbun* discontinued this question.)[53] This timing of this shift suggests that the Iraq War caused many Japanese to worry that ending the ban on the right to collective self-defence could lead to Japan becoming entrapped in an American-led war that would not be in Japan's national interest. It is also likely that more and more Japanese began associating a lifting of this ban with SDF combat overseas.

With such polling results, the LDP began to run away from constitutional reform. Even Abe himself began to limit the amount of time he spent talking about constitutional reform and security issues. During the first day after the official start of the 2007 Upper House election campaign, Abe spent only 11 per cent of his speaking time discussing diplomacy and security issues, and 2 per cent discussing constitutional reform. The DPJ's Ozawa essentially spent no time discussing either.[54] Many LDP candidates began distancing themselves from constitutional reform as well.[55]

Nonetheless, the LDP and Komei, its coalition partner, suffered a historic defeat during the 29 July 2007 election. The LDP had lost its stand-alone control of the Upper House in 1989 but it had remained the largest party in the Upper House until this defeat. With the LDP and Komei in the minority, the DPJ became the largest party, and in combination with other opposition parties, most notably the Social Democratic Party and the People's New Party, was able to form a working majority in the Upper House. This majority allowed the opposition to block ordinary legislation for a minimum of sixty days, or permanently unless the Lower House mustered a two-thirds majority to override the Upper House. Because of Koizumi's major victory in the September 2005 postal election, the LDP and Komei could, if they agreed, muster a two-thirds majority in the Lower House to override the Upper House.[56]

Why did the DPJ win such a sweeping victory? In *Yomiuri Shimbun* and NTV's joint exit polling during the July 2007 Upper House election, constitutional reform finished fifth, behind pensions, the economy and economic inequality, political corruption and education, but ahead of a possible rise in the consumption tax. However, it is not clear whether those selecting this as a priority in deciding their vote were opponents or supporters of revision. Given that the Social Democrats and Communists were the most active in campaigning against constitutional reform, it is likely that a large percentage of voters were opponents.[57] These results show that the public were not voting against constitutional reform or a greater overseas role for the SDF per se. Nonetheless, this exit poll and the overall results clearly show that voters punished Abe and the LDP for focusing on constitutional reform and international security rather than focusing on domestic insecurity issues that mattered to them more, such as pension reform and growing economic inequality.

Taken together with pre-election polling results, discussed above, the public's message that constitutional reform and an expansion of Japan's overseas security role should be taken off the agenda was heard loud and clear by politicians. The day after the election, the head of Komei bluntly warned Abe to stop focusing on constitutional reform and focus on bread-and-butter issues, growing economic inequality and political corruption.[58] The *Asahi Shimbun* reported the comments of senior LDP party leaders who admitted, 'the reason the LDP took such a battering [...] lay in a perception gap over what the public wanted and what Prime Minister Shinzo Abe's Cabinet pursued [...] While public attention was riveted on the debacle of millions of missing pension records, Abe kept harping on about making constitutional amendments a key issue of contention in the election.'[59]

In the wake of the LDP's massive defeat, a significant shift of opinion occurred in the Upper House against constitutional reform. An *Asahi Shimbun* poll of elected members after the 2004 election revealed that 71 per cent of Upper House members favoured constitutional reform of some kind, while 20 per cent were opposed, 7 per cent were unsure and 2 per cent answered otherwise. The July 2007 election produced a major drop in support for constitutional reform to 53 per cent, with 26 per cent opposing, 15 per cent undecided and 6 per cent answering otherwise. This drop was evident even in the LDP, with 89 per cent strongly supporting constitutional reform after the 2004 Upper House election, but only 62 per cent strongly supporting it after the 2007 election. Support for revising Article 9 fell even lower. The *Asahi* poll found that only 31 per cent of Upper House members favoured changing Article 9 after the July 2007 election, while 50 per cent opposed it.[60]

In the wake of the LDP's historic defeat, pressure on Prime Minister Abe to resign to take responsibility for the defeat was intense, and after six weeks he resigned. This paved the way for Yasuo Fukuda to become Prime Minister after defeating the more hawkish Taro Aso. Fukuda quickly made it evident that he did not share the Koizumi Doctrine's objectives of promoting constitutional reform or reclaiming the right to collective self-defence.[61] According to a senior LDP Lower House member, 'as a result of this election, the dominant view in the LDP has changed. The election was a red light [...] Even if we eventually change the interpretation of the Constitution we will not exercise this right for a long time into the future, if ever.'[62] Fukuda even scrapped Abe's proposal to create a strong US-style National Security Council.[63] Unlike his predecessor, the Fukuda Cabinet emphatically opposed dispatching the SDF to Afghanistan, citing the ban on collective self-defence as the reason.[64]

On the other hand, Fukuda did defend one of Koizumi's foreign policy accomplishments, namely the continuation of the MSDF Indian Ocean logistical mission to provide US and Allied naval vessels with fuel and water. This deployment had been the first step in the Koizumi Doctrine's goal of deploying Japanese troops globally in support of US military operations.

Fukuda tried to break up the public opinion majority opposing continuation of the MSDF refuelling mission by watering down the contents of the Anti-Terrorism Special Measures act. In the end, he decided on a new bill that eliminated almost all of the provisions of the previous law, including those allowing for the dispatch of P-3C planes and other assets for patrol and intelligence gathering, joint search and rescue activities, medical assistance for US military personnel, and the dispatch of the GSDF to refugee camps in Pakistan for relief activities, provisions that had never been exercised, but which remained in the law and reflected Koizumi's ambitions for expanding the mission. The stripped-down bill limited activities to providing US and Allied vessels with fuel and water only, and the new bill clearly stipulated that this fuel was supposed to be used only for counter-terrorism maritime interdiction missions related to the Afghan conflict, not for other conflicts such as the Iraq War. It also limited the size of the MSDF contingent to one refuelling vessel and one escort destroyer, significantly smaller than the MSDF contingent had been from November 2001 through summer 2005, but the same size as the MSDF contingent had been from summer 2005 through October 2007.[65]

Fukuda's decision to water down the bill and offers of compromise with the DPJ were initially successful in eliminating the opinion majorities opposed to extending the MSDF mission. Nonetheless, Fukuda was not able to build stable support for this mission, and an opposing opinion majority re-emerged in December 2007 and January 2008. This deterioration in support reflected growing mistrust in Prime Minister Fukuda himself. In the mid-December *Asahi* poll, Fukuda's overall support rate dropped by a whopping 13 per cent, down to 31 per cent. Among the 48 per cent who expressed non-support for the Fukuda Cabinet, 57 per cent cited opposition to its policies as the primary reason. The main reason for these results was growing anger over his handling of the missing pension account issue; 60 per cent of respondents said they thought the ruling Cabinet had broken its promise on this issue, versus 30 per cent who did not. Seventy-two per cent of respondents said they could not expect Fukuda to regain public trust regarding the pension issue. Asked which party they would vote for in the proportional representation contest if a general election were held now, 38 per cent picked the DPJ versus 23 per cent who picked the LDP. This was the largest gap in favour of the DPJ ever recorded in an *Asahi* poll.[66]

The DPJ was able to use its Upper House majority to force Fukuda to focus his political energy on extending the MSDF refuelling mission, making it his top priority rather than the pension issue that voters wanted him to focus on. In perception and probably in reality as well, Fukuda's focus on the refuelling mission contributed to his poor handling of the pension issue, such as his costly and uninformed remark questioning whether the LDP had actually promised to find all the missing pension accounts.[67] The DPJ managed to get Fukuda to change the channel back to international security and away from pensions, a move that created a major voter backlash. This backlash created downward momentum for Fukuda's public approval ratings, and indeed for the LDP's approval ratings as well, momentum that continued until Fukuda resigned the premiership in September 2008, only about a year after assuming the post.

In other areas, Fukuda acted to reverse some innovations of the Koizumi Doctrine, thereby returning policy to the Yoshida Doctrine status quo ante. Most notably, Fukuda dropped the 'arc of freedom' concept for containing China in favour of returning to the concept of economic development as the best way to promote peace and prosperity. Linguistically, the arc of freedom was replaced with 'strengthened' Asian diplomacy,[68] a concept that also refers to Fukuda's restoration of reassurance as a priority in diplomacy toward Asia, first and foremost by reining in the nationalist agenda domestically.

The retreat from the nationalist agenda had already begun under Abe. Koizumi's attempt to break the taboo on visits to Yasukuni was already a manifest failure by the time he left office. Had it worked, his successor, Abe, and indeed Abe's rivals for the top post, especially Taro Aso, would have run for office promising to visit Yasukuni as Prime Minister. The fact that they failed to do so, combined with Abe's adoption of a declaratory policy of ambiguity and then an actual policy of not visiting the shrine, demonstrated that a consensus had emerged among elites, if not mass opinion, against visits to Yasukuni.[69] This consensus was especially strong in the business community, which worried that Koizumi's Yasukuni visits were damaging economic ties with China, and possibly with other Asian countries.[70] With an implicit promise not to visit Yasukuni, Abe was able to begin mending political relations with China and South Korea, convincing the two nations to lift the diplomatic sanctions (i.e. the decision to suspend high-level diplomatic contacts with Japan, especially with Koizumi himself) they had imposed on Japan in late 2004.

While Abe sought to promote the nationalist agenda in other areas, Fukuda reversed these policies. In particular, Fukuda unambiguously reaffirmed the Kono apology regarding the so-called 'comfort women', and his Education and Technology Minister reversed the Abe Cabinet policy of instructing textbook authors to omit references to the Imperial Japanese Army forcing Okinawans to commit suicide during the battle for Okinawa. In retrospect, it is clear that Koizumi and Abe's attempts to promote patriotism undermined their goal of tightening the bilateral alliance with the United States, since American officials became increasingly opposed to these efforts.[71] It effectively produced a broader backlash in the US Congress, in Europe, and elsewhere.

The Fukuda Cabinet also displayed a willingness to tone down nationalist claims for the sake of reassuring neighbouring Asian nations. For example, the Ministry of Education, Science and Technology was ordered to delete portions of curriculum guidelines for junior high-school social studies students that instructed teachers to teach that Takeshima (Tokdo in Korean) is Japanese territory, despite Korea's own claims and its occupation of this set of rocks.[72]

Conclusion: an emerging Defensive Realism

One area where the Koizumi Doctrine has continued and appears to have long-term viability is in the area of missile defence. Indeed, in contrast to overseas deployments of the SDF for supporting US military deployments (and even the nationalist agenda), the striking characteristic of missile defence in Japan is the lack of controversy.[73] This reflects underlying support for missile defence and for homeland defence of Japan in general, including building up the capabilities of *Hoancho*, or the Maritime Safety Agency (coastguard).[74]

A reflection of this broad consensus was the overwhelming super-majority in the Diet, composed of the LDP, Komei and the opposition DPJ, that quickly repealed (in a mere two weeks) the ban on using outer space for 'military purposes' and replaced it with wording forbidding the use of space for 'aggression', thereby allowing the Defense Ministry to use space for defensive purposes. This decision cleared an important legal barrier for Japan to develop military-quality spy satellites with photographic resolution down to objects of 15 cm and heat sensors capable of detecting missile launches.[75] This decision is also significant because it suggests a desire to develop more autonomy from the United States in intelligence gathering and in missile defence, thus posing a challenge to the Koizumi Doctrine's goal of tightening the alliance. Indeed, US officials have been on record since the late 1990s discouraging Japan from developing independent reconnaissance satellites, criticizing them as a costly redundancy in the context of the alliance.

More than anything, the rapid lifting of the ban on using space for military purposes to allow the use of space for defensive purposes signalled the emergence of Defensive Realism as the dominant paradigm in Japan's grand strategy. The gradual recession of anti-militarist mistrust of the state by the general public and elites alike over recent decades has gradually revealed Defensive Realist attitudes. These attitudes are realist in that they entail recognizing war as an ever-present possibility for which states must prepare. They are defensive in that they recognize military power as having utility for homeland defence but not as a political instrument in foreign policy. In particular, there is broad scepticism about the utility of using offensive military force overseas to suppress terrorism or WMD proliferation or to promote democracy and human rights.[76]

Arguably, policy in democratic polities tends to flow like water, seeking the path of least resistance. If so, then Japanese security policy will likely show far greater innovation in missile defence and other aspects of homeland defence than in promoting an international security role for the SDF. Article 9 and the ban on the exercise of the right of collective self-defence will likely remain in place. United States expectations for Japan to assist in global conflicts will go unfulfilled, and Japanese homeland defence may gradually become more autonomous. If there is a major change between the Yoshida Doctrine as described above and this emerging Defensive Realism, it is this nascent trend for Japan to take greater responsibility for territorial defence.

While Japan shows heightened concern about missile threats and a growing desire to gather intelligence on China and North Korea, the continued stagnation of Japan's defence budget when Chinese defence budgets have been rising by more than 15 per cent per year over 2006–08 continues to raise questions about Japan's willingness to balance China. This raises the possibility that, to paraphrase David Kang, many Japanese elites and the public, like those elsewhere in East Asia, do not feel as threatened by China's rise as we think they should.[77] In other words, despite historical tensions and the suspicions of conservative Japanese elites, there is still little evidence to suggest that ordinary Japanese, or even many sections of the elites, see Chinese intentions as especially hostile, a clear contrast with their perceptions of North Korean intentions. Certainly, these perceptions of China are consistent with generally benign perceptions of Beijing in South Korea and much of South East Asia. Growing trade ties appear to be reinforcing these benign perceptions.[78] This relative lack of perceptions of Chinese malevolence in Japan is a major reason why the Koizumi Doctrine failed, in most respects, to be translated into policy.

Ambivalence about the United States and the alliance with the United States appears to be the second reason for the failure of the Koizumi Doctrine to take root. The Iraq War rekindled entrapment fears among many elites and especially the public. In the wake of the Iraq War the clear majority in Japan distrusts the United States.[79] Consequently, we will likely see a retrenchment in SDF support for the War on Terrorism coupled with significant development of missile defence and perhaps other elements of autonomous homeland defence. More than anything, we will likely see Japan retreat from international activism and turn more inward as it struggles to address aging society issues such as pension and health care reform, socioeconomic gaps, and attempts to increase productivity and technoeconomic competitiveness. The fact that even a North Korean nuclear test was not able to challenge the dominance of this agenda suggests that it would take an exceptionally large external shock to change this trajectory in Japanese foreign policy over the coming years. A new and distinct iteration of *Shōnihonshugi* (or Little Japanism) may be emerging,[80] although *Chūnihonshugi* (or Medium-size Japanism) might be a better description. Indeed, an increasingly influential elite view defines Japan's identity not as a great power but as a middle power.[81] Defining Japan as a 'middle power', rather than as a great 'normal' military power, appears to be the direction Japanese national identity and foreign policy are moving after the demise of the Koizumi Doctrine.

Notes

1 For a good example, see M. J. Green, *Japan's Reluctant Realism*, New York: Palgrave Macmillan, 2001, p. 1. Also see W. W. Grimes, 'Institutionalized inertia: Japanese Foreign policy in the Post-Cold War world' in G. J. Ikenberry and M.

Mastanduno (eds) *International Relations Theory and the Asia-Pacific*, New York: Columbia University Press, 2003, pp. 353–86.

2 Regarding the Yoshida Doctrine, see K. B. Pyle, *Japan Rising: The Resurgence of Japanese Power and Purpose*, New York: Public Affairs, 2007, pp. 241–77. One of the first to identify a distinct Yoshida Doctrine was K. Masataka, 'Genjitsushugisha no heiwaron', *Chuo Koron* 903, January 1963, 38–49.

3 The classic statement on antimilitarism is T. U. Berger, *Cultures of Antimilitarism: National Security in Germany and Japan*, Baltimore, MD: Johns Hopkins University Press, 1998. Whereas Berger conceptualizes anti-militarism as a political culture, I conceptualize it as cognitive mistrust of the state and its ability to control the military and wield the military instrument wisely.

4 Emphasizing this aspect is R. J. Samuels, *Securing Japan: Tokyo's Grand Strategy and the Future of East Asia*, Ithaca, NY: Cornell University, 2007, pp. 29–37.

5 Regarding alliance dilemma dangers of entrapment versus abandonment see G. H. Snyder, *Alliance Politics*, Ithaca, NY: Cornell University Press, 1997. Regarding fear of entrapment and anti-militarism in Japan see Y. Izumikawa, 'Unpacking Antimilitarism: Entrapment Fear, Domestic Liberal Ideology, and Pacifism in Japanese Politics', paper delivered at the annual conference of the International Political Science Association, Fukuoka, Japan, 9–13 July 2006.

6 T. Saki, '"Kyūjō-anpo taisei" no shyuen – sengo Nihon gaikō to seitō seiji', *Kokusai Mondai*, March 1991, p. 35.

7 S. Sudo, *The Fukuda Doctrine and ASEAN: New Dimensions in Japanese Foreign Policy*, Singapore: Institute of South East Asian Studies, 1992. For background see T. Fukuda, *Hoshu kakumei ni kakeru*, Tokyo: Yomiuri Shimbunsha, 1974, pp. 198–205.

8 P. Midford, 'Japan's leadership role in East Asian security multilateralism: the Nakayama proposal and the logic of reassurance', *Pacific Review* 13 (3), 2000, 367–97; Y. Satoh, '1995 nen no fushime ni mukatte: Ajia-Taiheyō chiki no anzen hoshyō', *Gaiko Forumu* 64, January 1994, 12–18; Ministry of Foreign Affairs, *Diplomatic Bluebook, 1991: Japan's Diplomatic Activities*, Tokyo: Ministry of Foreign Affairs, 1991, pp. 463–71.

9 Midford, 'Japan's leadership role in East Asian security multilateralism'; T. Kawasaki, 'Between realism and idealism in Japanese security policy: the case of the ASEAN Regional Forum', *Pacific Review* 10 (4), 1997; and C. W. Hughes, 'Japan's subregional security and defence linkages with ASEAN, South Korea and China in the 1990s', *Pacific Review* 9 (2), 1997, 229–50.

10 M. Green and B. Self, 'Japan's Changing China policy: from commercial liberalism to reluctant realism', *Survival* 38 (2), summer 1996, 35–58.

11 See M. Green and M. Mochizuki, *The US–Japan Security Alliance in the Twenty-first Century: Prospects for Incremental Change*, New York: Council on Foreign Relations, 1998, pp. 55–72, and Y. Funabashi, *Alliance Adrift*, New York: Council on Foreign Relations, 1999, pp. 436–7.

12 P. Midford, 'China views the revised US–Japan defense guidelines: popping the cork?', *International Relations of the Asia-Pacific* 4, 2004, 124.

13 Ibid., 113–45.

14 T. Berger, 'The construction of antagonism: the history problem in Japan's foreign relations' in G. J. Ikenberry and T. Inoguchi (eds) *Reinventing the Alliance: U.S.–Japan Security Partnership in an Era of Change*, New York: Palgrave Macmillan, 2003, pp. 63–84.

15 This phrase and the idea behind it originate with the so-called 'Armitage report' written by a group of Japan experts that would subsequently serve in the Bush administration. See Institute for National Strategic Studies, 'The United States and Japan: Advancing toward a Mature Partnerhsip', *INSS Special Report*, Washington, DC: National Defense University, 2000, available at www.ndu.edu/inss/press/Spelreprts/SFJAPAN.PDF (accessed 28 May 2007).

16 R. Samuels, *Securing Japan*, pp. 69, 84; IISS, *The Military Balance, 2005–2006*, London: Routledge, 2006, p. 260. Regarding the joint statement on Taiwan, see http://japan.usembassy.gov/e/p/tp-20050219-77.html (accessed 12 May 2008).
17 'Backing of U.S. revives debate on SDF', *Japan Times*, 28 September, 2001.
18 P. Midford and P. D. Scott, 'Japanese political parties face public opinion: leading, responding, or ignoring?' in R. Eldridge and P. Midford (eds) *Japanese Public Opinion and the War on Terrorism*, New York: Palgrave Macmillan, 2008, pp. 125–58, esp. pp. 142–5; and P. Midford, 'Japan's response to terror: sending the SDF to the Arabian Sea', *Asian Survey* 43 (2), March–April 2003, 329–51.
19 Cabinet Office, 'Prime Minister Junichiro Koizumi's Interview on the Issue of Iraq', 18 March 2003, www.kanteigo.jp/foreign/koizumispeech/2003/03/18interview_e.html (accessed 9 July 2007). Also see D. M. Kliman, *Japan's Security Strategy in the post-9/11 World: Embracing a new Realpolitik*, Westport CT: Praeger, 2006, p. 127.
20 *Yomiuri Shimbun*, 11 April, 2003.
21 G. Ito, 'Participation in UN peacekeeping' in T. U. Berger, M. M. Mochizuki and J. Tsuchiyama (eds) *Japan in International Politics: The Foreign Policies of an Adaptive State*, Boulder, CO: Lynne Reinner, 2007, p. 85, who cites D. Sakurada and G. Ito (eds) *Hikaku gaikō seisaku: Iraku sensō e no taiō gaikō*, Tokyo: Akashi Shoten, 2004.
22 T. Shinoda, 'Japan's top-down policy process to dispatch the SDF to Iraq', *Japanese Journal of Political Science* 7 (1), April 2006, 71–91. The September 2003 LDP leadership election was another reason for increasing opposition within the LDP. See R. Pekkanen and E. S. Krauss, 'Japan's "coalition of the willing" on security policies', *Orbis*, summer 2005, pp. 429–44, at p. 440; and 'Teiko seiryoku, oshikiri shusei,' *Asahi Shimbun*, 14 June 2003 (morning edition), p. 1.
23 'Diet opens debate on SDF, Iraq', *Asahi Shimbun*, 25 June 2003; 'Iraku shinpo giron honkakuka', *Nihon Keizai Shimbun*, 11 June 2003 (morning edition), p. 1; 'Jimin, Komei ni iron mo', *Kyodo Tsushin*, 10 June 2003, http://news.kyodo.co.jp/kyodonews/2003/ira2/news/0611-1140.html (accessed 12 July 2007).
24 Shinoda, 'Japan's top-down policy process', p. 79.
25 'Kōkyūho motome jokentsuki ryōshō', *Kyodo Tsushin*, 12 June 2003, http://news.kyodo.co.jp/kyodonews/2003/iraq2/news/0612-1149.html (accessed 7 July 2006); and Shinoda, 'Japan's top-down policy process', pp. 78, 80.
26 'Jimin haken zentei ni chūmon zokushutsu, rikuji tōnyū de Komei to masatsu mo', *Kyodo Tsushin*, 8 December 2003; and Shinoda, 'Japan's top-down policy process', p. 87.
27 C. Hughes, *Japan's Re-emergence as a 'Normal' Military Power*, p. 129; 'Nihon ni iraku de no "kiken junin" motomeru beikoku fuku chōkan', *Asahi Shimbun*, 11 June 2003; and '1,000 strong SDF division eyed for Iraq', *Daily Yomiuri*, 25 June 2003.
28 'Press Conference by Prime Minister Junichiro Koizumi', 9 December 2003, www.kantei.go.jp/foreign/koizumispeech/2003/12/09press_html (accessed 7 July 2006); Shinoda, 'Japan's top-down policy process', p. 87; and Hughes, *Japan's Re-emergence as a 'Normal' Military Power*, p. 130; *Asahi Shimbun*, 10 December 2003, p. 5.
29 P. Midford, *Japanese Public Opinion and the War on Terrorism: Implications for Japan's Security Strategy*, Washington, DC: East–West Center, 2006, pp. 35–46.
30 Ibid., pp. 36–40.
31 *Bōei Handobukku 2007*, Tokyo: Asagumo Shinbunsha, 2007, p. 818.
32 'Jieitai hirogaru kaigai ninmu', *Yomiuri Shimbun* (morning edition), 17 December 2006, p. 3.
33 'National Security Council plan urges streamlining, secrecy law', *Asahi Shimbun*, 1 March 2007; 'Shushō "higan" e ippo–kōshi yōnin taisei shimeru', *Asahi Shimbun*, 19 May 2007, p. 3.
34 M. Ito, 'Diet clears path to referendum on Constitution', *Japan Times*, 15 May 2007.
35 This arc of freedom is highlighted in Chapter 1 of the 2007 Diplomatic Bluebook; indeed, it is even featured in the title: *Diplomatic Bluebook 2007:* 'Arc of Freedom

and Prosperity: Japan's Expanding Diplomatic Horizons', available at www.mofa.go.jp/policy/other/bluebook/2007/html/index.html (accessed 16 May 2008).

36 Scepticism about reassuring East Asian states, especially China, emerges especially clearly in Abe's widely noted book, published just before he became Prime Minister: S. Abe, *Utsukushii Kuni e*, Tokyo: Bunshun Shinsho, 2006, pp. 68–9.

37 'New memorial for war dead planned after Yasukuni furor', *Japan Times*, 19 August 2001; 'An alternative to Yasukuni', *Japan Times*, 29 August 2001; 'Lawmakers discuss secular war memorial', *Japan Times*, 10 November 2005; 'Yasukuni mondai no kaiketsu o', *Asahi Shimbun*, 30 August 2003; 'Memorial pitch expected by year end', *Japan Times*, 19 August 2002. Regarding Nihon Izokukai and the Yasukuni issue see F. Seraphim, *War Memory and Social Politics in Japan, 1945–2005*, Cambridge, MA: Harvard University Asia Center, 2008.

38 Regarding this debate, see R. Yoshida, 'Koizumi's foreign policy: U.S. always comes first', *Japan Times*, 25 June 2006.

39 H. Tabuchi, 'Prime Minister denies women were forced into World War II brothels', *Washington Post*, 2 March 2007, p. A9.

40 Abe, *Utsukushii Kuni e*, pp. 69–74.

41 'Shushō: 'Ninkichū ni kaiken', *Asahi Shimbun*, 1 November 2006.

42 E. Prideaux and A. Nakamura, 'Education Bill shifts power to the state', *Japan Times*, 18 November 2005; and M. Ito, 'Education, defense Bills passed', *Japan Times*, 16 December 2006.

43 'Japan No. 5 ODA donor: OECD', *Japan Times*, 3 April 2008.

44 Chinese defence spending was USD 55.9 billion in 2003 and USD 62.5 billion in 2004 respectively, while Japanese spending was USD 42.8 billion, USD 45.1 billion, in 2003 and 2004 respectively. IISS, *The Military Balance, 2005–2006*, London: Routledge, 2005, pp. 270, 279.

45 Although continued modernization will expand ASW capabilities in some respects, the large cut in the number of destroyers (platforms) unambiguously reduces ASW capabilities below what they would have been without these cuts but continued modernization.

46 Kyodo, 'Extend MSDF Indian Ocean refueling duty: U.S.', *Japan Times*, 27 July 2006.

47 'Abe wants permanent law for SDF missions abroad, collective defence', *Japan Times*, 26 August 2006.

48 Kyodo, 'Bill to extend antiterrorism law clears Diet', *Japan Times*, 28 October 2006.

49 'Iraku shiji wa "zen shusho no kojinteki kenkai", bōei chyōkan', *Asahi Shimbun*, 7 December 2006 (morning edition); and Kyodo, 'Kyuma hedges support for the US', *Japan Times*, 8 December 2006; 'Kyuma: U.S. invasion of Iraq a mistake', *Japan Times*, 25 January 2007; Kyodo, 'U.S. protests Kyuma's criticism of Bush', *Japan Times*, 28 January 2007; 'Japan's FM calls US operation "naïve"', *AFP*, 3 February 2007; and K. Nabeshima, 'To move without US cues', *Japan Times*, 5 March 2007; Y. Kato and H. Kujiraoka, 'US peeved at Kyuma's attacks on policy', *Asahi.com*, 2 February 2007, available at http://asahi.com/english/Herald-asahi/TKY200702020103.html (accessed 5 February 2007).

50 'Shitsumon to kaito Asahi Shimbunsha Yoron Chōsa', *Asahi Shimbun*, 23 January 2007 (morning edition), p. 4.

51 'Poll: 66 per cent want Article 9 to stay as is', *Asahi Shimbun*, 5 May 2008.

52 'Pensions, health top LDP's platform for July election', *Asahi Shimbun*, 6 June 2007.

53 As cited by D. M. Kliman, *Japan's Security Strategy in the post-9/11 World: Embracing a New Realpolitik*, Westport, CT: Praeger and Washington, DC: Center for Strategic and International Studies, 2006, p. 55. In a differently worded poll by *Kyodo Tsushin*, 54.6 per cent of respondents opposed changing the current constitutional interpretation banning the exercise of the right of collective self-defence, versus 18.3 per cent who wanted to revise this interpretation. See Kyodo, 'Response to Abe's drive: support falls for amending Constitution', *Japan Times*, 17 April 2007.

54 *Yomiuri Shimbun*, 13 July 2007 (morning edition), p. 3.
55 E. Johnston, 'Shimane voters: Has Tokyo helped us?', *Japan Times*, 25 July 2007.
56 However, in the case of government appointments, such as the Governor of the Bank of Japan, an Upper House rejection cannot be overridden.
57 Johnston, 'Shimane voters: Has Tokyo helped us?'.
58 'Kenpō yori seikatsu jyushi o', *Asahi Shimbun*, 31 July 2007 (morning edition), p. 4.
59 'Abe plots new course without clear policies', *Asahi.com*, 29 August 2007, www.asahi.com/english/Herald-asahi/TKY200708290099.html (accessed 4 September 2007).
60 'Sanin kaikenha 3 bun no 2 wareru' and 'Sanin sameru kaiken netsu', *Asahi Shimbun*, 7 August 2007 (morning edition), pp. 1, 4.
61 'Shudanteki jieiken, kondankai no kaihai fukume kentō ... Sanin yosanin de shusho', *Yomiuri Shimbun*, 16 October 2007.
62 Author's interview of 8 August 2007.
63 'Fukuda officially scraps Abe's NSC plan', *Daily Yomiuri Online*, 26 December 2007; and 'Fukuda scraps Abe's security council plan', *Asahi Shimbun*, 26 December 2007.
64 M. Ito, 'Ozawa's Afghan gambit rejected', *Japan Times*, 10 October 2007. Regarding DPJ leader Ozawa Ichiro argued that Japan could dispatch troops to Afghanistan, and even participate in combat operations, if they were participating in a UN operation, but could not do so in support of the US alliance. See 'Ima koso kokusai anzenhoshō no gensoku kakuritsu o', *Sekai*, November 2007.
65 'Cabinet OK's Bill for fresh anti-terror law', *Daily Yomiuri Online*, 18 October 2007; 'Cabinet OKs new anti-terrorism Bill for MSDF', *Asahi Shimbun*, 18 October 2007; International Institute for Strategic Studies (IISS), *Strategic Survey 2006: The ISS Annual Review of World Affairs*, London: Routledge, 2006, p. 357; Kliman, *Japan's Security Strategy in the post-9/11 World*, p. 81; and E. Heginbotham and R. J. Samuels, 'Japan' in Richard J. Ellings and Aaron L. Friedberg (eds) *Strategic Asia, 2002–2003: Asian Aftershocks*, Seattle: National Bureau for Asian Research, 2002, p. 104.
66 'Cabinet support rate plunges to 31 per cent', *Asahi Shimbun*, 22 December 2007. The Kyodo poll cited above had similar results. See Kyodo Tsushin, 'Support rate for Fukuda sinks to 35 per cent over pensions', *Japan Times*, 17 December 2007.
67 Kyodo Tsushin, 'Support rate for Fukuda sinks to 35 per cent over pensions'.
68 '"Jiyu to hanei no yumi" kie "Ajia gaikō kyōka" e gaikō seisho', *Asahi Shimbun*, 1 April 2008.
69 Indeed, visits to Yasukuni by other Cabinet members began declining even during Koizumi's term as Prime Minister, and also vanished under Abe, with only one junior Minister making a last-minute visit to Yasukuni on 15 August 2007.
70 'How to be a good neighbor', *JongAng Daily*, 18 April 2006.
71 See, for example, 'US got Abe to drop denial over sex slaves', *Japan Times*, 9 November 2007.
72 Kyodo Tsushin, 'Schools to skip row on Takeshima', *Japan Times*, 28 May 2008.
73 For example, in the wake of North Korea's nuclear test in October 2006, Abe Cabinet plans to interdict and inspect ships travelling to and from North Korea went nowhere, but plans to speed up missile defence proceeded without any controversy. M. Nakamoto, 'Japan plans to speed up anti-missile programme', *Financial Times*, 26 October 2006.
74 Regarding Japanese missile defence, see 'North Korea's nuclear threat', *Yomiuri Shimbun*, 10 July 2007; 'Govt. OK's U.S. work on multiple warheads', *Yomiuri Shimbun*, 3 May 2008; 'Pentagon seeks second radar system to monitor missiles aimed at U.S.', *Asahi Shimbun*, 27 December 2006; and 'SDF plans PAC-3 redeployment drills', *Yomiuri Shimbun*, 25 November 2007.
75 'Diet enacts law on use of space for defence', *Japan Times*, 22 May 2008; and K. Kobayashi, 'New space policy result of regional tensions', *Japan Times*, 22 May

2008. Regarding the legislation, see 'Coalition to submit space-defence Bill', *Asahi Shimbun*, 7 June 2007; Jiyū minshūto seimu chōsakai, uchū kaihatsu tokubetsu iinkai, aratana uchū kaihatsu riyō seido no kōchiku ni mukete: Heiwa kokka Nihon toshite no uchū seisaku (An), September 2006, pp. 12–13; and Steven Berner, 'Japan's Space Program: A Fork in the Road', unpublished party document, Santa Monica, CA: Rand Corporation, National Security Research Division, 2005, pp. 4–37.

76 Defensive Realism is a school of thought within Realism and the study of international politics. What is referred to here is 'attitudinal Defensive Realism', a set of attitudes found in public opinion, and in this case Japanese public opinion. Academic Realism and attitudinal realism are distinct, but similar in some ways. For two of the most representative works of academic Defensive Realism see S. Van Evera, *Causes of War*, Ithaca, NY: Cornell University Press, 1999, and J. L. Snyder, *Myths of Empire*, Ithaca, NY: Cornell University Press, 1991. Regarding the role of attitudes in structuring public opinion, see J. Hurwitz and M. Peffley, 'How are foreign policy attitudes structured? A hierarchical model', *American Political Science Review* 81 (4), December 1987, pp. 1099–119. For more on attitudinal Defensive Realism in Japanese public opinion and the relationship with academic Realism see P. Midford, 'Japanese mass opinion and the War on Terrorism' in R. Eldridge and P. Midford (eds) *Public Opinion and the War on Terrorism*, New York: Palgrave, 2008, pp. 11–43.

77 D. Kang, *China Rising*, New York: Columbia University Press, 2007.

78 Ibid.

79 According to *Yomiuri Shimbun's* annual question asking respondents whether they trust America, a plurality has distrusted the United States since 2003, and since 2004 (at least through 2007) this plurality has expanded into an absolute majority. See P. Midford, *Japanese Public Opinion and the War on Terrorism: Implications for Japan's Security Strategy*, Policy Study 27, Washington, DC: East–West Center, 2006, p. 47, table 17. For the results for 2007 see 'Nichibei kyodo chōsa-Nichibei kankei ni futomekan', *Yomiuri Shimbun*, 14 December 2007, p. 12. For a discussion of entrapment fears see R. Samuels, *Securing Japan*, pp. 83–4.

80 On Small Japanism see S. H. Nolte, *Liberalism in Modern Japan: Ishibashi Tanzan and his Teachers, 1905–1960*, Berkeley, CA: University of California Press, 1987.

81 See Y. Soeya, *Nihon no 'Middle Power' gaikō: sengo nihon no sentaku to kōsō*, Tokyo: Chikuma Shincho, 2005.

Part II

Case studies

4 Shifting incentives for political leadership

Verena Blechinger-Talcott

Leadership in Japanese politics has been and still is a contested issue in academic and public debates.[1] Many studies on Japanese politics and political decision making explicitly or implicitly argue that Japanese politics is characterized by an absence of decisive leadership, and that not only the patterns of political decision making but also political recruiting and the importance of seniority practically prevent individual politicians from becoming charismatic, proactive leaders.[2] Others stress that leaders nevertheless matter in Japanese politics, although their leadership style is different from other democracies.[3]

Media images of Japanese leadership have been shifting quite dramatically since the late 1990s. Although the media in the United States and Europe (and to a certain degree also in Japan) seemed to agree that Japanese politics lacked leaders, things changed dramatically in 2001 when Prime Minister Junichiro Koizumi took over the reins of government. Koizumi's charismatic personality and assertive leadership style triggered a veritable Koizumi boom in Japan and internationally. The Liberal Democratic Party (LDP) headquarters in Nagatacho became, for several months, one of the city's main attractions. Tourist buses stopped there during their sightseeing programmes, and hundreds of shoppers crowded the LDP gift store to purchase Koizumi goods for themselves and their friends: T-shirts, mugs, stickers, calendars and posters. A cartoon character that depicted the new prime minister as 'Lion Heart' in an oversized lion costume with a big red pulsating heart became a 'must have' item, not only for young women. And for several weeks a huge Koizumi poster covered one of the sides of the LDP building. A Japanese publisher, Futabasha, even produced a Koizumi photo album (*shashinshū*), a genre usually featuring the private lives of pop stars and actors.[4] Foreign observers of Japanese politics became similarly excited about this new and seemingly innovative leader that had risen to power in Japan. Major international newspapers carried feature articles about the new man in Nagatacho, and Japan experts worldwide gathered in panels and workshops to analyse and understand the 'Koizumi phenomenon'.

The Koizumi boom lasted for about eighteen months. Thereafter, commentators both in Japan and abroad lost their enthusiasm and a more gloomy tone returned to Japanese political commentary. Three years after his leaving office,

Koizumi is portrayed no longer as the bright star in the Japanese political firmament, but as a politician with shortcomings and deficiencies who succeeded in maintaining a support rate of 50 per cent or more throughout his time in office[5] and who could secure a landslide victory for his party in the 2005 Lower House elections. In the end, however, Koizumi failed in his endeavour to produce sustainable economic and structural reforms, mostly due to resistance from within his own party. His successors, until they were voted out of power in August 2009 by the now ruling DJP party, had to confront a much more difficult situation in the Diet after losing the (coalition) majority in the Upper House in 2007. After this, media coverage of Japanese politics, both domestic and international, portrayed Japanese politics as characterized by a 'leadership vacuum'[6] that led to a situation where Japan had three prime ministers in three years, Shinzo Abe (September 2006–September 2007), Yasuo Fukuda (September 2007–September 2008), and Taro Aso (September 2008–2009), and where the prime minister faced ever dropping support rates.

Do we have a shortage of leaders in Japan and especially in the long-term ruling party, the LDP? Was Prime Minister Koizumi – who was long considered too radical by fellow party members and political observers and thus unlikely to become prime minister – the first of a new group of leaders in Japanese politics? Or was Koizumi's tenure as prime minister rather an aberration in Japanese politics? Does political leadership in Japan change? Can we see current developments in Japan in the context of similar developments in Europe, where political leadership turned away from media-oriented postures of leadership after the demise of the Blair and Schroeder governments?

In this chapter I analyse aspects of training and career development of Japanese politicians, especially within the LDP. I explain how leaders have emerged in the LDP and what effect the process of becoming a party leader has had on the leadership style in national politics. I point out incentives and opportunities for leadership embedded in the Japanese political system and especially in the relationship between politicians and voters, on the one hand, and within the LDP decision-making process on the other. The argument I make in this chapter consists of four points.

First, leadership in Japanese politics and especially within the LDP is the product of incentives and opportunities embedded in the mechanisms of political and party decision making. If we want to understand the core of political leadership in Japan, we have to turn to the distribution of power in the Japanese political system and to the relationship between politicians, their voters, supporters, and fellow party and Diet members. I argue that until the mid-1990s, politicians who wanted to make a career in the LDP and/or in government had to focus on two tasks: catering to the (often narrow) interests of their local support base (which was not necessarily the whole electoral district) and building a network among fellow LDP Diet members. This situation favoured political leaders that were highly skilled as mediators between often conflicting interests, but it penalized those who self-assertively took charge of policy issues or who singlemindedly proposed path-breaking new legislation.[7]

Second, incentives for leaders in Japanese politics are undergoing major changes. Japanese and especially LDP politicians today are confronted with social and demographic change that affects their voter base and thus presents them with a different set of choices than their predecessors. Whereas the LDP party leaders and prime ministers of the 1980s and 1990s could base their careers on strong and durable support networks in rural constituencies, today urban districts have become more and more important. These districts confront political leaders with different demands and opportunities, and they favour different leadership skills. Moreover, recent institutional changes, such as the introduction of a new electoral system for the Lower House in 1994, provided politicians with different incentives for career building.

Third, leadership in Japanese politics is changing as a result of these institutional and societal changes. Instead of political leaders who are highly skilled in mediating between often narrow specialized constituencies and who are experts in the push and pull of party politics, we will see more political leaders in the future who strive to appeal directly to a broader, more urban, voter base and to the media. Some of these new leaders might be populists, but we also see an increasing professionalisation among Japanese politicians. The new generation of political leaders is dominated in wide parts by second-generation Diet members or graduates of political training academies. These politicians are better prepared for political office, are better skilled in their handling of the media, and have more international experience than their predecessors.

Fourth, this change in personnel, together with the growing importance of urban voters and the changing incentives presented by new political institutions, will be difficult to reverse. This has to be seen as the core legacy of former Prime Minister Koizumi whose policies practically destroyed the established decision-making structures within the Liberal Democratic Party. New leaders may also attempt to invigorate the role of the Diet as the main generator of policy, as demonstrated by the rise in cross-party working groups staffed by young Diet members who are interested in fundamental change, including constitutional and administrative reform.

Leadership until the mid-1990s

Electoral victory in Japan has been and still is determined to a high degree by the quality of the personal connections of a Diet member with his or her core voters. For this reason, politicians spend much effort satisfying loyal voters, who are organized in Diet members' personal support groups (*kōenkai*), while intensively lobbying for new votes. *Kōenkai* members usually include local entrepreneurs, leaders of local associations, and religious institutions and influential constituents who are in a position to use their leading role within the local community to speak out in support of a candidate. One way to ensure the loyalty of the local electorate and to improve the chances of re-election has been the acquisition of public subsidies and funds for local infrastructure projects (roads, tunnels, bridges) from the national government for the constituency.[8] To satisfy demands from local interest groups and to thus ensure re-election, LDP Diet members in particular engage in cultivating ties with bureaucrats in the central government ministries. A candidate's contacts (*kone*) within the central bureaucracy and the quality of his or her service to the support group have been (and still are) a decisive factor in determining a politician's chance for re-election. Political actors gain status or influence not only from their position in their constituency, but also from their standing within the party hierarchy or their appointment to high-ranking posts in influential political and social organizations.

In the LDP, status gains within the party hierarchy were (and still are) frequently reached by building upon a support network within the party, in the often officially dissolved, but still active party factions (*habatsu*). While factions have lost some of their influence in LDP politics due to campaign finance reform and the change to single member districts in 1994, they still play a vital role in the selection of party officials and Cabinet members.[9] As the uproar about the appointment of Shinzo Abe to LDP Secretary General in the early 2000s illustrates, to rise within the party hierarchy, a leading position within a faction is usually a prerequisite. Senior faction leaders actively recruit new members for their intra-party groups among candidates for the Diet, and they provide candidates and junior Diet members with organizational (and often also financial) support and valuable contacts within politics, the bureaucracy, and business. In return, faction members support their candidacy for party leadership positions.

Like businesses, politicians also needed money to fund their activities. Until donations to individual politicians became illegal in 2000, Diet members drew the majority of their revenues from donations by corporations and interest groups. Since, many donors have shifted their payments to the local party chapter, which is run by the politician who used to receive individual donations directly. The relationship between politicians and their 'sponsors' was thereby determined by mutual obligations, which corresponded in essence to those in the 'service contract' between politicians and their supporters in the electoral district.[10] Local interest groups expected their Diet member to channel as many advantages as possible into their particular region. Corporations which financed individual politicians hoped for their backing in the central bureaucracy, which was difficult to access for businesses trying to push into a new market. The difference lay in the reward politicians received for their mediation. Whereas groups of supporters in an electoral district were able to mobilize great numbers of votes, sponsors from the private industry made political contributions. The quest for money and votes therefore bound politicians to their districts and to industry outside of their districts.

What did this mean for leadership? Up to the late 1990s, LDP politicians in party leadership positions excelled especially in two sets of skills: networking and mediating. In order to rise in the political hierarchy, it was important to build a vast network of contacts both within the central government ministries and with local and national businesses. These contacts helped politicians to mediate successfully between local interest groups from a Diet member's constituency and central government ministries, and they also ensured a flow of political donations that helped fund election campaigns. On the other hand, the same skills proved useful in lobbying other Diet members to expand politicians' support networks and thus to increase their chances in the race for party leadership positions.

The same skills were applied in policy deliberations within the party. Since the 1970s, all Cabinet-sponsored Bills have been subject to discussion within the committees of the LDP's Policy Affairs Research Council (PARC, *seisaku chōsa kai*). Only after the relevant subcommittee and the PARC's executive council have given their approval are bills introduced to the Diet. LDP Diet members usually vote unanimously in Diet deliberations.[11] In the party's policy committees, however, Diet members and especially expert politicians in a certain policy area (*zoku giin*) try to influence proposed legislation in the interests of their supporters outside the Diet. In this deliberation process, negotiating and mediating skills and also the ability to use a wide network of contacts within the party for bargaining purposes again prove useful in establishing support for or drumming up opposition against a certain policy agenda. The party policy subcommittees are also the areas where policy expertise can be useful in establishing a position of power within the party. In contrast to Cabinet members, who are frequently rotated in and out of their positions and who rarely have enough time to familiarize themselves enough with the issues and agendas of their respective ministries, party policy experts can exert long-term influence on policy making within their area of expertise.[12]

The consequences of this system for leadership in Japanese politics were (and to a certain degree still are) twofold. First, leadership was exercised outside of the Diet in the LDP party committees and thus behind doors closed to the public. Leaders usually did not distinguish themselves for their elaborate speeches in the Diet or their policy initiatives in Diet committees, but were respected for their ability to influence decision-making processes within the party policy subcommittees in favour of or against a certain bill. Second, this setting was useful for maintaining the status quo and for ensuring smooth decision-making processes, but it was less effective in times of crisis or rapid change that demanded quick decisions.

Pressures for change

With the 1994 political reforms, pressure for change rose in recent years induced also by social and demographic developments in Japan and brought with it demands for new and more proactive leadership. In 1994 a set of institutional reforms changed the Japanese electoral system, the mechanisms for political funding and the status of political parties. The old multi-member, medium-sized district system (*chūsenkyoku seido*) with a single non-transferable vote was changed into a parallel system (*heiritsusei*) of 300 single-member districts and 200 (later reduced to 180) seats decided by personal representation in eleven regional blocs. The new system and the related realignment of electoral districts affected both the campaigning within local constituencies and the role of LDP factions (*habatsu*).

Up to the 1994 electoral reform, Japanese Diet members were elected from multi-seat constituencies and therefore competed not only with candidates from other parties, but – at least in the case of the LDP – also with politicians from their own party. This system had the advantage that, especially in districts with one very strong competitor, a rather small number of votes was sufficient to win. Candidates could thus focus their attention at subconstituencies within their district, for example at a certain area within the district, or at a certain group of voters, and still have a good chance of getting elected. In the new single-member districts, however, candidates need to win a plurality of votes. This required a change in campaign strategy. Candidates now have to appeal to broader groups of voters and to pay attention to the demands of several groups within the constituency in order to maximize their chances of getting elected.[13] As each party is now allowed to field only one candidate per district (and therefore competition between candidates from the same party is limited to the nomination process), factions lost their previous pivotal role in organizing and supporting candidates' election campaigns. Campaigns are now coordinated between local politicians' district offices, LDP party chapters and LDP headquarters.[14]

The cultivation of personal votes and close ties between representatives and voters, both key elements in election campaign strategies, work best in rural settings. In urban areas, usually more diverse in their social structure, with a higher percentage of floating voters, and a higher fluctuation of voters due to people moving in and out of districts, it is nearly impossible to establish a personal support group that is as stable and works as efficiently as one in a rural district. Politicians in urban districts face a variety of demands from their voters, and they need to be more active to stay present in their voters' minds. They also need to embrace strategies other than the provision of public works projects and attracting government subsidies to appeal to the younger and mostly non-aligned voters in urban constituencies. Especially young voters often adopt a critical attitude towards the LDP due to its long hold to power, its perceived lack of transparency in decision making and frequent corruption scandals. Pre-election surveys in recent years frequently found that only a small percentage of voters in their twenties and thirties trust (LDP) politicians.[15] Diet members from urban areas generally have to campaign more intensely and regularly between elections than do representatives of rural constituencies in order to retain the name recognition that is critical to winning elections in Japan.

One more crucial aspect in this context is that electoral districts were insufficiently adjusted to population development. District lines were originally drawn in 1946 due to the fact that the majority of Japanese lived in the countryside. With subsequent high economic growth, many Japanese moved from country to urban areas where the jobs were located. In consequence, a major imbalance of district sizes and the number of voters emerged between the growing urban and the depopulating rural districts. The number of votes necessary to win an election was significantly lower in rural areas than in urban areas. While the imbalance between the most and the least densely populated electoral districts was as high as 4.98:1 in the 1998 Upper House election, in the Lower House elections the imbalance stabilized at about 2.4:1 from the 1980s due to district size adjustments ordered by the Supreme Court.[16]

Until the 1990s the prevailing strategy among LDP leaders was first to create a solid and lasting base in the constituency through an established support group and a track record of several successful re-elections, and then to shift the focus towards national politics gradually.[17] As representatives of urban constituencies were more engaged in campaigning and also more frequently ran the risk of losing an election than their colleagues from rural areas, the majority of LDP leaders throughout the post-war period came from rural constituencies.[18] This proved to be a challenge for the LDP after the 1994 electoral reform when single-member districts were introduced and district lines redrawn. Even today in the LDP there is still a slight imbalance between urban and rural areas favouring rural constituencies, nonetheless the importance of urban districts for winning a majority in the Diet increased. New strategies were needed to appeal to the diverse, critical and mostly disorganized group of urban voters who tended not to vote for the LDP, but to favour the opposition parties.

For LDP politicians, another challenge presented itself in the rise of anti-LDP movements in rural areas from the late 1990s. Voters became increasingly critical of the infrastructure projects initiated by LDP Diet members. Since the major burden of the cost for such investments has to be shouldered by local authorities, centrally initiated public works projects significantly weakened the financial stability of local communities. As a consequence, in several rural areas, citizens organized protest movements against such projects. This movement reached a high degree of popularity when in 2000 postmodernist author Yasuo Tanaka, a non-political, won the race for Governor of Nagano on a policy platform that explicitly criticized the often wasteful public works projects. For LDP politicians, this development implied the need to rethink and redesign election campaigns and also constituency relations in order to address the new demands from rural voters. In the following years, at the local level, a number of referenda against unpopular large-scale public works projects made national headlines and further illustrated the increasing dissatisfaction of rural voters with their LDP representatives.[19]

As a consequence of the apparent dissatisfaction among voters, the leaders of LDP prefectural chapters showed increasing signs of nervousness. In the 1996 and 2000 Lower House elections (held after the introduction of the new electoral system in 1994) the LDP lost dramatically in urban areas, while the main opposition Democratic Party of Japan (DPJ) managed to establish itself as a new grassroots-style party with a strong urban appeal. After losing numerous urban districts to the DPJ in the 2000 Lower House election, unrest grew among prefectural LDP members, especially in metropolitan areas. They feared that the LDP leadership under then Prime Minister Yoshiro Mori was not taking the situation seriously enough and that another defeat in the 2001 Upper House elections would be unavoidable.

Prior to and at the beginning of the 2001 LDP party convention, angry representatives from urban prefectural party organizations staged protests in front of the convention centre and handed out flyers asking for immediate reform. LDP leaders responded to the uproar among the party's rank-and-file members and agreed to change the election mode for the LDP party president. While in earlier times the party's top leader was selected almost entirely by the LDP representatives in both houses of the Diet, under the new system the prefectural party chapters were included in the selection process. Nationwide primaries on the prefectural level were held for the first time in 2001, and in a final vote 346 LDP members of both houses of the Diet and three representatives from each prefectural chapter (all together 141 delegates) cast a vote on the new party leader. The outcome of this leadership election led to the victory of Junichiro Koizumi, a candidate who previously qualified as an outside contender due to his maverick views.[20] In addition, Koizumi was the first LDP president and prime minister representing an urban district. So long as this mechanism for the party's presidential election is maintained an urban strategy will increasingly become important for candidates considering a bid for a party leadership position.

As a consequence of these demographic and institutional changes, the incentives for political leaders within the LDP have been modified. Political leaders are now under higher pressure than before to accommodate the demands of an increasingly urban electorate, and they have to adapt to new demands from rural voters. As demographic change advances and politicians face the rapid ageing of rural constituencies, this issue becomes even more important. On top of the urban–rural divide, politicians also face increasingly diverging demands of a majority elderly voter base in the countryside and younger urban voters. Instead of providing pork to specialized groups of long-time supporters with whom a close relationship could be formed, politicians now face the challenge of appealing to a much broader and more diverse group of voters. Moreover, while it was sufficient until 2001 to appeal to other LDP Diet members in order to be elected party president, now candidates for party leadership also have to demonstrate to rank-and-file party members that they are able to ensure electoral victory on the regional and national levels. New qualities, such as abilities to speak in public or make expert use of the media, have become increasingly important. (See P. Midford's chapter in this volume on the growing importance of opinion polls in politics.) The emergence of Junichiro Koizumi as party president and the ensuing eighteen months of 'Koizumi boom' in Japan represent this new kind of leadership, not because of his personal charisma, but for his usefulness in the altered electoral environment.

Naturally, Koizumi was not the first leader the LDP ever produced, but he was a different kind of leader. What made him so special to voters and the Japanese and foreign media alike was his declared willingness to take charge of Japanese politics, to enact political and structural reforms 'without sacred cows' and to even destroy his own party if it resisted his call for structural reforms in Japan. After ten years of economic crisis, political stagnation and missed opportunities that made commentators characterize the 1990s as a 'lost decade' for Japan,[21] the populist and media-savvy Koizumi seemed to many like a long-awaited hero who would help the country to get back on track and tackle economic and structural reforms.

The reforms initiated by Prime Minister Koizumi did in fact lead to major changes, especially within the LDP. Building on reform efforts started by his predecessors Yasuhiro Nakasone (1982–87) and Ryutaro Hashimoto (1996–98), Koizumi's efforts focused on establishing an independent leadership role for the prime minister within the government and especially within his own party. Nakasone's reforms were inspired by neo-liberal paradigms of a small state and wide-scale privatization. This agenda was widely contested within the LDP and the central government bureaucracy. In order to achieve his goal, Nakasone introduced wide-ranging administrative reform, accompanied by a system of special advisory committees staffed by experts from business and academia, and he strategically used the media as an instrument to increase support for his policies against resistance within the LDP. Both strategies gave the prime minister more control over information, both towards the public and within party decision-making processes, and therefore strengthened the role of the prime minister. Similarly, Hashimoto strove to establish independent decision-making capabilities within the Prime Minister's Office by launching a large-scale administrative reform and a reorganization of government ministries.[22]

Koizumi actively used these new structures and established a governance system that practically bypassed the previously dominant decision-making institutions within the LDP. He created the Council on Fiscal and Economic Reform (*keizai zaisei shimon kaigi*), which then was entrusted with producing policy proposals that were directly introduced in the Cabinet. Only after Cabinet discussion were the proposals forwarded to the LDP PARC for deliberation. By then at least parts of the reform proposals were already publicized and debated in the media, which made it difficult for anti-reformists among LDP Diet members to prevent reforms or even to introduce major changes. At the same time, Koizumi's core reforms, the privatization of postal services, reduced the amount of funds available for public investment programmes, thus eliminating the power base of most rural-based LDP heavyweights. While Koizumi's rhetoric focused on the reduction of public debt, he also made it clear to his own party and the public that postal service reforms were an intrinsic part of his strategy to revive and change his own party.[23] In consequence, while most observers agree that Koizumi failed in achieving his broader objective to revitalize politics and political economy, I argue that the changes he introduced to LDP decision-making institutions and processes are sustainable and have significantly affected the inner workings of the LDP leadership.

The new generation

Koizumi first entered office in the 1960s. He was the chief lieutenant of the Mori faction and resembled in other ways the pedigree of a 'traditional' LDP party president. At least two of his three successors since 2006 list personal and career elements in their political portfolios that would easily have qualified them for leadership during the 1990s. As one example, Taro Aso, the Prime Minister (2008–2009), was a contender for the LDP presidency for a long period of time.

At the lower stages in the party hierarchy, however, new groups of politicians are entering the political arena who seem to be well qualified to adapt to the new incentives. Within both the LDP and the DPJ we find an increasing number of well trained and highly professional politicians with a strong orientation towards grass-roots activities and policy consultation beyond party lines. The majority of these new types of politician belong to two groups: second and third-generation politicians who 'inherited' their seats from their fathers, grandfathers or uncles; and trained politicians who graduated from 'political training academies' such as the Matsushita Institute of Government and Management (*Matsushita seikei juku*).

As of autumn 2008, 131 of 480 members of the Lower House (about 25 per cent) were second or third-generation politicians. Within the LDP the share of political heirs is even higher; 108 out of 303 LDP Lower House members (about 30 per cent) won their mandates as successors to their fathers, grandfathers, fathers-in-law, uncles or other family members. The second largest group of political heirs could be found among the members of the present governing party, the DPJ; sixteen of 113 DPJ representatives in the Lower House (around 15 per cent) are political heirs. Further political 'heirs' can be found in the Clean Government Party (Komei Party), one representative out of thirty-one; the Japan New Party (Kokumin Shin Party) two representatives out of seven; and among independents three representatives of nine.[24]

To illustrate the importance of political heirs within the LDP, it has to be pointed out that second and third-generation Diet members are more prominent in leading party and Cabinet positions than their colleagues without a 'political' family background. Of the twelve Japanese prime ministers since 1991, five were second or third-generation politicians (namely Miyazawa, Hata, Hashimoto, Obuchi, Koizumi, Abe, Fukuda and Aso).[25] In the former Aso Cabinet twelve out of eighteen members (or about 60 per cent) were political heirs. Four of the Cabinet members, Prime Minister Aso, Foreign Minister Hirofumi Nakasone, Minister of Internal Affairs and Communication, Kunio Hatoyama, Minister of State for Decentralization Reform and Yuko Obuchi, Minister of State for Social Affairs and Gender Equality, all are children of former prime ministers.[26] A similarly high rate of political 'heirs' can be found when one looks at the Koizumi, Abe and Fukuda Cabinets.

Second and third-generation Diet members have a career advantage over their peers without a political family background due to their relatively young age and high public exposure. They all start their political careers drawing on an already existing and strong support structure that other Diet members have to start building upon election. This advantage leaves second and third-generation Diet members more time for career planning and related activities in their party and in parliament. As a consequence, they reach leading party and government positions at a comparatively younger age than their peers without this background and thus have a better chance to reach top positions during their time in office. The significance of this was mentioned above: five of the last nine prime ministers were political heirs, and many second and third-generation Diet members hold Cabinet and LDP leadership positions.

Political heirs have generally better knowledge of the political world than newcomers at the start of their careers. Most of them have prepared themselves for taking over the 'family business', have worked as political secretaries and thus have built up extensive and useful networks that their peers without such a background cannot rely on. In the Japanese press such politicians are therefore often called 'political thoroughbreds' (*seikai no sarabureddo*).

Some scholars, such as Norihiko Narita, president of Surugadai University and former executive secretary to Prime Minister Morihiro Hosokawa, pointed out that second and third-generation Diet members do not automatically win elections, and that after electoral reform in 1994 the competitive advantage of name recognition has been reduced due to the introduction of single seat constituencies. According to Narita, the current 'boom' of political 'heirs' is mostly determined by decisions voters made under the old system, as most of the current leaders who come from political families were first elected prior to 1996.[27] However, the fact that the majority of political 'heirs' succeeded in retaining their seats, and also that the number of candidates in national elections with a political family background is regularly continuously high, shows that this trend is not likely to end in the near future. Moreover, the career advantages outlined above, such as younger average age, better knowledge of political affairs, and an existing network within the Tokyo power elite, are not affected by the electoral system and will still enable political 'heirs' to pursue a faster career track than their competitors without this background.

We can expect that the increase in second-generation politicians will cause a higher degree of professionalization in Japanese politics. These politicians are well trained and prepared for their positions when they come into office. Many of them have studied abroad or have worked as interns in the offices of politicians in the US Congress, and they thus have experience with a distinctively American style of leadership. While this will of course not instantly transform Japanese politics, it is certainly a different format of leadership. Many young second-generation Diet members, such as Junichiro Koizumi or former Minister Nobuteru Ishihara, the latter of whom is well known as a promoter of reforms, expressed dissatisfaction with the 'traditional style' of leadership within the LDP. The emergence of young Diet members' inter-party working groups critical of the slow pace of reform and the strong influence of vested interests in Japanese political decision making illustrates this trend for change on the supply side of leadership.

A second group of politicians that seems to be well prepared for the new challenges and opportunities for leadership in Japanese politics is the graduates of political training academies such as the Matsushita Institute of Government and Management (Matsushita seikei juku). Founded in 1979 by the founder of Matsushita Electric, this institution trains future leaders in politics, business and the media. Of the 230 graduates the Institute had produced by 2008, about 44 per cent (100 graduates) were active in the field of politics. Of them, sixty-nine held public office; thirty were Diet members (twenty-seven in the Lower House and three in the Upper House), and the others were representatives in prefectural or local assemblies.

The Matsushita Institute's three-year programme includes, among others, leadership training, internships at national and international political organizations, training in public speaking, work experience on a factory assembly line, intensive language training in English, Chinese or Korean, and the infamous 100 km march lasting twenty-four hours, an exercise that is meant to test the endurance and willpower of future political leaders. After graduation, alumni tend to keep a close relationship with the Institute, and since its graduates can be found in all major parties, alumni groups also form the basis for regular policy study groups that cross party lines.[28] While the Institute is the best known and so far the most effective of the political training academies in Japan, similar initiatives have been developed by political parties, especially the DPJ and the LDP, in recent years. Professionalization has clearly become a trend in Japanese politics.

Conclusion

In conclusion, it can be stated that, despite media reports and the rather gloomy image of the Japanese political leadership reflected in media polls, there is no shortage or 'vacuum' of leaders in Japan today. What we find, however, is a change in leadership style. Incentives for leadership that brought the LDP party officials of the 1990s into power did not make them effective in dealing with the need for quick decisions and bold reforms. Former Prime Minister Mori, for example, has an excellent reputation as a mediator between competing groups within his party and is still an important faction leader whose influence became visible in the Koizumi, Abe and Fukuda Cabinets. But as prime minister he encountered serious problems addressing the need for structural reform or interacting with the media, which led to his reputation as one of the least popular prime ministers in Japan's post-war history. Similarly, Prime Minister Aso rose in the ranks of the LDP responding to the incentives for leadership set in the political system of the 1980s and 1990s.

Changes in the country's demographics and in important institutions in political decision making have led to a shift in these incentives. LDP presidential candidates no longer need merely to appeal to fellow Diet members or supporters in their constituencies with whom they have established long-term relationships, but are now required to present themselves as personable, professional and able to win elections in order to secure the votes from the party's rank-and-file members. The increasing importance of success in urban districts will further raise the incentive for politicians of all parties to increase their media skills. The major problem Japanese political leaders are facing today is the fact that Prime Minister Koizumi, during his tenure, removed or considerably weakened the last elements of incentives for political leaders, that is, the mediating vote. As he was (and still is) a very skilled communicator and enjoyed relatively high support rates among the public, even towards the end of his administration, Koizumi could use new instruments for leadership, such as personal advisory councils and frequent media appearances, very effectively and to his benefit. His successors, however, are not as skilled in the use of such Koizumi techniques to appeal to both the party and the public. At the same time, the old institutions within the LDP that allowed leadership by mediation and behind-the-scenes negotiations were considerably weakened by Koizumi. The media and public now expect good communication. The current leadership crisis perceived by Japanese and foreign media is a symptom of the shift in incentives detailed in this chapter. Among the younger LDP Diet members we find new groups who entered Japanese politics in recent years and who can be considered to be highly professional politicians with the potential to communicate and to lead. It remains to be seen whether party members vote one of them into party leadership, as was the case with Koizumi.

Acknowledgements

An earlier version of this chapter was presented at the Woodrow Wilson Center in Washington, DC in 2003 and published as part of the report *Learning to Lead: Incentives and Disincentives for Leadership in Japanese Politics*, Special Report No. 117, Washington, DC: Woodrow Wilson International Center for Scholars, Asia Program, 2004, pp. 20–5.

Notes

1 Leadership in this chapter is understood as including both characteristics of the office and characteristics of the person. Leaders are actors in high-ranking positions within an organization, such as a political party or government, which come with their own sets of responsibilities and opportunities. We can also consider leadership as a quality that characterizes outstanding politicians and as their ability to initiate change in policies, political processes, and institutions by, as R. Samuels put it, 'inspiring', 'buying' or 'bullying' those around them. See R. Samuels, *Macchiavelli's Children: Leaders and their Legacies in Italy and Japan*, Ithaca, NY: Cornell University Press, 2003, p. 8.

2 See, for example, K. Hayao, *The Japanese Prime Minister and Public Policy*, Pittsburgh, PA: University of Pittsburgh Press, 1993; A. George Mulgan, 'Japan's political leadership deficit', *Australian Journal of Political Science* 35 (2), 2000, 183–202; and I. Ozawa, *Blueprint for a New Japan: the Rethinking of a Nation*, Tokyo: Kodansha International, 1994.

3 Examples for this line of argument are Samuels, *Macchiavelli's Children*, or A. Gaunder, *Political Reform in Japan: Leadership Looming Large*, London: Routledge, 2007.

4 Futabasha (ed.) *Koizumi Junichiro Shashinshū*, Tokyo: Futabasha, 2001.

5 *Japan Times*, 6 April 2006.

6 *New York Times*, 3 September 2008.

7 One example would be Makiko Tanaka's appointment in the Ministry of Foreign Affairs, which lasted from April 2001 to January 2002. Tanaka started out as a strong critic of the ways in which political and bureaucratic decision making had been conducted and promised major reforms and new style in politics. While she was widely popular prior to and in the early stages of her tenure as Foreign Minister, her harsh treatment of high-level bureaucrats and her frequent and biting criticism of the administration she was then a part of, among other factors, led to her early dismissal.

8 See, for example, E. Scheiner, *Democracy without Competition in Japan: Opposition Failure in a One-party Dominant State*, Cambridge and New York: Cambridge

University Press, 2005; G. Curtis, *The Logic of Japanese Politics: Leaders, Institutions, and the Limits of Change*, New York: Columbia University Press, 1999; or H. Fukui and S. Fukai, 'The informal politics of Japanese Diet elections: cases and interpretations' in L. Dittmer, H. Fukui and P. N. S. Lee (eds) *Informal Politics in East Asia*, Cambridge and New York: Cambridge University Press, 1997, pp. 23–41.

9 See, for example, E. Krauss and R. Pekkanen, 'Explaining party adaptation to electoral reform: the discreet charm of the LDP?', *Journal of Japanese Studies* 30 (1), 2004, 1–34.

10 See, for example, V. Blechinger, 'Cleaning up politics and revitalizing democracy? A European view of the new system of political finance in Japan', *European Review* 8 (4), 2000, 533–51; for a more detailed account see V. Blechinger, *Politische Korruption in Japan. Ursachen, Hintergründe und Reformversuche*, Hamburg: Institute of Asian Affairs, 1998.

11 See, for example, E. Sakakibara, *Structural Reform in Japan: Breaking the Iron Triangle*, Washington, DC: Brookings Institution, 2003.

12 A concise account of LDP party decision-making processes can be found in A. George Mulgan, *Japan's Failed Revolution: Koizumi and the Politics of Economic Reform*, Canberra: Asia Pacific Press, 2002, pp. 129–41.

13 For an empirical test of the geographical effects of electoral reform see S. Hirano, 'Electoral institutions, home towns, and favoured minorities: evidence from Japanese electoral reforms', *World Politics* 58, 2006, 51–82.

14 While their influence in election campaigning seems to be reduced, factions still are major actors in LDP leadership decisions. For more details see Krauss and Pekkanen, 'Explaining party adaptation to electoral reform'; C. H. Park, 'Factional dynamics in Japan's LDP since political reform: continuity and change', *Asian Survey* 41 (3), 2001, 428–61; P. Köllner, *Die Organisation japanischer Parteien. Entwicklung, Wandel und Konsequenzen formaler und informeller Institutionen*, Hamburg: Institute of Asian Affairs, 2006.

15 For a discussion of the issues of trust and corruption in Japanese politics see for example S. Pharr, 'Public trust and corruption in Japan' in A. J. Heidenheimer and M. Johnston (eds) *Political Corruption: Concepts and Contexts*, New Brunswick, NJ: Transaction Books, 2002, pp. 835–60.

16 An adjustment of electoral districts was made possible in the Public Office Election Law, but it would have required legal action. As the imbalance between rural and urban areas favoured until the 1990s not only the LDP but also the largest opposition party, the Japan Socialist Party, no such law was introduced to parliament. For a detailed discussion see A. George Mulgan, *The Politics of Agriculture in Japan*, London: Routledge, 2000, pp. 368–74.

17 See, for example, Hayao, *The Japanese Prime Minister and Public Policy*.

18 Among the post-war prime ministers, since the 1950s, Junichiro Koizumi was the first to be elected from an urban constituency, Yokosuka, in Kanagawa prefecture, in the Tokyo metropolitan area. All other prime ministers come from rural constituencies, among which Gunma prefecture stands out, with four prime ministers: Takeo Fukuda (1976–78), Yasuhiro Nakasone (1983–87), Keizo Obuchi (1998–2000) and Yasuo Fukuda (2007–08). Two prime ministers come from rural Hiroshima, Hayatō Ikeda (1960–64) and Kiichi Miyazawa (1991–93).

19 For a detailed discussion see, for example, P. E. Lam, 'Local governance: the role of referenda and the rise of independent governors' in G. Hook (ed.) *Contested Governance in Japan: Sites and Issues*, Abingdon and New York: Routledge, 2005, pp. 71–89.

20 For further details see, for example, V. Blechinger, 'Reformland Japan?', *Blätter für deutsche und internationale Politik* 6, 2001, 653–7.

21 For the term 'lost decade' and related discourses see for example A. Komorida (ed.) *Ushinawareta jūnen o koeru*, Tokyo: University of Tokyo Press, 2005.

22 For Nakasone's reforms see for example M. Muramatsu, 'In search of national identity: the politics and policies of the Nakasone administration', *Journal of Japanese Studies* 13 (2), 1987, 307–42; or J. Iio, *Min'eika no seiji katei. Rinchō kaikaku no seika to genkai*, Tokyo: University of Tokyo Press, 1993. For the Hashimoto reforms see J. Campbell, 'Administrative reform as policy change and policy non-change', *Social Science Japan Journal* 2 (2), 1999, 157–6; K. Mishima, 'The changing relationship between Japan's LDP and the bureaucracy: Hashimoto's administrative reform effort and its politics', *Asian Survey* 38 (10), 1998, 968–85.

23 For a discussion of Koizumi's strategy and reforms see for example I. Kabashima and G. Steel, 'How Junichiro Koizumi seized the leadership of Japan's Liberal Democratic Party', *Japanese Journal of Political Science* 8 (1), 2007, 95–114; P. MacLachlan, 'Post office politics in modern Japan: the postmasters, iron triangles, and the limits of reform', *Journal of Japanese Studies* 30 (2), 2004, 281–313; T. Shinoda, 'Koizumi's top-down leadership in the anti-terrorism legislation: the impact of political-institutional changes', *SAIS Review* 23 (1), 2003, 19–34.

24 *Yomiuri Shinbun*, 24 October 2008.

25 Former Prime Minister Yoshiro Mori's father and grandfather were mayors in his home town in Ishikawa prefecture; thus he can also be described as a descendant of a political family.

26 For a detailed account of the Hatoyama family as one example for a political dynasty in Japan see M. Itoh, *The Rise and Fall of the Hatoyama Dynasty: Japanese Political Leadership through the Generations*, New York: Palgrave Macmillan, 2003.

27 *Yomiuri Shinbun*, 24 October 2008.

28 For details see the Matsushita Institute's Website at www.mskj.or.jp. While the English site provides aggregated data, the Japanese version lists the names and current positions for all graduates.

5 The construction of citizenship through volunteering

The case of lifelong learning

Akihiro Ogawa

On 19 February 2008 the Central Council for Education submitted a policy proposal to the Education Minister, Kisaburo Tokai. The proposal followed the revision of the Fundamental Law on Education in December 2006, and encouraged the incorporation of lifelong learning as an integral part of the national education policy. In fact, in this amendment process, the first since the enactment of the policy in 1947, the Japanese government added the term *shōgai gakushū*, or lifelong learning, to the national educational charter. Nowadays, lifelong learning has rapidly become one of the topmost priorities on the national policy agenda as Japan seeks to create a dynamic, sustainable, knowledge-based society in a constantly changing world.

As a general concept, lifelong learning encompasses all aspects of learning, starting from infancy and continuing into adult life. It includes the learning received in families, at schools, vocational training institutions, universities, workplaces and in communities. The Japanese concept of lifelong learning is traditionally considered to be a cultural construct that revolves around personal learning: it is a process in each individual's life. This process is aimed at self-actualization through exposure to the liberal arts and the enjoyment of hobbies and sports,[1] and at the achievement of a society that is continuously learning,[2] primarily in the context of an aging society.[3] Furthermore, Japan's model neither advocates a social policy nor contains utilitarian elements: it is simply designed to promote learning for learning's sake and oriented toward the attainment of cultural ends and the enjoyment of leisure time.[4] The Social Education Law (*Shakai kyōiku hō*) of 1949 and the Law on the Promotion of Lifelong Learning (*Shōgai gakushū shinkō hō*) of 1990 have guaranteed these learning opportunities.

New perspectives on the development of the concept of lifelong learning in Japan are presented in the 131 page policy report prepared by the task force on lifelong learning at the Central Council for Education. At the very beginning, the report states the key conceptual framework of lifelong learning in Japan, linking traditional personal learning with knowledge production that contributes positively to society:

> Learning is an individual activity based on a person's own interests and motivations. Promoting such learning activities makes it possible for people

to have healthy, sound lives. Also, acquiring and updating skills and knowledge for a working life makes it possible to have an economically stable life. At the same time, this kind of learning activity should contribute to the development of an individual's abilities. Such individuals will ultimately contribute to the overall activation of society and the sustainable development of this country.[5]

The current policy discussion is actually beyond the scope of the conventional cultural model focusing on learning at the individual level. This is because the newly advocated knowledge is disciplinary in nature: lifelong learning is primarily argued to contribute to the quality of the public sphere, which is called *atarashii kōkyō* or a New Public, a concept presented during the discussion on the revision of the Fundamental Law on Education in the early 2000s. A New Public is a foundation of solidarity that can enable good citizens to promote a better society; it is defined as increased civic engagement, which in itself would help society. It is a sphere in which people in general or people who are interested in a cause can voluntarily participate.

In this chapter, I argue that people at the grass-roots level attempt to support and enrich this public sphere – a New Public – through lifelong learning initiatives. Their learning is a medium of social construction: personal learning is translated into collective learning through social institutions. By locating their learning as a reformulation of the conventional rigid relationship between the state and society, which has been described as a strong state,[6] lifelong learning participants realize learning as a step toward achieving active 'citizenship'.

My argument on citizenship resonates strongly with the interpretation of citizenship as a constructivist process.[7] I will restrict the construction of citizenship to a learning process that involves volunteering for activities in the field of lifelong learning, as suggested by Gerard Delanty.[8] The assumption is that learning citizenship entails learning to volunteer. In 1992 the National Council for Lifelong Learning (NCLL), an advisory body to the Education Minister, stated that volunteering is integral to lifelong learning.[9] This was one of the key developments in Japanese lifelong learning. More specifically, the policy report claims the conceptual equalization of lifelong learning with volunteering activities in such local lifelong learning facilities as libraries and museums. The logic is that personal learning on skills and knowledge could be essential resources for volunteering. Equipped with these skills and knowledge, by supporting public lifelong learning facilities as volunteers, individuals could also achieve a crucial objective of lifelong learning activities in the form of self-actualization. Further, these volunteer activities are expected to contribute to the enhancement of local cultures.

I start my argument with an analysis of the production of new knowledge through lifelong learning initiatives proposed by the Central Council for Education. Second, I document narrative accounts of people at the grass-roots level who are trying to construct citizenship through dynamic, spontaneous participation in lifelong learning activities at public lifelong learning facilities. Together with an analysis of the policy documents on new knowledge generation through lifelong learning, I employ the narrative model of citizenship,[10] because citizenship consists of narratives, both individual and collective, and consists of memories, shared values and experiences. I examine the manner in which people construct personal biographies and narratives through the learning process as an active step toward participation in society, an important dimension of citizenship. Lastly, I introduce the current development of networking activities called *bunka borantia* (or culture volunteers) among volunteers in the field of lifelong learning in order to enhance their own citizenry. To support my argument, ethnographic examples are introduced from my fieldwork in Japanese society since September 2001. I have extensively documented community-oriented lifelong learning activities created by civic groups as well as the nationwide lifelong learning practices and policies.[11]

Generating new knowledge

One of the major new points in the ongoing discussion on lifelong learning in Japan is symbolically represented by the term *sōgōteki na chi*, 'comprehensive knowledge'.[12] The policy report prepared by the Central Council for Education describes knowledge as something inevitable in the contemporary world, which is constantly changing. Further, comprehensive knowledge is described as not being simple knowledge and skills in a narrow sense. Rather, it refers to the 'abilities to identify problems as well as to think things flexibly', and the report further claims that knowledge plays a significant role in the negotiation of the complexities of everyday life and the establishment of networks with others.[13]

Interestingly, the report emphasizes the role of local communities in this production of knowledge. The policy rationale is presented as below:

> Japanese society is currently experiencing dramatic changes as administrative reform as well as the deregulation process is implemented across the country.... As a result, social services formerly furnished by the government are now transferred to the private sector. Under the circumstances, as part of self-responsibility, each individual is expected to decide by him/herself what he/she needs to know. Thus, learning opportunities should be guaranteed and supported by the state so that Japanese people can decide what they need to know.... Now, local communities will be expected to set up their agendas and achieve them on their own. Instead of the government, local people will be expected to play the role of service providers. Not only individuals but also the community needs to enhance learning capabilities in order to respond to the changes we are now facing.[14]

Furthermore, with regard to this point, the interim report, which was submitted to the Education Minister in January 2007, provides extremely relevant insights.[15] The report discusses a distinctive view on the new Japanese concept of lifelong learning:

> It is now expected that people who have knowledge, skills, and experiences spontaneously and actively participate in agenda-setting and problem-solving activities in local communities; in order to facilitate these activities, the government needs to support learning about history and culture in the communities. Also, in collaboration with schools, public lifelong-learning facilities, businesses, and NPOs [non-profit organizations, a newly created third sector under the 1998 NPO Law], local residents are expected to jointly develop their own learning toward problem-solving activities. The government needs to support these efforts.[16]

In the above quotation, personal learning as a cultural construct is directly linked to the new lifelong learning initiative as a tool for active participation in Japanese social and political spheres. Through lifelong learning activities, Japanese people are encouraged to be involved in something that has a positive impact on society. These activities will allow them to use their knowledge, skills, and experience for improving their society.

This policy trend is in fact confirmed by the new Fundamental Law on Education, which was revised in December 2006. The revised educational charter advocates the purpose of education as follows: 'nurturing attitudes, which spontaneously participate in society and contribute to its development, based on the public spirit'. The background of this argument lies in the introduction of the concept of a New Public, mentioned at the beginning of this chapter. In Japanese society, the term 'public' has usually meant the state or something related to the state. However, the concept of public has been strategically expanded through education policy. The discussion record for the revision of the Fundamental Law on Education explains it as follows:

> Now we [Japanese people] are stepping into a new era in which we are supporting a sense of values that we now call a New Public. That is, we try to solve the social problems we face by ourselves, including life improvement issues in the daily lives of the local community as well as matters related to the global environment and human rights. It is expected that people will try to use their abilities and time for others, for the local community, and for society, based on their own will. For supporting a New Public, what one needs is self-awareness as an active participant in the making of state and society, bravery for practicing social justice, and an attitude of respect for traditional Japanese social norms.[17]

The backdrop of this policy making could be located in global neo-liberalism. It is the conservative market-oriented ideology seeking 'small government' by sponsoring the devolution of social services to civil society.[18] Since the early 2000s the ruling Liberal Democratic Party, led by the then Prime Minister, Junichiro Koizumi, has accelerated this political trend.

The trend supporting a New Public is also realized in policy making in the field of lifelong learning. In early September 2008 the National Institute for

Educational Policy Research in Tokyo held a three-day seminar. The primary topic was the means for developing lifelong learning policies and programmes which would be aimed at contributing to the generation of and support toward a New Public. The seminar targeted government officials and researchers in the field of lifelong learning. It began with a keynote speech on the significance of lifelong learning for the creation of a New Public by a former professor at the University of Tokyo. Three lectures were provided on the promotion of lifelong learning activities. The first lecture was on the role of local communities and was delivered by an education ministry official; the second was on the role of NPOs and was given by a well known NPO practitioner. The third lecture was on how personal learning activities should be linked in order to promote a New Public. Through the seminar, the participants confirmed that lifelong learning would be integral to the national policy effort for the molding of a New Public at the grass-roots level. One local civil servant in charge of lifelong learning policy in a small city of northern Japan commented that he wanted to generate a grand strategy under which civic learning (supporting a New Public) could be directly connected to society. In order to do so, first of all, the current lifelong learning policy making (supporting personal learning related to hobbies and the liberal arts) must be changed.[19]

Constructing citizenship through volunteering

With respect to volunteering, social welfare and disaster relief are traditionally popular fields in Japanese society. Meanwhile, since the NCLL statement in 1992, volunteering opportunities in public facilities such as libraries and museums have been gaining attention among people at the grass-roots level. One of the volunteers explained the differences between the two types of volunteering to me. While volunteers at libraries and museums mainly attempt *to create something new*, social welfare volunteers are merely expected to help others. The volunteers considered in this chapter belong to the former category. These volunteers try to organize creative activities that contribute to the public good. They serve as guides at museums by contributing their knowledge, skills and experience as docents. Moreover, they are assistants at libraries and course planners for community-oriented lifelong learning programmes. According to the latest statistics available, of the 4,000 museums across the country, 750 have begun to accept volunteers, an increase from 139 in 1993, with some 200 additional museums considering the introduction of volunteers.[20]

These volunteers might realize that they are simply complementing work originally done by the government as part of cost-cutting policies in public administration, a political preference advocated by neo-liberalism, as I briefly mentioned in the previous section. This is indeed true. I confirmed several cases in my previous studies wherein administrative costs, including personal expenses, were halved by introducing volunteers and simultaneously replacing bureaucrats in order to implement the publicly financed lifelong learning programme.[21] Under the laws related to lifelong learning (e.g. the Social Education

Law of 1949 and the Law on the Promotion of Lifelong Learning of 1990), Japanese government bodies at various levels are indeed required to make every possible effort to set up and operate public facilities for lifelong learning. This is in keeping with the policy whereby the state allows everyone to benefit from the opportunities to enhance their lives by cultivating themselves.

Meanwhile, I observe that volunteer activities in the field of lifelong learning are effecting a change in contemporary Japanese society through collaborative engagement in the formulation of the state discourse on a New Public. Volunteers I met during the course of my fieldwork often used the term *manabi* (translated as 'learning') to describe their work. Each individual sees her/his volunteering activities as a learning opportunity. However, their activities are not limited to personal learning. Rather, as Gerard Delanty points out, their 'learning involves agency on the part of the learning subject'.[22] The notion of agency recognizes that social action occurs in a context marked by a constant interplay of autonomy and domination, of liberating forces and structures of control, of possibility and limitation. Through such learning, people are expected to participate in a New Public and learn more about themselves and others. Ultimately, such learning entails empowerment, which enables the development of active citizenship. With regard to this aspect, I shall employ an argument by Delanty: 'it [citizenship] entails both personal and cognitive dimensions that extend beyond the personal to the wider cultural level of society. It is possible to relate this understanding of citizenship to "life-long learning", as citizenship is an on-going process that is conducted in communicative links.'[23]

The following sections present narrative accounts by ordinary citizens who actively participate as volunteers in public facilities for lifelong learning across the country. Nowadays, the volunteers are expected to contribute to spontaneous agenda setting and problem solving at the grass-roots level, and respond to a constantly changing social and political life that is represented as a New Public in contemporary Japan. Meanwhile, they will be armed with new knowledge, which I would call 'civic knowledge' (*shimin chi*), a tool for participating in a New Public. Further, the new knowledge is a foundation of citizenship building.

Starting with newspaper clippings

In the late 1970s, Keiko Suzuki, who is now in her late sixties, began her long career as a volunteer. Her first volunteering experience involved the archiving of news clippings at the library of the women's center that was newly established in her neighbourhood. Around that time, she had fulfilled her duties toward the raising of her children and wished to undertake some new responsibility. She had also considered entering college again. However, the volunteer opportunity appeared to be more attractive because she could immerse herself in a vast amount of information, thereby satisfying her intellectual curiosity. In simple terms, the work Ms Suzuki and her peers performed involved the clipping of articles from newspapers and magazines. Together, they read, organized, classified and archived news articles. Ms Suzuki stated that during the course of their work she and her colleagues tried to understand the nature of volunteering activities. As a research agenda, they were interested in exploring their role as volunteers; in other words, they wished to understand how they could locate volunteers/themselves in society and their reason for participating in volunteering activities.

Ms Suzuki was born in Taiwan during World War II, and returned to a prefecture in Kyushu, southern Japan, after the war. Her father taught ethics at a high school. She stated that she was used to discussing social and political affairs with her father since childhood. Although Ms Suzuki's mother attended a college in Tokyo, she withdrew owing to illness. At that time (that is, before the war), it was extremely rare for women from the countryside to attend college in Tokyo. Further, her mother's marriage was arranged by her parents without her consent. Ms Suzuki, who dreamt of becoming a designer, attended a fine arts college in Tokyo. When she was a junior, she witnessed Anpo (the anti US–Japan Security Treaty movement in 1960). She told me that this experience was one of the most influential in her life: 'At that time, actually, I did not know what I should do. I just knew something important had happened in this country. But I didn't know what I should do. So I wrote to my father, and he wrote back with only one line on a postcard: "Think and decide for yourself".' After Ms Suzuki received the postcard, she willingly started participating in demonstrations. On the day the security treaty was ratified at the National Diet, she spent a night on the railroad at Shinagawa station. On the journey home, feeling very tired and despairing over the hopeless situation, she thought of becoming a journalist instead of a designer. She wished to have a job that could make it possible for her to convey her opinions to society.

After graduating from college, Ms Suzuki joined a publishing company that specialized in women's fashion. A couple of years later, she married a co-worker and quit the job. In the 1960s it was a social practice for Japanese women to leave their jobs at the time of marriage. Hence, although Ms Suzuki believed women should continue working after marriage, she merely followed the custom. She also confessed that she was a little frustrated with her job. Instead of pursuing the fashions in vogue, she felt a need to do something different: she would prefer to write stories that could bring about social change. After marriage, another mode of life became available to her, as she became very active in her son's school PTA. On the other hand, as a freelance writer, she continued to develop her career.

Her motivation for participating in volunteer activities is to problematize issues in everyday life (*kurashi no nakano tēma o shakaika suru*) via selecting problems we face in our daily lives and visualizing them. Gaining a variety of information through volunteer activities was, as I mentioned earlier, a personal motivation for satisfying her intellectual curiosity. In addition, she felt that it was important to listen to the voices of people at the grass-roots level and let them be heard in society. With regard to volunteering, she does not believe in working according to the instructions of higher authorities (or the government). She explained herself as follows: 'When we volunteer, we should not simply accept and follow the requests from the government. We need to understand what we are expected to do and then reflect on the meaning of what we are doing. Otherwise, we just become subcontractors of the government.' She continued, 'Just supporting the government's work is not enough and means nothing to us.' For her, it was important to reflect on how she was involved with society through volunteering and how she transformed herself as well as society.

She often describes her reflections by using two Japanese words: *manabi* and *kizuki*. I have already mentioned the term *manabi* earlier. Ms Suzuki also uses the Japanese term *kizuki* (becoming aware of) when she refers to the act of learning something new. Repeated exposure to such *kizuki* also leads to personal development. She then tries to convert what has been learned into a new volunteering opportunity. For Ms Suzuki, volunteering is a great learning opportunity available to everybody: volunteers, officials of public facilities, as well as users. All of the stakeholders can adopt the same standpoint, while working with volunteers could provide new perspectives to public officials. Further, it could serve as a learning experience for the officials.

Twenty years after she started working with volunteers on the archiving of news clippings, Ms Suzuki stopped the activities at the women's centre and created an independent network with other volunteers in public facilities for lifelong learning. The major motivation was to build a collaborative relationship with the government at various levels. Through the network, each volunteer is expected to become aware of what she/he is doing. Ms Suzuki's network has now transformed into a social movement called *bunka borantia*, literally translated as 'culture volunteers.'[24]

Bunka borantia

Bunka borantia is a relatively new term in Japanese society. The term was originally advocated by Hayao Kawai, a former chief of the Agency for Cultural Affairs (Bunkachō) and a well known Jungian psychologist, when he assumed this position in January 2002. Kawai describes the term *bunka borantia* as follows.

> I am often asked what *bunka borantia* means. Recently in this country volunteering has begun to gather much attention. Many people might associate volunteering with social welfare activities. There is no formal definition of the term *bunka borantia* in policy documents. I believe that it is not necessary to define the term strictly as that would limit the scope of activities. *Bunka borantia* broadly means volunteering that helps others enjoy cultural activities, while volunteers themselves enjoy the activities.[25]

Bunka borantia initially targeted volunteers working in public facilities for lifelong learning, such as libraries and museums. The meaning of the term has been expanded to include community development (*machi zukuri*) through dramatic and musical performances and cultural resource management (*bunkazai hogo* in a broader sense). Since February 2002 the Agency for Cultural Affairs has published ten newsletters over a period of four years; the newsletters introduced activities conducted by the *bunka borantia*, namely sixty-two activities, launched across the country.[26]

Since 2005 people connected to Ms Suzuki's network have been organizing an annual series of national gatherings of the *bunka borantia* in association with the Agency for Cultural Affairs. For the past four years, a total of some 1,000 people have attended the gatherings. Instead of institutionalizing their network as a corporate entity such as an NPO (which they also consider to be regulated), they prefer to remain a social movement so that they can enjoy maximum flexibility. One of the group members compares the flexible nature of their activities to that of amoeba. Without any articles of association or membership system, they are simply bound together by a mission: constructing citizenship through volunteering under lifelong learning initiatives. The network participants are connected by a blog on the Internet so that they can easily communicate with each other. Thus, they can share and update information about their activities.

People participating in this network reveal an interesting trend of demographic diversity. I came across three categories: women (or housewife volunteers), local civil servants and youth. Women are a major category of participants supporting this network, as they have long been the backbone of social movements in Japan.[27] If I have to categorize the female participants by occupation, then they are mainly housewives in their fifties and sixties. Second, civil servants, who are mostly from the prefectural and municipal levels and are in charge of affairs related to lifelong learning, participate in these gatherings as part of their business. Some of the retired civil servants who were previously engaged in lifelong learning policy making remain active participants. Lastly, people in this network are making serious efforts to attract the youth. As a result, the number of young volunteers joining this network gradually but steadily increased. For example, in the 2006 meeting, more than half (53 per cent) of the participants were in their twenties (18 per cent) and thirties (35 per cent),[28] and this is a major difference in the demographic data of Japanese volunteerism, which is mostly dominated by retired seniors.[29]

Through networking at the national gatherings, the participants intend to accumulate grass-roots knowledge generated by volunteers through their daily volunteering activities at public lifelong learning facilities. The new knowledge deals with the coordination skills of volunteer activities, collaboration techniques with the government at various levels, capacity of involvement in community development as volunteers, and decision-making tools for diversified stakeholders, all of which are practical knowledge that I would call 'civic knowledge' (*shimin chi*) for active participation in a New Public. If I have to select key words from the records of the national gathering, I find that civic knowledge is represented by such words as management, coordination, partnership with the government, and quality of volunteerism.[30] Civic knowledge is a tool for ordinary citizens to participate in the public sphere. For them, volunteering at libraries and museums is a means to support and enrich a New Public from below. It is an opportunity to better society through civic engagement. Through the networking of *bunka borantia* the participants are trying to institutionalize civic knowledge as a result of collective learning as a social institution.

A key member of this network and a director of a community development NPO in north-eastern Japan, Ms Sato, a woman in her sixties, told me:

> What we are trying to do is simple: recognizing each other, trying to make an agreement among diversity, and building and solving our own agenda; such kinds of knowledge have not been accumulated in public administration, which prefers uniformity or trying to deal with its population in the same way. Our networking sheds light on each individual, supporting him or her. Our networking backs up their empowerment through new knowledge production.

Ms Sato was a former deputy mayor in her municipality and is organizing an NPO that promotes grass-roots empowerment through gender equality. She added, 'Collaborating with citizens armed with such knowledge is probably the only way that the government can survive. Collaboration might take a lot of time, but it is worth while.'

Mr Iwata, who is an engineer in his thirties and active as a course planner at a local lifelong learning centre in Tokyo, had the following to say: 'Within our network, for example, I enjoy the fact that everybody is different. It might be difficult to reach an agreement in such situations. But I appreciate the fact that we enjoy the process. We are changing, and the government is trying to change, too.' Activities like *bunka borantia* are not merely aimed at helping others enjoying cultural activities, as I cited earlier as a statement by Mr Kawai, the former chief of the Agency for Cultural Affairs. The production of civic knowledge through volunteer activities at public lifelong learning facilities is a solid foundation for reshaping the conventional discourse on the Japanese state–society relationship. It generates new dynamism and a flow of energy at the grass-roots level. Ultimately, civic knowledge production is a crucial part of the construction of citizenship based on active participation in society.

Conclusion

In this chapter, I examined the development of Japan's lifelong learning policy. In fact, the nature of lifelong learning in Japan is dramatically changing. It has been interpreted as a cultural construct revolving around personal learning related to hobbies and the liberal arts. Currently, however, the state promotes lifelong learning as the foremost item on the agenda of the national education policy; in particular, it intends to support a New Public. The state discourse on lifelong learning is expected to produce disciplinary knowledge, presented as *sōgōteki na chi*, in order to primarily contribute to the quality of the public sphere.

I have documented a grass-roots response to this macro political discourse through the lens of lifelong learning practice. Volunteers in the field of lifelong learning are collaboratively engaging with the state in the formulation of the discourse on a New Public. They are participating in volunteer activities at public facilities – for instance, libraries, museums and lifelong learning facilities – as a core part of their lifelong learning activities. In contemporary Japanese society, new knowledge or civic knowledge production under lifelong learning initiatives is indeed significant in supporting the devolution process of social services or the withdrawal of the state from social services – a key feature of neo-liberal governmentality – primarily aimed at cost cutting in public administration.[31] This policy, characterized by 'a "folding back" of the objectives of government upon its means' entails breaching the conventional divisions between the state and society.[32] In fact, policy collaboration between the state and the third sector is popularly known as *kyōdō* (or collaboration in Japanese), and has become a fashionable administrative technique in Japanese local politics.

Meanwhile the volunteers see the collaboration process with the state as an opportunity to construct their citizenship from below, while producing practical civic knowledge. Such knowledge empowers people; further, the accumulation of civic knowledge leads to active citizenship based on social participation. By consolidating such empowerment of individuals at the grass-roots level, civil society in Japan would in fact be strengthened. Related to this point, as Aihwa Ong notes, citizenship is indeed a dual process of self-making and being-made, with webs of power linked to the nation-state and civil society.[33] The exercise of citizenship occurs in concrete social relations mediated by power.

Civic knowledge generation is the result of a countrywide network that operates as a social movement called *bunka borantia*, involving participants with diverse demographic profiles. Through networking, it becomes possible for people at the grass-roots level to bravely and flexibly challenge new systems and break conventional norms and practices where bureaucratic rationality dominates. Furthermore, *bunka borantia* participants are expected to be key players in local public facilities and galvanize their local neighbourhood from the grass-roots level.[34] They are at the forefront of a change in contemporary Japan.

Acknowledgements

Earlier versions of this chapter were presented at the Stockholm Workshop on Japan's Political Economy at the European Institute of Japanese Studies on 14 June 2008, and at the twelfth international conference of the European Association for Japanese Studies in Lecce, Italy, on 22 September 2008. I thank all the participants who were interested in my chapter. In particular, I appreciate the insightful comments of Glenn D. Hook and Sherry Martin. No identifying information, including personal names, is provided because of the confidential nature of the material this chapter draws upon. Except where indicated, all quotations are taken from my fieldnotes and all translations are mine.

Notes

1 See H. Watanabe, 'Changing adult learning in Japan: the shift from traditional singing to karaoke', *International Journal of Lifelong Education* 24 (3), 2005, 257–67; A. S. Rausch, 'Lifelong learning in rural Japan: relevance, focus and sustainability for the hobbyist, the resident, the careerist and the activist as lifelong learner', *Japan Forum* 16 (3), 2004, 473–93; J. D. Wilson, 'Lifelong learning in Japan: a lifeline for a

"maturing" society?', *International Journal of Lifelong Education* 20 (4), 2001, 297–343.

2 See Y. Sawano, 'The learning society in Japan' in M. Kuhn (ed.) *New Society Models for a New Millennium: The Learning Society in Europe and Beyond*, New York: Peter Lang, 2007, pp. 471–88; K. Fuwa, 'Lifelong education in Japan, a highly school-oriented society: educational opportunities and practical educational activities for adults', *International Journal of Lifelong Education* 20 (1–2), 2001, 127–36; S. Kawanobe, 'Lifelong learning in Japan', *International Review of Education* 40 (6), 1994, 485–93.

3 See S. Ogawa, 'Lifelong learning and demographics: a Japanese perspective', *International Journal of Lifelong Education* 24 (4), 2005, 351–68.

4 See K. Okamoto, 'Lifelong learning and the leisure-oriented society: the development and challenges in the Far East', in D. Aspin, J. Chapman, M. Hatton and Y. Sawano (eds) *International Handbook of Lifelong Learning*, Part One, Dordrecht: Kluwer, 2001, pp. 317–28.

5 Central Council for Education, *Atarashii jidai o kirihiraku shōgai gakushū no shinkō hōsaku nit tsuite, chi no junkangata shakai no kōchiku o mezashite*, Tokyo: Central Council for Education, 2008, p. 3, http://211.120.54.153/b_menu/shingi/chukyo/chukyo0/toushin/080219-01.pdf (accessed 27 May 2008).

6 For example, see C. Johnson, *Japan: Who Governs? The Rise of the Developmental State*, New York: W. W. Norton, 1995.

7 I employ the concept of cultural citizenship for my argument on new knowledge production through lifelong learning. Cultural citizenship is very different from the older liberal notion, or what British sociologist T. H. Marshall in his *Citizenship and Social Class* (London: Pluto Press, 1992 [1950]) describes as rights or formal membership in a polity. In the post-welfare, neoliberal advanced industrial societies, including Japan, the idea of citizenship is best conveyed through responsible consumers of social services, and the role of the state is but to facilitate this consumption, preferably through the use of private providers. In keeping with this view, greater emphasis has been placed on the responsibilities of citizens for maintaining order in society at large. Nowadays, citizenship is considered to have a major impact on the cultural processes of society. It is argued as a dynamic, contextual, contested, and multidimensional notion. The meanings of the concept of citizenship have indeed generated different interpretations and applications. Citizenship is about status (membership), identity (belonging), civic virtue (dispositions, values, and behaviors), and agency (engagement and political efficacy). In particular, my focus is on citizenship as agency, which refers to the state of being in action or exerting power. See, for example, L. Pawley, 'Cultural citizenship', *Sociology Compass* 2, 2008, 1–15; T. Miller, *Cultural Citizenship: Cosmopolitanism, Consumerism, and Television in a Neoliberal Age*, Philadelphia, PA: Temple University Press, 2007; N. Stevenson, *Cultural Citizenship: Cosmopolitan Questions*, Maidenhead: Open University Press, 2003; G. Delanty, 'Citizenship as a learning process: disciplinary citizenship versus cultural citizenship', *International Journal of Lifelong Education* 22 (6), 2003, 597–605; A. Ong, *Flexible Citizenship: The Cultural Logics of Transnationality*, Durham, NC: Duke University Press, 1999; and R. Rosaldo, 'Cultural citizenship, inequality, and multiculturalism' in W. Flores and R. Benmayor (eds) *Latino Cultural Citizenship: Claiming Identity, Space, and Rights*, Boston, MA: Beacon Press, 1997, pp. 27–38.

8 G. Delanty, 'Citizenship as a learning process: disciplinary citizenship versus cultural citizenship', *International Journal of Lifelong Education* 22 (6), 2003, 597–605.

9 National Council for Lifelong Learning, *Kongo no shakai no dōkō ni taiōshita shōgai gakushū no shinkō hōsaku ni tsuite*, Tokyo: National Council for Lifelong Learning, 1992.

10 See M. R. Somers, 'Narrating and naturalizing civil society and citizenship theory: the place of political culture and the pubic sphere', *Sociological Theory* 13 (3), 1995, 229–74.

11 See A. Ogawa, *The Failure of Civil Society? The Third Sector and the State in Contemporary Japan*, Albany, NY: State University of New York Press, 2009.
12 Central Council for Education, 2008, p. 3.
13 Ibid.
14 Ibid., p. 4.
15 Central Council for Education, *Atarashii jidai o kirihiraku shōgai gakushū no shinkō hōsaku ni tsuite*, Tokyo: Central Council for Education, 2007, http://211.120.54.153/b_menu/shingi/chukyo/chukyo0/toushin/07020806.htm (accessed on 27 May 2008).
16 Ibid.
17 Central Council for Education, *Atarashii jidai ni fusawashii kyōiku kihonhō to kyōiku shinkō kihon keikaku no arikata ni tsuite*, Tokyo: Central Council for Education, 2003. http://211.120.54.153/b_menu/shingi/chukyo/chukyo0/toushin/030301.htm (accessed 27 May 2008).
18 Neoliberalism is a politico-economic ideology centered around the values of a global economy represented as a free market, free trade, and unrestricted flow of capital. It became widespread during the last quarter of the twentieth century. See, for example, D. Harvey, *A Brief History of Neoliberalism*, Oxford: Oxford University Press, 2005.
19 *Shaken tsūshin* 61. Mail magazine distributed by the National Institute for Educational Policy Research on 16 October 2008. Special permission from the institute to quote the comment on 29 October 2008.
20 *Musée*, 'Myuziamu borantia ni kansuru jittai chōsa', *Musée* 68, 2005, 12.
21 See Ogawa, *The Failure of Civil Society?*.
22 Delanty, 'Citizenship as a learning process', 601.
23 Ibid., 602.
24 See K. Okubo, *Bunka borantia gaido: hajimeyō! Enjoi deizu*, Tokyo: Nippon hyōjun, 2004; A. Ogawa and K. Okubo, 'Dento bunka to bunka borantia', *Shakai Kyōiku* 734, 2007, 55–61.
25 Agency for Cultural Affairs, *Bunka borantia tsūshin dai 2 gō*, Tokyo: Agency for Cultural Affairs, 2002.
26 Ibid.
27 See, for example, R. LeBlanc, *Bicycle Citizens: The Political World of the Japanese Housewife*, Ithaca, NY: Cornell University Press, 1999.
28 Bunka Volunteer National Forum, *Bunka borantia, asu kara no dezain: tokoton, kiite, hanashite, kangaeta*, Tokyo: Um Promotion, 2007, p. 20.
29 See, for example, Ogawa, *The Failure of Civil Society?*, pp. 57–8.
30 Bunka Volunteer National Forum, *Bunka borantia*, 19.
31 I have identified the phenomenon from a viewpoint heavily influenced by Michel Foucault's notion of governmentality, which refers not only to political processes or state agencies but also, in a more general sense, to the art of guiding people. See M. Foucault, *Discipline and Punish: The Birth of the Prison*, New York: Vintage Books, 1977; M. Foucault, 'Governmentality' in G. Burchell, C. Gordon and P. Miller (eds) *The Foucault Effect: Studies in Governmentality*, Chicago: University of Chicago Press, 1991, pp. 87–104; See also T. Lemke, '"The birth of bio-politics": Michel Foucault's lecture at the Collège de France on neo-liberal governmentality', *Economy and Society* 30 (2), 2001, 190–207; M. Dean, *Governmentality: Power and Rule in Modern Society*, London: Sage Publications, p. 199.
32 Dean, *Governmentality*, p. 174.
33 Ong, *Flexible Citizenship*, p. 738.
34 Regarding the development of *bunka borantia*, see also T. Hirose, 'Bunka borantia to gyōsei no kyōdō', *Shichōson kyōi*, November 2007, 2–4.

6 Foreign aid as a tool for peace building

Is the goal security or poverty reduction?

Marie Söderberg

'Extreme poverty and the proportion of people suffering from hunger shall be halved by 2015.'[1] This was the first of the development goals in the UN Millennium Declaration signed by 190 nations at the turn of the century. The rich countries, including Japan, promised to increase foreign aid to assist in eradicating world poverty. Recently there have on the contrary been severe cuts in Japanese ODA[2] and aid in general is becoming more and more entangled with issues of peace and security, not only in Japan but among most of the OECD Development Assistance Committee (DAC) members[3] in general.

Even if peace is a necessary ingredient for development and poverty reduction it is not evident that ODA used for peace actually reduces poverty. Somehow it seems that aid has been 'hi-jacked' in Japan and is increasingly being used for ensuring Japan's own security and prosperity. The securitarization of aid that has occurred since 9/11 and the 'War on Terror' that followed in Afghanistan and Pakistan, as well as the invasion of Iraq in a trial run of forcible disarmament of weapons of mass destruction, poses special problems for Japan that, through its so-called 'Peace Constitution', has clear limitations to what the country can do in the field of peacekeeping with its Self Defense Forces. To cover up for that, ODA is getting an enhanced role. The revised Japanese ODA Charter of 2003 thus does not note poverty reduction up front but states that 'the objectives of Japan's ODA are to contribute to the peace and development of the international community, and thereby help ensure Japan's own security and prosperity'.

The aim of this chapter is to answer the questions: What is happening with the Japanese policy of peace building through ODA at the implementation level? What are the challenges? And is poverty reduction really its main aim? It starts off by recapping how the policies of linking security and development originally developed and the basis upon which such links were created. It should be noted that conflict prevention, peace building or peace preservation are complex areas that to a large extent are not issues of ODA but also incorporate peacekeeping operations (PKO) and other issues. There is a mixture of civil and military dimensions to such missions as the Japanese reconstruction efforts in Iraq, where the Self Defense Forces (SDF) worked side by side with aid workers. ODA and SDF are thus being launched as 'two wheels of the same cart'. This makes things all the more complex in Japan from a legal point of view.

We trace the Japanese policy of peace building to the implementation level, putting the main emphasis on the ODA part but also touching on the non-ODA part, and research the difficulties that arise due to Article 9, the so-called peace clause, of the Japanese Constitution that forbids Japan to make military contributions to solve conflicts abroad. Afghanistan is taken as a case study to show how Japanese policy works, beyond the policy rhetoric, on the ground. Some comparison will be made with Swedish action in Afghanistan to make clear what peace-building measures are being used by other nations that do not have a peace clause. The aim here is to research what the link between security and development looks like at the implementation phase, since a number of policy documents both within the UN system and from the DAC Network on Conflict, Peace and Development Cooperation[4] have worked to establish the importance of this link. Finally some conclusions will be drawn concerning the goal of Japanese ODA.

The origins of the link between security and development in the present discourse

Reducing poverty and achieving the Millennium Development Goals are the objectives of the DAC countries. At the same time peace building is now seen as a prerequisite to reach those goals. There is an increased securitarization of aid and the DAC members have declared their aims to support security system reform (SSR) in the developing world and stated that they might even draw on sources other than aid to do so.[5] The importance of peace and security is all part of a broader 'human security' agenda developed under the leadership of the UN Development Programme (UNDP).

It was UN Secretary General Boutros Boutros-Ghali who, after the end of the Cold War in his famous report to the Security Council *An Agenda for Peace*[6] in 1992, initiated the new discourse linking security and development. He reported on peacekeeping, peace making and preventive diplomacy and how the UN could work in this field, but he also added the element of 'post-conflict peace building', which he defined as 'actions to identify and support structures which will tend to strengthen and solidify peace in order to avoid a relapse into conflict'. The innovative part of Boutros-Ghali's policy was that organizations such as UN agencies in the economic and social fields, which had not hitherto been recognized as peace organizations, were considered to have an important part to play in the post-conflict phase.[7]

This way of viewing security, which was different from the traditional military one, overlaps with the concept of 'human security' introduced in the 1994 *Human Development Report* of the UNDP.[8] That report challenged the traditional notion of national security and argued that the proper referent for security should be the individual rather than the state. Ensuring 'freedom from want' and 'freedom from fear' for all people was necessary for national, global and regional stability. In this multidisciplinary understanding of security threats such as hunger, disease and oppression, protection from sudden disruption of people's daily life should be assured. Social peace was considered as important as strategic military or political peace.

Another important work in this debate was UN Secretary General Kofi Annan's 1998 report *The Causes of Conflict and the Promotions of Durable Peace and Sustainable Development in Africa* in which, after the bitter failure of a number of UN peacekeeping missions in Africa, he concluded that there were not only external factors behind the armed conflicts in Africa but also internal causes such as fragile state mechanisms. To Annan, 'good governance' was thus indispensable for a durable peace and he pointed to four areas of importance: 'securing respect for human rights and the rule of law'; 'promoting transparency and accountability in public administration'; 'enhancing administrative capacity'; and 'strengthening democratic governance'.[9]

The so-called Brahimi report of the Panel on United Nations Peace Operations, issued in 2000, stands as a symbol of the doctrinal shift in peacekeeping operations that included all categories of peace operations such as peace making, peacekeeping and peace building. Traditional peacekeeping, which according to Brahimi treats the symptoms rather than the sources of conflict, was seen as having no exit strategy. A shift was required in how civilian police were conceived and utilized, how the rule of law was upheld, and respect for human rights.[10]

From a development point of view, the importance of security for all people also became evident during the 1990s. Security was seen as a prerequisite for poverty reduction. Again and again it had been proved that years of development could quickly be wiped out by internal fighting as well as war with neighbouring states. In the mid-1990s the Development Assistance Committee formed the DAC Network on Conflict, Peace and Development Cooperation. In 1998 it published the first guidelines for donors on conflict, peace and development cooperation. A second report, entitled *Helping to Prevent Violent Conflict*, in 2001 and the security system reform (SSR) was endorsed by ministers and agency heads at a high-level meeting in 2004. The DAC Guidelines specify a number of recommendations for action in order to promote peace and security as fundamental pillars of development on both a personal and the state level. These include supporting country-owned and country-led reform efforts and making necessary institutional changes to promote people's security in their daily lives. To work effectively on SSR, 'whole of government' approaches are needed both in donor and developing countries. This implies that a range of policy and funding instrument such as development cooperation, diplomacy, trade, finance and investment as well as defence should be coordinated to increase effectiveness.

Japan's approach to peace building: historical background

The Japanese Constitution adopted in 1946 set certain restrictions on the role Japan has been able to play in the international community. In Article 9 of the Constitution 'the Japanese people forever renounce war as a sovereign right of the nation and the threat or use of force as a means of settling international disputes'.[11] This was Japan's first experience of a democratic constitution. It was adopted during the Occupation (1945–52), when for the first time Japan had been conquered by a foreign country and the population had suffered great human as well as material losses. Since then the Japanese people have been extremely sensitive to military issues.[12]

Initially, the purpose of the Occupation forces was to move Japanese society away from possible rearmament. With the communist take-over in China in 1949 and the Korean War (1950–53), however, the plans were changed. Conditions in Japan were unstable and when most of the Occupation forces left for South Korea, since both the Japanese military and the police forces had been disbanded after the war, there was no one left to take care of the internal security of the country. The Occupation forces, headed by General Douglas MacArthur, ordered the Japanese government to establish a National Police Reserve Force in 1950, which later developed into the present Self Defense Forces (SDF) in 1954. When Japan signed the peace treaty it also signed a Security Treaty with the United States that is still in force today. Both the SDF and the Security Treaty have been among the most controversial issues in post-war Japanese politics; the opposition, under the leadership of the Social Democratic Party, considered the SDF unconstitutional and until the 1980s constantly advocated unarmed neutrality and the abolition of the Security Treaty.[13]

According to the Japanese government's interpretation of Article 9, Japan has the right to defend itself if attacked, although it is not allowed to participate in collective defence, which is considered to go beyond the minimum necessary use of force to defend the country.[14] Before the 1990s, sending the Self Defense Forces abroad for peacekeeping missions was considered unthinkable. There was even a considerable political debate over whether the SDF should be allowed to conduct joint training together with US forces based in Japan. When the Japanese trade surplus with the United States increased during the 1970s, and especially during the 1980s, accusations grew that Japan was a 'free rider' on US military defence spending and, rather than bearing the cost of its own defence, used the money instead to fund its own economic development.[15] The increase in Japanese ODA spending, with a number of plans which doubled the amount of its aid from the end of the 1970s and onwards, was seen as one way for Japan to fulfil its obligation to international society.[16] The increase was partly explained in terms of 'burden sharing' (*yakuwari buntan*) according to which Japan should take greater responsibility in the field of aid in order to compensate for the United States' expenditure on the global security umbrella.[17]

In a speech in London in 1988 Japanese Prime Minister Noboru Takeshita explained Japan's international cooperation initiatives:

> As you may know, Japan is firmly committed to the furtherance of world peace, and its Constitution does not permit it to extend any military cooperation. This does not mean, however, that Japan should stand idly by with regard to international peace. I believe that Japan, from a political and moral

> viewpoint, should extend cooperation to the utmost of its ability. I will pursue 'Cooperation for Peace' as a new approach toward enhancing Japan's contributions to the maintenance and reinforcement of international peace. This will include positive participation in diplomatic efforts, the dispatch of necessary personnel and the provision of financial cooperation, aiming at the resolution of regional conflicts.[18]

According to Takeshita, ODA was the most valued aspect of Japan's international contribution and he would continue to improve both its quality and its quantity.

During the Gulf War (1990–91) Japan was not part of the thirty-four-nation-strong Allied forces, led by the United States, which fought under the UN flag to get Iraq out of Kuwait. To send troops there was considered to be against the Constitution. At first, Japan offered a minor financial contribution, but after strong criticism from the United States, among others, it ended up committing USD 13 billion, more than anyone else, to the Gulf War and to support specific Middle Eastern countries affected by the conflict. Still, Japan was criticized for so-called 'chequebook diplomacy', just providing money and no human contribution in the form of personnel.

The International Peace Cooperation Law

The Gulf War was an eye-opener to the Japanese public and somehow there emerged a kind of consensus among the population that Japan should contribute not only with money but also by the dispatch of human resources for peacekeeping.[19] Efforts to pass new legislation with this purpose, which had failed in 1990, succeeded two years later. The resulting International Peace Cooperation Law (1992) embodied severe restrictions in the sense that Japanese personnel were not to be involved in armed conflict.

The law stipulates five principles for Japanese participation in UN peacekeeping operations: (1) an agreement on a cease-fire shall have been reached among the parties to the armed conflict; (2) consent for the undertaking of UN peacekeeping operations as well as Japan's participation in such operations shall have been obtained from the host countries as well as all the parties to the armed conflict; (3) the operations shall maintain strict impartiality, not favouring any party to the armed conflict; (4) should any of the requirements in the above-mentioned guidelines cease to be satisfied, the government of Japan may withdraw its international peace cooperation corps; and (5) the use of weapons shall be limited to the minimum necessary to protect the lives of the personnel.

This legislation made some limited[20] Japanese cooperation in UN peacekeeping operations possible for the first time in the post-war period. The first PKO deployment was Cambodia, where Japan sent 1,300 people, including SDF personnel (1,200 people from engineering units), civilian police officers and election monitors in 1992. Up to 2007 this had been followed by the dispatch of personnel to Mozambique, the Golan Heights, East Timor and Nepal.

Other legislation

Operations for disaster relief activities, for example, following the major earthquake off Sumatra in Indonesia or the tsunami in the Indian Ocean, where the Japanese Self Defense Forces were dispatched, were not covered by the International Peace Cooperation Law. Nor was the reconstruction work in Iraq, which was not being conducted under the UN banner. The operations in the Indian Ocean in connection with the anti-terrorist operations in Afghanistan are not covered either. For these types of operations, except the tsunami, which was a rescue effort from natural catastrophe, a number of special measures laws are required. The Anti-Terrorism Special Measures Law (November 2001) for the dispatch of SDF vessels for refuelling missions in the Indian Ocean was extended three times before it expired in 2007. It was later replaced by the Replenishment Support Special Measures Law in 2008. (See also Chapter 3 by P. Midford in this volume.) In July 2003 the Special Measures Law on Humanitarian and Reconstruction Assistance in Iraq was enacted.

These laws all have to do with the Self Defense Forces, whose dispatch abroad requires a legal basis provided by acts of the Diet. In some countries, any military activity ordered by the head of state or the commander-in-chief is allowed unless these activities are specifically prohibited by legislation. In Japan, it is exactly the opposite. No activities that do not follow the principles of the international peace cooperation law are allowed unless they are specifically authorized by Acts of the Diet. Examples of how this works in the implementation phase are the SDF refuelling missions in the Indian Ocean. When the Anti-Terrorism Special Measures Law regulating their activities could no longer be extended in 2007, the SDF vessels had to go home. It took a new law and a considerable amount of political discussion in the Diet before the vessels could return to refuelling duty. This system has made it extremely difficult for Japan to take any flexible approach in peace building when it comes to the use of the SDF.

In a major policy speech on peace building in 2008, Minister of Foreign Affairs Masahiko Koumura explained his aim to change the system and to promote the adoption of 'a general law' on cooperation for international peace that would make it easier to dispatch the Self Defense Forces.[21] Since the transition of the Self Defense Agency to the Ministry of Defense, international peace is now also stipulated as one of the prime missions for the SDF besides the defence of Japan.[22]

There are, however, also other tools that can be used in peace cooperation. It is the Prime Minister who formally heads the International Peace Cooperation headquarters and its secretariat is located in the Cabinet Office. The secretariat consists of around fifty people. Most of the officials are seconded from various ministries, of which some of the most important are the Ministry of Foreign Affairs (MOFA) and the Ministry of Defense, but officials also hail from the Ministry of Interior Affairs, the coastguard and so on. Cabinet Office officials are in a minority. Diplomacy and ODA are other ways for Japan to promote peace building or peacekeeping. I will discuss each of these in some detail below.

Diplomacy and ODA

In a policy speech entitled 'Arc of Freedom and Prosperity' delivered on 30 November 2006, the then Minister of Foreign Affairs, Taro Aso, pointed out that peace building is important to expand freedom and prosperity and that creating affluent, stable regions grounded in such universal values as freedom and democracy is a new pillar of Japanese diplomacy. In the conceptual framework developed for peace building by the Japanese government (see also Chapter 7 by N. Palanovics in this volume) the consolidation of peace and nation building are the key concepts. The consolidation of peace consists of the promotion of peace processes, securing domestic stability and security, and humanitarian and reconstruction assistance. Nation building deals with issues such as building a structure for better governance and the development of economic as well as social infrastructure.

ODA is seen as a key instrument of peace building, and the revised ODA Charter of 2003 clearly states that 'The objectives of Japan's ODA are to contribute to the peace and development of the international community and thereby to help ensure Japan's own security and prosperity'. The ODA Charter of 2003 set out four priority issues: (1) poverty reduction; (2) sustainable growth; (3) addressing global issues; and (4) peace building.

In 2007, MOFA formulated a new and expanded priority policy for international cooperation based upon a strategy formulated by the Overseas Economic Cooperation Council[23] and the International Cooperation Planning Headquarters established in MOFA in 2006. The following are now the five priority issues in implementing international cooperation:[24] (1) addressing environmental and climate change issues; (2) realizing the economic growth of developing countries and furthering economic prosperity in Japan; (3) democratization and assisting market-oriented economic reforms; (4) peace building and the fight against terrorism; and (5) ensuring human security.

Japan's policy regarding peace building with ODA is 'to support the response to humanitarian emergencies and to provide counter-terrorism capacity-building assistance, as well as address projects that contribute to consolidation of peace and post-conflict nation building, including disarmament, demobilization and reintegration (DDR) of former soldiers, the collection of small arms, demining and related activities and improving governance'.[25] Although the ODA Charter is still valid, the current priority issues have seemingly changed. Notably, poverty reduction is no longer a priority issue on its own. In short, the fight against terrorism has been added to the part on peace building, and human security has become a priority issue in its own right.

An intellectual contribution and human resource development for peace building

Japan likes to emphasize its intellectual contribution to peace building. According to Minister of Foreign Affairs Masahiko Koumura, 'Japan must demonstrate leadership in building peace in the world.'[26] One way of doing this is by chairing the newly established Peace Building Commission at the UN. The purpose of this commission is to bring together all the relevant actors (including international donors, financial institutions, national governments and troop-contributing countries), marshal resources and advise and propose integrated strategies for post-conflict peace building.[27]

At the 'New JICA' (Japan International Cooperation Agency), which was formed in October 2008 as the result of a merger between Japan's two implementing agencies for ODA (the Japan Bank of International Cooperation and JICA), the plan is to establish a high-level international think tank on ODA. However, apart from Sadako Ogata, the head of JICA, there are few internationally known Japanese who are working with peace building. At the moment there is a lack of people with capabilities at the policy level.[28] (See also Chapter 7 by N. Palanovics in this volume.)

One project that is often cited in connection with the promotion of Japan as a leader of peace building that is aimed also at building policy-level capacity among Japanese is the new pilot programme of education for peace building at Hiroshima University. This programme is partly modelled on the Swedish Folke Bernadotte Academy,[29] which is a government agency with the mission to improve peace operations.[30] In the first round of applications in 2007, fifteen Asians and fifteen Japanese were accepted into the programme and in a second round in 2008 the same number of students. The Asian trainees included one each from the ASEAN countries. These belong to a variety of organizations such as the Ministry of Foreign Affairs, the Ministry of the Interior, think tanks and NGOs. After a few weeks in Japan, the participants are sent out on overseas on-the-job training. The programme is intended to develop human resources in Japan and other Asian countries with the practical capabilities required when they are engaged in peace-building activities in various parts of the world.

Comparing Japanese and Swedish peace-building efforts: the case of Afghanistan

When it comes to peace building, policy rhetoric is one thing, most developed countries have policies that are rather similar in content. In DAC a set of mutually guiding principles for security system reform and governance have been issued. Still, how the member countries apply those may differ considerably, depending on their legal framework at home, interest in the issue as well as their historical and cultural background. There is not just one way of peace building but the various countries have their own models for how it should be done. This is very often mediated by their own experience. Concerning the non-ODA part, that is, peace building by the use of military forces, this will also vary depending on the situation on the ground as well as which country that is involved, whether the operations are conducted under the UN flag, under the NATO banner, a coalition of the willing or by an individual country alone. It will also depend on legal framework in the individual countries, the level of threat perceived, the external environment as well as the domestic opinion.

In the twenty-first century there have so far been two major interventions, both with strong US leadership, the one in Iraq and the other in Afghanistan. The Iraq one was hotly contested and even divided the European countries into two camps, with NATO allies such as Norway against an invasion. The Iraq war was not sanctioned by the UN Security Council. Neither was the military campaign in Afghanistan. Operation Enduring Freedom was launched by the United States with the United Kingdom in October 2001 in response to the 11 September 2001 attacks. The stated purpose of the invasion was to capture Osama bin Laden, destroy al-Qaeda and remove the Taliban regime, which had provided support and safe harbour to al-Qaeda. As the Taliban regime fell in December 2001, the UNSC did, however, authorize the creation of an International Security Assistance Force (ISAF) with authority to take all measures necessary to assist the Afghan Interim Authority in maintaining security. The UN authorizations as well as a great amount of acceptance of the actions in Afghanistan are reasons for choosing it as a case study.

Why then make a comparison between Japan and Sweden? In contrast to the United Kingdom, another US ally that is often one of the first to support US actions by military means, Sweden is a non-allied country that has not used military force on its own during the last century and is generally considered as a peaceful country with a strong ODA profile. It shares an interest in preventive diplomacy and disarmament with Japan and one could expect the two countries to conduct similar policies towards Afghanistan. The time period over which their respective initiatives in Afghanistan are compared is from December 2001 (the UNSC authorization of ISAF) until the present.

Japanese initiatives

Japan hosted the International Conference on Reconstruction Assistance (ICRA) to Afghanistan in 2002. At that time, Japan pledged USD 500 million over two and a half years. At later conferences in Berlin (2004) and London (2006), Japan announced its intention to extend an additional USD 400 million and USD 450 million. By November 2007, USD 1.24 billion worth of Japanese ODA had been implemented (see Table 6.1).[31] ODA to Afghanistan has, however, always been a small percentage of Japan's total ODA during recent years. According to OECD DAC, *Development Co-operation Report, 2007*, Afghanistan was not even on the list of the top ten recipients during the period 2005–06 (see Table 6.3). According to the Japanese Development Assistance White Paper 2007, aid to Afghanistan was 1.58 per cent of the total Japanese grant aid and 1.03 per cent of the technical cooperation. No loan aid was provided.[32] In total 0.53 per cent of Japanese bilateral ODA went to Afghanistan.

Humanitarian aid has taken the form of support for refugees, food aid and so on, but most of the money has been spent on support for reconstruction (USD 710 million). Highways and secondary road construction account for around one-third of this, but there are also regional comprehensive development projects targeting local communities (the so-called Ogata initiative). There is health,

Table 6.1 Breakdown of Japanese ODA support for Afghanistan as of November 2007 (USD million)

Type of support		*Value*
Humanitarian		175
Reconstruction:		
(a) Political process and governance	165	1,068
(b) Improvement of security	193	
(c) Reconstruction	710	
Total		1,243

Source: compiled from Ministry of Foreign Affairs, *Japan's Official Development Assistance White Paper 2007*, Urban Connections, Tokyo, 2007, pp. 218–19.

education and agriculture and rural development aid as well as grant assistance for grass-roots and human security projects.

A total of USD 193 million has been spent on improving security. Of this, USD 140 million went to DDR activities and USD 43 million to land-mine countermeasures. Japan has also supported a crackdown on narcotics and provided the Afghani police with vehicles and wireless devices. Support for political processes and governance amounted to USD 165 million, the main part going to administrative expenses and support for the provisional and transitional government before the elections. Japan provided assistance for voter registration and the conduct of the elections.

In the field of diplomacy Japan also hosted two conferences in Tokyo on the consolidation of peace in Afghanistan. Because the country has now passed the stage of requiring emergency humanitarian assistance, recovery and reconstruction, it should now move on to full-scale development assistance, although it still faces severe security problems.[33] To deal with the latter, Japan supports programmes for the disbandment of illegal armed groups.

At the Japan–NATO High Level Consultation in March 2007, Japan agreed to cooperate with the NATO provincial reconstruction teams (PRTs) through Japanese grant aid for grass-roots projects. The cooperation with NATO clearly represents a widening of Japan's range of cooperation partners.

Besides the different initiatives in the field of ODA, Japan also conducts refuelling missions for US vessels conducting anti-terrorism activities in the area. This has been allowed through the adoption of the controversial Anti-Terrorism Special Measures Law adopted in November 2001. After three extensions this was replaceded by the Replenishment Support Special Law in 2008. (See also Chapter 3 by P. Midford in this volume.)

Swedish initiatives

By comparison, Swedish ODA support for Afghanistan during the three-year cooperation strategy, in effect until 1 July 2009, provided a total of SEK 1 billion (USD 162 million). With a 2007 budget of SEK 380 million (USD 61 million), this makes Afghanistan one of the largest recipients of Swedish bilateral ODA, in fact the eighth largest. Still, as a percentage of Swedish bilateral ODA, aid to Afghanistan is no more than slightly over 1 per cent of total Swedish ODA. In November 2008 the Swedish government announced that it would increase the annual budget to SEK 500 million.[34] The aims of Swedish development cooperation in Afghanistan are: (1) reducing poverty; (2) promoting democracy and human rights; (3) developing civil society; and (4) strengthening cross-border and national security. All Swedish aid is given with particular regard to the situation of women and girls.[35] Aid is channelled via the United Nations or via Swedish or international non-governmental organizations (NGOs).

Human rights and democratic governance are the fields to which the largest share of the money is allocated (see Table 6.2). The Swedish International Development Cooperation Agency (Sida), similar to Japanese and other aid agencies, under the heading 'human rights and democratic governance', has facilitated the conduct of general elections, supported the training of members of parliament (MPs) and organized the building of infrastructure needed to carry out training organized by the UNDP. Education is the second largest field, where support is given to the Swedish Committee for Afghanistan (SCA) for basic education (nine years of compulsory schooling) projects in rural areas. Other education projects in Afghanistan through the United Nations Children's Fund (UNICEF) are also supported. Sida also contributes to mine clearance programmes and to anti-drug campaigns through the UNDP's Counter Narcotics Trust Fund (CNTF).

In the coming three-year country assistance plan starting from 1 July 2009, there will be a concentration of ODA to three areas, namely: (1) democracy; (2) education, with a special emphasis on women; and (3) different activities for promoting trade and business. As we can see from Table 6.2, not much Swedish aid money goes to peace-building measures in a narrow sense. Instead, what Sweden is doing in this field falls mainly outside the ODA budget.

Table 6.2 Swedish ODA to Afghanistan in 2007 (SEK 000)

Type of support	*Amount*
Human rights and democratic governance	146,048
Education	131,169
Infrastructure	36,027
Humanitarian assistance	23,632
Health	18,566
Conflict, peace and security	14,323
Natural resources and environment	2,555
Research	2,000
Trade, business and financial system	515
Other	5,847
Total	380,682

Source: Sida Annual Report 2007.

According to Sweden's Global Development Policy, development cooperation projects should be coordinated with other activities that Sweden supports. In Afghanistan, Sweden supports the International Security Assistance Force (ISAF), which is there to help the Afghani government maintain security in the country. The forces are NATO-led under a commission of the UN Security Council. Sweden leads the ISAF unit responsible for four provinces in northern Afghanistan. Since 2006 it has also led a PRT in Mazar-e Sharif, one of the main cities in northern Afghanistan. There are roughly 350 Swedish soldiers and a few civilians stationed there. The number of soldiers would be increased to 500, according to an announcement by the government.[36] Sweden also contributes to the work being done by the European Union (EU) to support the police and judicial sectors in the region. In 2007 Sida received a directive from the Swedish government that included the demand that 15–20 per cent of its development cooperation with the country should be concentrated in the north where the Swedish military are concentrated. This is a new policy for Sweden, where ODA is being disbursed in connection with military activities. The Moderate Party, that is, the leaders of the Swedish governing coalition, declared that it would like to lower ODA in general to be able to use money more freely and take other measures than the ones strictly classified as ODA in for example northern Afghanistan.[37]

Comparing Japan and Sweden

Comparing the Swedish and Japanese contributions to support for peace building in Afghanistan, the biggest difference is unsurprisingly Sweden's dispatch of troops, who are working under dangerous conditions to build peace on the ground. A certain amount of the Swedish aid money (15–20 per cent) is used in the area where the Swedish troops are working. In this sense there is a certain level of coordination between the civilian and the military sides of Sweden's contributions to peace in Afghanistan.

In the Japanese case, the SDF mission of refuelling the vessels of the Coalition falls outside the ODA budget. Otherwise, most of Japan's missions in Afghanistan are within the ODA budget. In the Japanese case, the key concepts are the political process and governance as well as the improvement of security and reconstruction. In the Swedish case, at least for the ODA part, poverty reduction is still a key concept.

Military–civilian cooperation

One of the problems with the implementation of various peace-building measures through ODA is that of security. Many of the missions take place in insecure areas. ODA is by definition not to be used for military actions and in Japan the implementing agencies for ODA, such as JICA, have been very reluctant to cooperate with the Self Defense Forces. Their opportunities to take flexible action are also limited due to the legal limitations pointed out above. Take the so-called Disarmament, Demobilization and Reintegration (DDR) activities as an example.

Japan took the lead in the DDR process in Afghanistan. The government supported the DDR programme, which completed the disarmament and reintegration of 60,000 members of the Afghan Military Force. The Japanese also created the International Observer Group (IOG) to observe the DDR process on behalf of the international community. The IOG headquarters were initially established in the Japanese embassy. It was argued within the embassy that the IOG should be a neutral third party, not directly governed by the lead donor country. As their task required military knowledge, the members of the IOG all had a military background. Due to legal considerations the Self Defense Forces could not be assigned the mission. Thus a Japanese NGO called the JMAS (Japan Mine Action Service), consisting of retired SDF officers, was assigned to take over the leadership of the IOG. One characteristic (or it could be a limitation) was that IOG observers were not allowed to carry weapons for any purpose, including self-defence. They were responsible for their own safety and had a contract with the Afghanistan police for their protection.[38]

This group also came to function as something of an informal coordination centre for other ODA activities. When they heard about needs on the ground they tried to establish links between local people and other NGOs working on development.[39] That there was no one who knew anything about development issues was pointed out as a weakness in the final report of the IOG's activities. There was a heavy focus on observation in disarmament and demobilization activities but reintegration was rarely in focus.[40]

A third-party evaluation of Japanese peace-building assistance, commissioned by MOFA, pointed out that DDR activities that include a disarmament process implemented by an army or one that presupposes the reuse of arms collected goes against the ODA Charter, and that ODA could not be used for military purposes. Budgets other than ODA should be used for such purposes in the future, the report concluded.[41] Another weakness pointed out in the report was that security measures for NGOs working in the field cannot be covered by the ODA budget.

Peace building and ODA budget allocations

Japanese ODA to Afghanistan has been the second largest, after the United States', in terms of budget allocations.[42] The amount of ODA channelled to the reconstruction efforts in Iraq during 2006, when Iraq was Japan's top recipient of ODA (Table 6.3), indicates that peace building and the fight against terrorism were given considerable space within Japanese ODA allocations. Japan was second only to the United States in its size of ODA to Iraq.

Putting this in perspective, however, Japan and Sweden were not alone in providing large amounts of ODA to Iraq in that year. In the 2005–06 period, nine DAC countries had Iraq as the largest recipient of ODA. In 2005, a record high for a single country, Iraq received USD 22,052 million (USD 14 billion was in the form of debt cancellation) and, in 2006, another USD 8,661 million. The same was true for many of the other DAC donors; 2005–06 must be considered an exceptional year.[43]

Table 6.3 Top ten recipients of Japanese and Swedish gross ODA, 2005–06 (USD million)

Rank	*From Japan*	*%*	*Rank*	*From Sweden*	*%*
1	Iraq	12.1	1	Iraq	4.0
2	China	8.6	2	Tanzania	2.8
3	Indonesia	6.6	3	Mozambique	2.3
4	Nigeria	6.2	4	Uganda	1.5
5	Philippines	4.2	5	Ethiopia	1.5
6	Viet Nam	3.7	6	Kenya	1.3
7	India	3.3	7	Sudan	1.3
8	Thailand	2.7	8	Afghanistan	1.2
9	Zambia	2.2	9	Palestinian Admin. Areas	1.2
10	Sri Lanka	1.9	10	Bosnia-Herzegovina	1.2
	Total of top ten	57.7		Total of top ten	23.7
	Multilateral ODA	18.5		Multilateral ODA	30.2

Source: OECD DAC, *Development Co-operation Report 2007*, Vol. 9, No. 1, pp. 211, 216.

What is more remarkable is that Afghanistan is not at all on Japan's list of top ten recipients (Table 6.3). Eleven DAC countries had Afghanistan among its top ten recipients. In all ODA from DAC countries Afghanistan ended up in fifth place, receiving 2 per cent of the total amount.[44] The list of top recipients of Japanese as well as Swedish ODA (Table 6.3), on the contrary, indicates that most of the aid is given for purposes other than peace building. The revised Japanese ODA Charter designated Asia as a priority area, but with the termination of the yen loans to China this year, plus the fact that many of the Asian countries have now reached such a level of development that they no longer need aid or have indicated that they do not want to take any more ODA (e.g. India and Thailand), the share of Japan's ODA that goes to Asia is likely to decrease while the share that goes to Africa is likely to increase. At the Tokyo International Conference on African Development in May 2008, Japan committed itself to doubling its aid to Africa by 2012.

Although the Japanese Foreign Minister indicated that Japan will increase its capabilities in peace building, from a budget point of view there are few examples of new initiatives.[45] Most examples of Japanese contributions to peace building in the past are old, such as the Cambodian case, which occurred almost twenty years ago. Although Japan is shouldering a significant part, 16.6 per cent, of the overall budget for PKO worldwide, its human contribution is still very meagre. According to UN statistics, Japan has dispatched only thirty-six military and police personnel, 0.04 per cent of the total, which gives it a low rank position in the world community. Even Cambodia has now dispatched three times as many military and police personal to PKO activities as Japan has.[46]

There is also the problem that the Japanese ODA budget as such has been steadily decreasing. In fact, it shrank by 40 per cent between 1997 and 2007 (from JPY 1,168 billion to JPY 729 billion). According to recent DAC statistics, Japan, which was the largest donor during the 1990s, has now fallen to fifth place after the United

States, which is the biggest contributor, followed by Germany, and then France and the United Kingdom. At the annual meeting of the World Economic Forum in Davos in January 2009, Prime Minister Taro Aso, however, announced that he expected Japanese ODA to increase by approximately 20 per cent on a net basis.[47] Moreover, in the Japanese ODA budget, aid for peace building does not have a prominence that distinguishes Japan from other donors. The specific characteristics of Japanese ODA are rather the belief in development through economic growth and the fact that as much as 61 per cent of the ODA is connected with aid for trade, whereas the OECD average is 30 per cent.[48]

Conclusion

Since the end of the Cold War there have been an increasing number of conflicts both within countries and between countries. Globalization has made the world more interconnected and what happens in one part can affect another. At the same time it has also become obvious that there is a link between security and development and that security threats do not always come from outside a country but can also be caused by so-called 'fragile state' mechanisms. The DAC recommends its members to promote peace and security as fundamental pillars of development both on a personal and on the state level and to push for security system reform, implying increased transparency, good governance, the protection of human rights and institutional change in the developing countries. There is currently huge pressure to make security the key foreign policy objective of donor countries. This is happening on a worldwide basis, and not only in Japan.

To understand Japan's efforts to build peace through ODA, one also has to put them in the wider context of security-related efforts, such as US military strategy and the US–Japan defence cooperation. In the 'two plus two' meeting in October 2005 (that is, the meeting of the Foreign and Defense Ministers of the United States and Japan), the US and Japanese governments confirmed 'their close and continuous policy and operational coordination' that would evolve as the global and security environment changes. The specific areas for cooperation included counter-terrorism, humanitarian relief operations and reconstruction assistance operations.[49] The major ODA contribution Japan has made to Iraq must be understood within this framework. Here security concerns prevail over poverty reduction and other development issues. Iraq is not a poor but a middle-income country. In a sense, the situation resembles that of the 1980s, with 'burden sharing' whereby Japan should provide assistance in the form of aid to compensate for what the United States contributes by providing a global security umbrella. Afghanistan on the other hand is one of the poorest countries in the world. It is the second biggest recipient of aid from the United States. Still it is not among the top ten recipients of Japanese ODA. Here the argument of burden sharing does not seem to apply.

Since the 9/11 incident the fight against terrorism has become a priority for many donors, including Japan. Usually this is not done via the ODA budget but through other means. In its present situation, due to constitutional restraints, Japan cannot use its Self Defense Forces, at least not in combat areas, for either peace building or fighting terrorism. The domestic political situation makes it difficult to expect any changes to the Constitution at present. This means that Japan has to find other ways, such as development aid.

The question must be raised, however, what kind of counter-measures against terrorism as well as peace building can be achieved in what type of situation with the help of diplomacy and ODA. Japan could certainly not work on the ground in areas of conflict and unrest where peace-building efforts might be very important. This sets certain limits to Japanese peace-building efforts. It also makes ODA policy unclear in the sense that it has to take a larger role in the fight against terrorism and in peace-building efforts, as Japan does not have much else that it can contribute.

ODA is a flexible tool that historically Japan has used for many different purposes, such as war reparations, promoting economic growth and securing natural resources. It is always seen as a two-way trade, as it is today, when Japanese contributions to peace and development are also seen as ensuring Japan's own security and prosperity. To a certain extent, the present ODA contribution to peace building must be seen as partly belonging to the field of rhetoric and a defence against pressure on Japan to do more in the security field. After all, peace building is a small part of the ODA programme and ODA itself has been shrinking by 40 per cent in the course of the last ten years.

In the UN Millennium Development Goals, poverty reduction is the most important issue. That is also what really counts for many of the people in the developing countries. What does this fight against terrorism then imply for them? Recent experience suggests that in putting security issues at the forefront, there is a danger that the interests of poorer countries will be conflated with the interests of richer countries, when in fact the problems that most concern richer countries (such as terrorism) are not always a priority concern of the developing countries. The link between security and development has been proved. This does not, however, mean that security is more important than development in the face of the huge poverty reduction challenges that the poor countries and their inhabitants are facing.

The main aim of peace building through ODA should be poverty reduction. The fact that this has been dropped as a priority issue in the latest White Paper on ODA in Japan should be seen as a worrying sign for the developing world. Especially since the Japanese ODA budget has been shrinking per se, poverty reduction can be considered to have been hi-jacked by security considerations in Japanese development policy.

Notes

1 www.sida.se/sida/jsp/sida.jsp?d=1350&a=4853&language=en_US (accessed 6 December 2008).

2 Official development assistance (ODA) is foreign aid as defined by DAC. It has to be government-to-government, for development purposes, and with a grant element of at least 25 per cent. Explicitly excluded from these criteria are military aid and the enforcement aspects of peacekeeping. But donors are allowed to include a number of related areas such as rehabilitation assistance to demobilized soldiers, training in

customs and border control procedures, counter-narcotics activities, disposal of weapons and land mines, and the training of police forces in civil police functions (but not in counter-subversive methods or suppression of political dissent).

3 The following are DAC members: Australia, Austria, Belgium, Canada, Denmark, Finland, France, Germany, Greece, Ireland, Italy, Japan, Luxembourg, the Netherlands, New Zealand, Norway, Portugal, Spain, Sweden, Switzerland, the United Kingdom, the United States and the Commission of the European Communities.

4 The first was *DAC Guidelines: Conflict Peace and Development Co-operation* (1998) and the most recent *Security System Reform and Governance* (2005).

5 DAC Guidelines and Reference Series, *Security System Reform and Governance*, Paris: OECD, 2005, www.oecd.org/dataoecd/8/39/31785288.pdf (accessed 19 January 2009).

6 B. Boutros-Ghali, *An Agenda for Peace*, UN Document A/47/277-S/24111, 1992.

7 H. Shinoda, 'Toward a sustainable strategy of peace building: an examination of negative and positive justifications of Security Sector Reforms (SSR)', *Hiroshima Peace Science* 29, 2007, 92.

8 UNDP, *Human Development Report*, New York and Oxford: Oxford University Press, 1994. Also available at http://hdr.undp.org/en/reports/global/hdr1994/ (accessed 14 December 2008).

9 K. Annan, *The Cause of Conflict and the Promotion of Durable Peace and Sustainable Development in Africa: Report of the Secretary General*, UN Document A/52/871-S/1998/318, paras 71–8, as cited by Shinoda, 'Toward a sustainable strategy of peace building', pp. 94–5.

10 *Report of the Panel on United Nations Peace Operations*, UN Document A/55/305-S/2000/809, as cited by Shinoda, 'Toward a sustainable strategy of peace building', pp. 95–8.

11 An English translation of the Japanese Constitution can be found at www.solon.org/Constitutions/Japan/English/english-Constitution.html (accessed 6 December 2008).

12 M. Söderberg, 'Japan's Military Export Policy', Täby: Akademitryck, 1986 (Ph.D. thesis), p. 9.

13 Ibid., pp. 32–4.

14 *Japan Times*, 'Collective Defense: What it Means to Japan', 19 May 2007, http://search.japantimes.co.jp/cgi-bin/nn20070519f1.html (accessed 1 June 2008).

15 This was a view explained among others by John H. Holdridge, Assistant Secretary of State for East Asia and Pacific Affairs in *United States–Japan Relations Hearing before the Committee on Foreign Affairs House of Representatives and its Subcommittees on International Economic Policy and Trade and on Asia and Pacific Affairs, 97th Congress, 2nd session*, Washington, DC: Government Printing Office, 1982, p. 79.

16 M. Söderberg (ed.), *The Business of Japanese Foreign Aid: Five Case Studies from Asia*, London and New York: Routledge, 1996.

17 See for example M. Hanabusa, 'A Japanese perspective on aid and development' in S. Islam (ed.) *Yen for development: Japanese Foreign Aid and the Politics of Burden-Sharing*, New York: Council on Foreign Relations Press, 1991; or D. Yasutomo, *The Manner of Giving: Strategic Aid and Japanese Foreign Policy*, Lexington, MA: Lexington Books, 1986.

18 Statement by Prime Minister Takeshita in London in 1988, www.mofa.go.jp/policy/other/bluebook/1988/1988-appendix-2.htm (accessed 19 January 2009).

19 N. Suto, 'Japan: accepting the challenges of conflict prevention and peacebuilding' in A. Heijmans, N. Simmonds and H. van de Veen (eds) *Searching for Peace in Asia Pacific: An Overview of Conflict Prevention and Peace-building Activities*, London: Lynne Rienner, 2004.

20 The cooperation was limited to non-combat positions.

21 Speech of 28 January 2008 by M. Koumura, 'Japan: A Builder of Peace', www.mofa.go.jp/policy/un/pko/speech0801.html (accessed 19 January 2009).

22 Ministry of Defense, *Defence of Japan 2007* (White Paper), Tokyo: Intergroup, 2007, p. 157.
23 This council is chaired by the Prime Minister. Other members are the Chief Cabinet Secretary, the Minister of Foreign Affairs, the Minister of Finance and the Minster of the Economy, Trade and Industry. This council was established as a 'control tower' to strengthen the strategic aspects of overseas economic cooperation.
24 Ministry of Foreign Affairs, *Japan's Official Development Assistance White Paper, 2007*, Tokyo: Urban Connections, 2007, pp. 4–5.
25 Ibid., p. 4.
26 Koumura, 'Japan: A Builder of Peace'.
27 Web page of the Commission: www.un.org/peace/peacebuilding (accessed 19 January 2009).
28 Interview with Sachiko Ishikawa, Senior Adviser, Institute for International Cooperation, Tokyo: JICA, May 2008.
29 The Folke Bernadotte Academy is a Swedish government agency, created in 2002 and dedicated to improving the quality and effectiveness of international conflict and crisis management, with a particular focus on peace operations. The Academy functions as a platform for cooperation between Swedish agencies and organizations and their international partners. The home page of the organization can be found at www.folkebernadotteacademy.se/roach/rootpage.do?pageId=1 (accessed 14 December 2008).
30 Interview with one of the initiators, Professor Nakamitsu Izumi of Hitotsubashi University, November 2007.
31 Ministry of Foreign Affairs, *Japan's Official Development Assistance White Paper, 2007*, p. 142.
32 Ibid., p. 223.
33 Ibid., p. 142.
34 *Svenska Dagbladet*, 14 November 2008, p. 8.
35 See the Sida Web information, www.sida.se/sida/jsp/sida.jsp?d=245&a=853&language=en_US (accessed 14 December 2008).
36 *Svenska Dagbladet*, 14 November 2008, p. 8.
37 *Dagens Nyheter*, DN debate, 27 November 2008.
38 UNDP, International Observer Group, JMAS Final Programme Report: International Observer Group for DDR in Afghanistan ref.: C04-074, pp. 2–5.
39 Interview with Hiroaki Sonobe, JMAS, May 2008, in Tokyo. (Sonobe Hiroaki was the leader of the IOG in Afghanistan.)
40 UNDP, International Observer Group, 'Final Report: International Observer Group for DDR in Afghanistan' ref.: C04-074, p. 21.
41 Ministry of Foreign Affairs, Third Party Evaluation of Japan's Peace Building Assistance Policy – A Case Study: Afghanistan Summary Report, March 2006, www.mofa.go.jp/policy/oda/evaluation/2005/afghanistan.txt (accessed 4 June 2008).
42 Ibid.
43 OECD DAC, *Development Co-operation Report, 2007*, Vol. 9, No. 1.
44 Ibid., pp. 206–19.
45 Koumura, 'Japan: A Builder of Peace'.
46 www.mofa.go.jp/policy/un/pko/symposium0803-s.html (accessed 14 December 2008).
47 Ministry of Foreign Affairs, www.mofa.go.jp/policy/economy/wef/2009/address.html (accessed 2 February 2009).
48 The high Japanese figure is mainly due to the focus on infrastructure development: OECD DAC, *Development Co-operation Report, 2007*, Vol. 9, No. 1.
49 Security Consultative Committee Document 'U.S.–Japan Alliance: Transformation and Realignment for the Future', www.mofa.go.jp/region/n-america/us/security/scc/doc0510.html (accessed 19 January 2009).

7 Peace diplomacy by ODA

Rhetoric and reality

Norbert Palanovics

A survey of 28,000 people across twenty-seven countries found that Japan was seen as one of the most positively influential countries. Respondents were asked if twelve countries of high international importance had positive or negative influence in the world. The research concluded that people around the world tend to look negatively on countries that used or pursued the use of military power. However, countries with high soft power-projecting capabilities were perceived well.[1] Perceptions of Japan as a peace country were based predominantly on its stance in international relations.[2] These perceptions fall in line with Japan's own, desired international role. In a survey conducted by the Cabinet Office of Japan, the second most popular answer among the Japanese respondents was that they would like their country to contribute to maintaining world peace and cooperating toward peaceful resolutions of regional conflicts, disarmament, and non-proliferation.[3]

Japan's tools of soft power, such as culture and economic diplomacy – including products and brands, but also development aid – have elevated the country into one of the most positively perceived actors of the international scene, especially when seen away from North East Asia.[4] Nevertheless, contemporary Japan is still struggling to find its place in world politics. The country that transformed from an expansionist but defeated power to a peaceful global economic power has been seeking ways to locate itself in the international community of the twenty-first century. In the post-Cold War and post-9/11 world, Japan's leaders have been working to redefine Japan's international image and its role. In this light, in the 1980s and 1990s, the concept of peace diplomacy emerged. Capitalizing on the concept of peace diplomacy, Japan started taking a more active role in international peace-related operations. The Koizumi era that coincided with the post-9/11 period brought new changes in Japan's diplomacy and foreign policy. These changes were triggered both by internal and external factors.

In addition to reforming the US–Japan relationship, the rhetoric of satisfying national interests was used to justify Japan's participation in various international peace-related activities, including the US-led War against Terror and sending troops to various conflict regions, including Iraq and Afghanistan. Japan declared that it would play a larger political role via ODA and peace building. Utilizing this tool, Japan has been active in trying to provide humanitarian and reconstruction assistance to various conflict-torn countries or regions.

The purpose of this chapter is to illustrate how Japan conducts its ODA-based peace diplomacy. This chapter focuses on Japan's rhetoric to foreign policy, particularly of development assistance and peace building, and examines the link between rhetoric and action. While the focus is on the twenty-first-century developments in Japan's peace-building activities and foreign policy, we emphasize the achievements of the Koizumi and Abe administrations.

The analysis is done by exploring Japan's participation in Sri Lanka. Sri Lanka is regarded as a model case for Japanese ODA as a diplomatic tool for peace and the first instance where Japanese ODA was used to explicitly support the diplomatic aspects of the peace process. The Sri Lankan case is better understood if seen together with an earlier occurrence of Japan's participation in Cambodia. The two cases show many similarities and points of contrasts, and they are both regarded as reference cases and both indicate milestones for Japanese peace-related activities.

This chapter begins with an introduction to the whole-of-government approach to peace building that has become one of the influential approaches to development aid and consolidating peace in post-conflict (and conflict) zones. Thereafter, we discuss the degree to which Japan has adopted this approach. In the next two sections, we examine the latest developments in Japan's ODA policies, including the interpretation of the concepts of peace building and human security and the relationship between ODA and peace building. Next, we analyse Japan's peace building-based ODA diplomacy with an emphasis on the case of Sri Lanka, which is compared with Japan's participation in Cambodia's peace process in the early 1990s. In conclusion, we make some recommendations as to how Japan could improve its peace diplomacy.

The whole-of-government approach

Global interdependence has resulted in conflicts having international spill-over effects that manifest themselves in, among others, migration, crime, health issues, environmental problems, terrorism and human trafficking which all concern the national security of the developed countries.[5] The terrorist attacks on US targets on 11 September 2001 and the political, economic and security consequences of those opened a new chapter in numerous countries' foreign policies. Political, defence, diplomatic and economic instruments of national power have started to move towards a common direction with the aim to provide a secure environment, make and keep peace, restore and develop economies and social structures and institutions in unstable or conflict-torn regions around the world.

In a 2006 speech, Bernard Bot, the Dutch Foreign Minister, called the overall political framework encompassing political, military and developmental efforts a 'trinity'. According to Bot, security and foreign policy cannot be separated from development cooperation, and these are the three keys to success in conflict prevention and conflict resolution.[6]

The trinity of political, military and developmental efforts has manifested in policy initiatives such as the 'Defence, Diplomacy and Development' (the 3D approach) and 'whole of government' approaches. Both initiatives aim to tackle security challenges that affect the donor country and the aid recipient countries, and they are based on the notion that in order to respond properly to challenges of national interest and stability, intergovernmental coordination is needed, and all the relevant actors (including the fields of security, economy, social services, and humanitarian relief) should work together. The result of this thinking is that foreign aid and ODA became major elements of the national security and foreign policy strategies of many countries. In Canada or in Australia, for example, this coherent and integrated approach is called 'whole-of-government coherence.'[7]

The donor community accepted the whole-of-government approach in April 2005, when the Organization for Economic Co-operation and Development's Development Assistance Committee (OECD DAC) outlined a set of principles. They define the whole-of-government approach as 'one where a government actively uses formal and/or informal networks across the different agencies' to plan and execute a 'range of interventions [...] in order to increase the effectiveness of those interventions in achieving the desired objectives'.[8]

The whole-of-government approach gives elevated political attention to conflicted and developing countries. This political attention, however, stems from the national interest of the donor country, which is often received with ambivalence in the developing countries, thus there is a risk of the core development agenda being subordinated to other, political issues.[9] In such circumstances, the whole-of-government approach can become a 'Trojan horse' for the politicization of aid.[10] Cammack *et al.* noted that if donors use this approach, aid loses its autonomy.[11]

The whole-of-government approach defined by OECD DAC is similar in many ways to the Goodhand *et al.* multi-track approach to peace building and conflict resolution (see Table 7.1).[12] Goodhand's three-track peace diplomacy framework is a modified version of the original Track One, Track Two paradigm coined by Montville.[13]

Goodhand *et al.* understand official negotiations between political and military actors as Track One diplomacy. Track Two means non-official mediation, for example among civil society actors or behind-the-scenes communication of political representatives. Track Three is defined by humanitarian and development

Table 7.1 Parallels between the multi-track and the whole-of-government approaches

Goodhand et al.*'s multi-track approach*	*Whole-of-government approach*
Track One (official negotiations)	National security (defence) and political efforts (diplomacy, economy)
Track One-and-a-half (peacemaking between official and non-official)	Political (diplomacy) and development efforts (confidence building, building economic ties)
Track Two (non-official mediations)	Political and development efforts (social services, linking civil societies)
Track Three (humanitarian and development assistance)	Development efforts (humanitarian relief)

Sources: adapted from Goodhand *et al.*, p. 27, OECD, 2006, p. 4, and Bot, 2006.

assistance. Goodhand *et al.* also introduced Track One-and-a-half, which refers to peacemaking efforts that occupy the terrain between official and non-official confidence building.[14]

Defence, security guarantees and cease-fire monitoring can all be classified as Track One using Goodhand's framework. The 'three tracks' concept calls for convergence and synergies among the tracks and between development and security. Like Goodhand's backchannel track, the peace-building Track Two serves as a rather informal backchannel for Track One. The actors in the peace building process depend on what is happening in Track One.

Japan implemented a government reform in 2001, moving it toward better policy coherence. Scholars noted that closer cross-agency cooperation and the whole-of-government approach are new challenges for governments worldwide, and while it was not being discussed much in Japan at the present, the 2001 government reforms marked the way forward.[15]

When Junichiro Koizumi took up the premiership in 2001, one of his goals was to transform and revitalize Japan's internal and foreign affairs. Koizumi brought a new style of popular politics into Japan's political scene and, among many other actions, also began to centralize decision-making, including development aid issues, resulting in the creation of the ODA Strategy Council in 2006. The Japanese government set up the ministerial Council on Overseas Economic Cooperation, chaired by Koizumi, to 'flexibly discuss key issues of ODA and ensure its strategic and efficient implementation' and to 'act as the headquarters for strategic overseas economic cooperation'.[16]

The reformist-minded Koizumi inherited a changing foreign policy. The aid budget, a major tool for Japan's internationalization in the twentieth century, was shrinking while greater emphasis was being placed on peace cooperation, with human security and peace building at its core. Koizumi was keen to use the peace rhetoric to team up with the United States in the War against Terrorism after 9/11.

During and since the Koizumi administration, anti-terrorism and development assistance rhetoric has been frequently used in documents published by the Japanese government as well as in policy makers' speeches. These underline the fact that the government tried to link the various diplomatic tools that could effectively serve the country's broad range of national interests. MOFA's English-language home page listed as of the end of 2007 at least twenty-eight press releases, comments or speeches that mentioned Japan's participation in the 'War against Terrorism'.[17] In a January 2006 speech, then Minister of Foreign Affairs Taro Aso declared ODA a political policy measure that should also favour the donor nation. Consequently, Japan's ODA should serve as a tool to enhance ties between Japan and other countries with similar interests.[18]

Background to Japanese ODA in the twenty-first century

Aid had long been a cornerstone of Japan's internationalization, and long been linked to the foreign – especially Asian – expansion of Japanese companies. After the bursting of the economic bubble in the early 1990s, Japan experienced aid fatigue, which eventually led to ODA budget cuts and adjustments to its administration. The changes in ODA were fostered not only by the changes in the international environment, but also by growing criticism of Japan's international cooperation and aid policies, its maturation as a donor and the rapid development of South East Asian countries that had 'graduated' from Japan's aid. Japan gradually realized that it could not ignore the forces of globalization as it became clear that Japan's economy was highly intertwined with the globalized world economy. There was a discussion among policy makers and bureaucrats in Japan about whether aid should be extended to such issues as democracy, human rights, good governance, human resource development and institution building in recipient countries.[19] These developments and the new challenges posed by, among others, the post-9/11 world order had a large impact on the aid administration, and provided an opportunity to reinvent Japanese ODA.

The determination to address critiques of ODA combined with the fact that MOFA became the main administrator of ODA in 2001 contributed to the revision in 2003 of the original 1992 ODA Charter. The changes were officially attributed to the need to address the dramatic domestic and international changes that had occurred since the ODA Charter was first adopted, and the increased need for strategic, more effective and efficient implementation of ODA.[20] The most important elements of the second, revised ODA Charter included supporting the self-help efforts of developing countries and the introduction of human security among its basic policies. Peace building also became the new Charter's priority issue in addition to poverty reduction, sustainable growth and addressing global issues.[21]

The objectives of the new ODA Charter are 'to contribute to the peace and development of the international community, and thereby to help ensure Japan's own security and prosperity'.[22] The establishment of MOFA's International Cooperation Bureau in August 2006 enhanced the strategic aspects of economic cooperation and also provided an opportunity to better integrate ODA into MOFA's various diplomatic tools. The launch of the new Japan International Cooperation Agency (JICA) (by merging JICA and much of the Japan Bank for International Cooperation, JBIC) in 2008 has strengthened this approach.

The role of ODA as a means of healing the wounds caused by conflicts and building peace has become increasingly important in recent years. It is due to the fact that conflicts have been a major obstacle of development. There has been a growing awareness that conflicts which have occurred frequently since the end of the Cold War ruined in a short time what long-term development had achieved.[23]

The 2006 ODA White Paper related ODA to the country's national security goals and declared, 'utilizing ODA to contribute to peace building plays an important role in ensuring Japan's own security and prosperity'.[24] Because the JICA and MOFA definitions of peace building encompass peacekeeping military operations, the new ODA Charter opens the possibility of using ODA for peace-related military activities. Nevertheless, we should not forget to highlight the legal – and psychological – constraints imposed by Article 9 of the Constitution on Japan's international activities that involve the Self Defense Forces (SDF).

Documents in the field of defence view ODA as a tool to contribute to Japan's defence. *The Defense of Japan, 2007*, the Ministry of Defense's (MOD) White Paper, stated that the improvement of the international security will occur via ODA.[25] According to the White Paper, 'humanitarian and reconstruction operations can be conducted with the assistance of Japanese ODA, and consequently, Japan can better contribute to the security and the international fight against terror'.[26] In line with Japan's National Defense Programme Guidelines, ODA is to be used to support international cooperation activities.

Japan's peace-building policies

Peace building can be said to be a result of Japan's peace evolution and soul-searching on the international stage. Japan is, nonetheless, a relative latecomer to active, participative international peace initiatives, and is moving forward slowly. This hesitating and relatively indecisive behaviour was clear in the early 1990s, when Japan had an opportunity to become a world-leading promoter of peace. Legislation was changed, peacekeepers were sent abroad and Cambodia was regarded as a reference case for Japan's new type of international cooperation.

These developments gave Japan an opportunity to show its peace orientation and peace-supporting activities to the world while justifying the existence of the SDF. The Cambodian operations allowed Japan to address critiques of its so-called 'chequebook diplomacy' (after its widely criticized Gulf War participation), but in spite of the relative success there, Japan did not manage to achieve international recognition as a top peace promoter. This was partly due to the constitutional constraints and consequently to Japan's hesitant attitude.

The events of 9/11 gave Japan another opportunity to provide a conspicuous answer to acts that concerned the global community, and as some say to avoid the same humiliation as following the Gulf War.[27] The answer served the purpose of satisfying the US–Japan alliance, while also giving Japan a chance to enhance its international role with global visibility. The Anti-Terrorism Special Measures Law passed in 2001 allowed Japan to send troops to volatile areas to exterminate terrorists (which mainly involved only logistical missions), and the consequent decision to deploy SDF forces to the Indian Ocean to assist the international forces in Afghanistan seemed to be a another revolutionary step since it went close to or beyond the limits of the Constitution.[28] (See also Chapter 3 by P. Midford in this volume.)

Japan built up its peace-related activities step by step between the end of the 1980s and the beginning of the new millennium. It was only after Koizumi came to power in 2001 that Japan's peace-building approach began to be explicitly linked to various foreign policy goals manifested in policy documents and speeches. In May 2002 Koizumi delivered a speech in Sydney on the consolidation of peace and nation building.[29] The announcement was new, but Japanese experts had been using the concepts of peace and nation building for several years.[30]

Japan's idea of peace building was somewhat influenced by international trends, but the government introduced its own interpretation in 2000. Japan proposed a comprehensive approach to include politics, security, economy, society and development under the framework of peace building at the G8 Foreign Ministers' meeting in Miyazaki, Japan. This was the first time that an overall philosophy of Japan's support for conflict-affected countries and areas was presented. The approach was in line with a 2001 JICA document, as both provided an extensive definition of peace building that went beyond the original idea of post-conflict peace building.[31] The latter defined peace building in a broad sense, including military, political and development frameworks – similar to the three tracks of Goodhand *et al.* – and encompassing the whole time scale of the conflict from the pre-conflict stage to the post-conflict reconstruction (see Figure 7.1).[32]

A broad definition was very appealing to the Koizumi government, as it meant that political support *and* military participation could be linked to peace building. Japan could theoretically use the concept of peace building for a more active foreign policy, and also send troops abroad in the name of peace. This phenomenon was not without precedent in the international community. Government rhetoric of peace promotion became popular among international actors, including Canada and the United States in the post-Cold War period. Countries and organizations used the idea of peace in order to reach and achieve various, political, developmental or economic goals.[33]

Since the late 1990s, Japan has increasingly utilized the concept of human security as an approach to development and conflict. The first Prime Minister to use the words 'human security' was Keizo Obuchi in 1998. In 2001 the formation of the Commission of Human Security chaired by Amartya Sen and Sadako Ogata was announced. The Commission developed the concept of human security further, and created a definition and discussed methods of utilizing it.

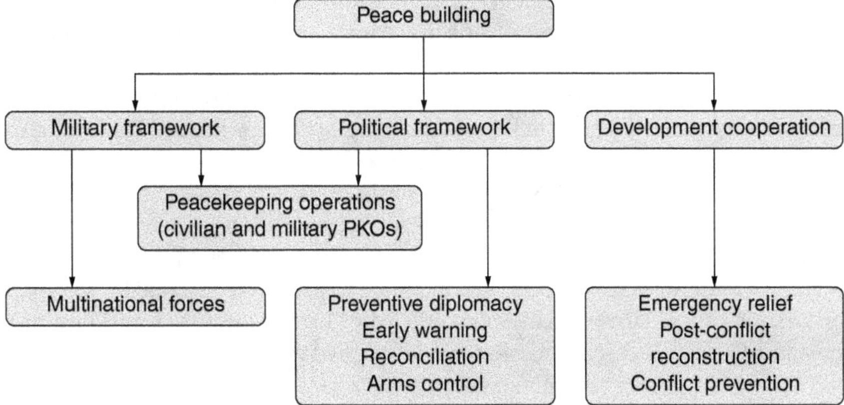

Figure 7.1 The major elements of the Japanese peace-building framework (source: adapted from JICA, 2001, p. 7).

The Japanese definition and interpretation of the concept of human security have not changed significantly since its introduction, although it has been partly revised. It encompasses primarily freedom from want, but to an extent freedom from fear as well. According to Fukushima, human security has been considered a foreign-policy catch phrase to refer to Japan's role in ensuring international peace and security.[34] Lam counted sixteen speeches between 1998 and 2004 using human security,[35] while Fukushima lists forty-four given by Japanese prime ministers, foreign ministers and their top representatives on Japanese aspects of human security.[36]

Among them, Koizumi went the furthest using the original meaning of human security and applying it as a concept to respond to 9/11. Human security became accepted as one of the means to justify Japan's participation in the War against Terrorism (in Iraq and in Afghanistan).[37] The phrase is thus used to demonstrate the 'honourable' nature of Japan's participation in the war. Also under Koizumi, human security became a key pillar of Japan's ODA diplomacy. In a Diet speech of January 2003 Koizumi mentioned human security as part of ODA reform, and said that ODA should be strategically extended with an emphasis on human security.

Former Foreign Minister Yoshiko Kawaguchi also highlighted the role of human security in ODA and as a foreign policy tool. She linked 'creative foreign policy' to this concept, and emphasized Japan's efforts to consolidate peace via the human security approach in Sri Lanka and Afghanistan.[38] The inclusion of human security meant that Japan could dilute its growing international political activities by using a new security phrase, which was seen as having a positive and honourable role, because it focused on individuals as opposed to the traditional concepts of security.

Human security provides a soft approach to linking security and development, as it embraces 'hard' traditional security issues that involve military participation (peacekeeping, for example) in an appealing package. The political meaning of the concept does not refer only to the security of the developing, conflicted countries but also to the security of the donors, and hence it serves national interests.

Within its approach to human security, the Japanese government used the rhetoric of anti-terrorism to link peace building to foreign policy. This included the revision of the Peacekeeping Operations (PKO) Law and the introduction of the Anti-Terrorism Special Measures Law in 2001. In practice, the latter law influenced the previously mentioned Indian Ocean mission to provide logistical support to the US and multinational forces in Afghanistan, and the 2005 deployment of the Ground SDF to Iraq. The mentioned cases were referred by Koizumi and the Japanese government using the new rhetoric of peace building and human security. The Iraqi mission was also governed by the Law Concerning the Special Measures on Humanitarian and Reconstruction Assistance adopted in July 2003. The mission was a major shift away for Japan's peace diplomacy, since Japan acted for the first time on the ground not as part of the UN forces, as in previous occasions, but as 'Japan'.

Besides terrorism, another important part of the new rhetoric attached to peace building was the concept of consolidation of peace. The emergence of the concept of consolidation of peace came after Koizumi's Sydney speech. A government-established study group called the Group on International Peace Cooperation chaired by Akashi Yasushi further elaborated it, and Sri Lanka was chosen as one of the projects under this concept. The Japanese government was aware of the need to make active efforts for successful peace negotiations and to look beyond post-conflict peace building.[39] This policy shift resulted in that Japan moved towards providing assistance for peace building even before a formal peace agreement was concluded, which was in line with JICA's recommendations. Table 7.2 summarizes the internal and external factors influencing Japan's peace building-based ODA diplomacy.

In the Japanese context, consolidation of peace and nation building are the two major pillars of peace building. The two pillars provide a holistic approach to peace building as they encompass the whole system rather than emphasizing selected elements. Consolidation of peace consists of the promotion of peace processes, securing the domestic stability and security of the recipient countries and the humanitarian and reconstruction assistance, while nation building encompasses building a structure for better governance, development of economic and social infrastructure.[40]

Japan's concept of peace building by ODA is understood as 'seamless support'.[41] It means that ODA to peace building is provided in a broad and comprehensive manner, starting from conflict prevention throughout the consolidation of peace until the nation-building activities. This concept resonates with the previously discussed peace-building framework of JICA, as both take a broad approach and both include several different tools (military, diplomacy, development

Table 7.2 External and internal influences on Japan's peace building-based ODA diplomacy

External factors

- The Gulf War and the new post-Cold War world order
- PKO, peace building and human security initiatives of the international community
- Changing Asian geopolitics
- Terrorist acts of 9/11, new challenges to world security and the responses of the international community (War on Terror, failed states, whole-of-government approaches)
- US desire to redefine the US–Japan alliance

Internal factors

- Searching Japan's new political role in the post-Cold War and post-9/11 world (including the debate on the Constitution)
- Japan's desire to redefine the post-Cold War US–Japan alliance
- Influence of individuals (among others Koizumi, Ogata, Akashi)
- Search for a new role for the SDF after the Cold War
- Budget constraints of the Japanese government (shrinking ODA budget)
- Administrative reforms (centralized decision making)
- Japan's notion of a peace country

Source: author's research.

and humanitarian assistance) of peace support, thus making the peace building activities comprehensive.

The 2005 Medium-Term Policy (which outlines the actions, priorities and key regions for the next five years) on ODA further emphasized the comprehensive, human security and peace building aspects of Japanese ODA. The 2006 ODA White Paper published by MOFA devoted almost twenty pages to explaining the importance of peace building combined with ODA.[42] The White Paper emphasized that Iraq, Afghanistan, Sudan, Cambodia, Sri Lanka, Kosovo, East Timor and Palestine are among the best illustrations of peace building through ODA.

According to MOFA, Japanese ODA was used for the first time in Sri Lanka as part of the country's proactive foreign policy to support the diplomatic efforts of the peace process.[43] The Japanese government regarded it as a 'model case' in which aid would be used as a diplomatic tool and as a catalyst for building and consolidating peace. In this context, Japan went so far as to send a peace envoy.

On paper, Sri Lanka looked very good and promising for Japanese diplomacy. The case is interesting from several viewpoints: it could provide a good example for international community for the War against Terror, but at the same time, and importantly for Japan, it is not a showcase daily in the spotlight, but a relatively low-profile case; Sri Lanka also has a strategic geopolitical location and its importance has not been fully exploited. When Japan started to provide aid to Sri Lanka, the country seemed to be a friendly and easy case for Japanese diplomacy.[44] Relations between the two countries were nurtured by personal networks, and at the time of the changing Japanese foreign policy of the first years of the twenty-first century, Sri Lanka looked good from the viewpoint of the 'consolidation of peace' and seemed to become a good place where Japan could show its achievements not only at the grass roots, but also on the political level using peace building-based ODA policies.

Based on the above, Sri Lanka could be regarded as a representative case for Japan's peace-building diplomacy with ODA. As a representative or most likely case, it is well suited to provide a generalization characteristic.[45] In order to better understand the Sri Lankan case, it is important to touch upon the case of Cambodia, as it is one of the most commonly used reference points of Japanese peace diplomacy.

Cambodia compared with Sri Lanka

In 1988 Japan's government under Prime Minister Takeshita launched the 'International Cooperation Initiative', and set three pillars. These pillars were to strengthen cooperation to achieve peace; to promote international cultural exchanges; and to expand ODA. The pillar of peace cooperation would then be conducted within the framework of the United Nations and its peacekeeping operations.

Japan hosted a UN-backed conference to resolve the thirteen-year civil war in Cambodia, and in February 1991 the country proposed a modification to the UN peace plan. As Takeda noted, Japan did not have to worry about losing face as it did not take part in drafting the original plan.[46]

After the peace treaty, Japan was involved in numerous informal dialogues regarding Cambodia, mainly because the process was strongly backed by the United Nations. At home, as a consequence of Japan's hesitation whether to actively participate in the Gulf War in 1991 (which led to international criticism), Japan enacted the strict but simultaneously breakthrough PKO Law in 1992. The five principles of that law enabled the Japanese Self Defense Forces to take part in the Cambodian peacekeeping mission. For the first time since World War II, Japan sent 700 personnel to contribute to Cambodia's reconstruction. The troops served under the United Nations Transitional Authority Mission in Cambodia (UNTAC). Japan also granted economic assistance to finance UNTAC, the reconstruction and rehabilitation of Cambodia, and sent two key people to take up high-ranking UN positions related to the Cambodian process: Yasushi Akashi became the head of UNTAC and Sadako Ogata was the High Commissioner for the United Nations High Commission for Refugees (UNHCR). Japan had a separate budget for the Cambodian PKO, and development assistance, which had been stopped in 1974 and was resumed after the peace treaty of 1992. It refocused on agriculture, energy supplies and basic infrastructure. In 1993 Japan provided close to 62 per cent of all ODA to Cambodia. That happened parallel to the adoption of the first structured Japanese ODA policy document, the ODA Charter.

What makes the Cambodian case very similar to the Sri Lankan one is that in both cases multinational diplomacy played an important role in the peace process, and in both cases Japan made an attempt to catalyse the peace negotiations. In both instances, Japan did not have a decisive role, but was seen as an honest broker. The major difference, however, is that, unlike in Sri Lanka, Japan was backed by the United Nations in Cambodia. Japan did not emphasize ODA to influence the peace process in Cambodia, and restarted ODA only when the peace treaty was concluded. There was, however, an expectation that Japan would be the largest contributor of economic assistance during the negotiations and that gave Japan leverage to influence the Cambodian peace and reconstruction process.[47]

As we further elaborate in the following sections, Japan – acting without the direct backing of the United Nations in Sri Lanka – attempted to use an already existing, large ODA contribution as a political tool to influence the peace. The legal and policy background of the Sri Lankan participation was also different, as it was built on the second ODA Charter, ODA as a tool in the hands of the Japanese Ministry of Foreign Affairs and also on Koizumi's Sydney speech. There was no involvement of peacekeeping forces in Sri Lanka, but there was an involvement of a facilitator, Yasushi Akashi. The major similarities and differences between the Sri Lankan and the Cambodian case are summarized in Table 7.3.

The case of Sri Lanka

Sri Lanka is a strategic place that has raised the attention of the big powers for decades. It can provide resources for energy security, access to monitor shipping routes, and opportunity to reach the big markets of South Asia. Moreover, it has a strategic location for those wanting to control the Indian Ocean, and could provide a world-class harbour – Trincomalee – for military activities.

Sri Lanka has experienced a bloody, multi-faceted and intertwined conflict for the last few decades that has claimed tens of thousands of lives. The ethnic tension between the Tamils and the Sinhalese has its roots in the distribution of state patronage, government policy, official language, regional devolution, demographic encroachment and the availability of university places and public sector jobs in a prolonged clash that affects human lives.[48] A number of Tamil nationalist militant groups including the Liberation Tigers of Tamil Eelam (LTTE) sought to establish a separate Tamil state, and to achieve this they relied on guerilla tactics that included suicide bombers targeting key government and military personnel.

Table 7.3 Major similarities and differences between Japan's involvement in Cambodia and in Sri Lanka

	Cambodia	*Sri Lanka*
Modus operandi	Japan backed by and part of the UN force	Japan as one of the international donors, acting as an individual
Milestone year	1992	2002
Major external factor	Gulf War	9/11
Japan in the peace negotiations	Yes, but no ODA and not as a facilitator	Yes with ODA
Peace Treaty	Yes	No
Peace framework	International peacekeeping activities	Peace building and human security, consolidation of peace
UN PKOs	Yes, Japan with SDF	No
Legislation	PKO law	Anti-terrorism law, second ODA charter
Japanese ODA budget	Still increasing	Constantly shrinking
Japanese proactive diplomacy	Not part of the government's rhetoric	Part of the government's rhetoric
What makes it special	First large-scale SDF participation in UN PKOs	First time a peace envoy is dispatched before a peace accord is signed; first instance of ODA explicitly used as support for peace
Reference case	For Japan's PKO operations	For Japan's new proactive foreign policy that uses ODA as a political support for peace

Source: author's research.

Peace attempts since the 1980s have ranged from a failed Indian PKO to quasi-cease-fire agreements. The peace negotiations gained a new momentum in the early 2000s, and it seemed that Norway as a top mediator could achieve success there. Nevertheless, it was not the case, and the violence escalated again after a few years of relative calm. The Sri Lankan government claimed victory by military means in May 2009.

Sri Lanka is one of the largest recipients of per capita Japanese bilateral aid (see Table 7.4). According to the Japanese government, Sri Lanka is among the first countries where Japan promoted its new international role, which we elaborated earlier in this chapter. Following the 1954 launch of the Japanese cooperation programme, Japan gradually increased its contribution to Sri Lanka. Besides the strong personal networks of Japanese academics and diplomats, the reason

Table 7.4 Top recipients of Japanese bilateral ODA ranked by ODA per capita, 2007

Rank	*Recipient country*	*Japanese ODA by country (per capita, USD)*	*Average annual Japanese bilateral ODA, 2003–06 (USD million)*	*Population (million)*
1	Mongolia	20.37	59.08	2.9
2	Laos	10.60	68.93	6.5
3	Sri Lanka	10.38	216.86	20.9
4	Iraq	8.82	242.54	27.5
5	Cambodia	7.48	104.79	14.0
6	Viet Nam	6.65	566.29	85.2
7	Kazakhstan	5.85	89.52	15.3
8	Malaysia	5.40	133.86	24.8
9	Tunisia	5.22	53.73	10.3
10	Afghanistan	3.80	121.35	31.9
11	Philippines	3.52	320.06	91.0
12	Romania	3.25	72.50	22.3
13	Azerbaijan	3.13	25.44	8.1
14	Uzbekistan	2.12	59.01	27.8
15	Indonesia	2.10	493.11	234.7
16	Peru	2.08	59.43	28.6
17	Nepal	1.86	53.64	28.9
18	Ghana	1.84	42.25	22.9
19	D.R. Congo	1.71	112.13	65.7
20	Kenya	1.57	57.83	36.9
21	Pakistan	1.06	174.79	164.7
22	Morocco	1.02	34.51	33.8
23	China	0.64	839.52	1,321.0
24	Brazil	0.20	37.91	190.0
25	Bangladesh	0.16	23.73	150.5
26	Egypt	0.14	11.31	80.3
27	India	0.08	86.20	1,130.0

Source: author's calculations, based on MOFA's ODA White Papers 2005, 2006, 2007 and CIA World Factbook, 2007.

Note
countries with a population of less than one million people were excluded. ODA excludes debt relief.

for the large amount of Japanese aid given to Sri Lanka was the relatively easy access to an Asian Buddhist country where Japan could prove its determination to promote peace. Following 2002, Japan further deepened its involvement in Sri Lanka and made attempts to play a crucial role in resolving the conflict.

International donors in Sri Lanka follow different approaches when administering aid, but they do coordinate their activities through donor conferences. Among them, Japan was long the single largest donor to Sri Lanka, but it got involved directly in the peace process and started to act as a secondary facilitator only in 2002. The appointment of Special Envoy Akashi and becoming a co-chair of the donor conferences signified new waves in Japan's aid and foreign policies, where ODA was more closely related to the political project of peace building.

Initially, before 2002, Japan remained neutral in relation with the conflict and the domestic affairs of Sri Lanka. As part of the Japanese aid philosophy, non-economic issues and ethnic problems were detached from development issues and treated as internal political problems. As a MOFA document points out, 'internal political problems [...] should be handled by the recipient government itself',[49] therefore the conflict itself was not then a target of Japan's aid to Sri Lanka.

With the advent of a possible peace treaty in 2002, Japan saw opportunities for its new, 'consolidation of peace' policy in Sri Lanka. Therefore, peace promotion became a part of the Japanese aid rhetoric and to a limited extent, action, and besides bringing Akashi's participation in the peace process (which was in fact a result of the above-mentioned personal networks), it was pointed out that the proximity of the peace also 'brought a new page in Japan's assistance to Sri Lanka'.[50]

According to a major study of aid, conflict and peace building in Sri Lanka (by the governments of United Kingdom, the Netherlands and Sweden together with the Asia Foundation and the World Bank), Japanese ODA was long conflict-neutral, as Japan was unwilling to attach true political or conflict-related conditions to its assistance.[51] The study also supports the notion that Japan traditionally had scarcely been involved in governance-related issues.

Japan's projects undoubtedly have affected the grass-roots level in Sri Lanka. However, holistic Japanese peace diplomacy which could have impacted the Sri Lankan peace process did not exist in the way it was hoped. Although Japan has held several donor conferences, acting as a co-chair, increased its aid projects in the northern and eastern areas, and Akashi travelled more than a dozen times to Sri Lanka, Japan's role and achievements – since the commencement of the new Japanese policy towards Sri Lanka – regarding the promotion of the peace process remained marginal or at best, unclear.

In spite of the fanfares and the rhetoric surrounding Akashi and the promises by him to engage actively in brokering a solution, Japan did not achieve significant status as a facilitator on the side of Norway. As some MOFA and JBIC[52] officials mentioned, Akashi did not have the necessary resources for such an undertaking, and Japan did not have either the networks or the experience to deal with the Tamils and with the LTTE. High-ranking Japan experts in Washington

DC's Congress posit that current Japanese peace negotiators simply do not have the skills to actively broker a deal. JICA's president and one of Japan's most prominent people, Sadako Ogata, had an interesting comment about Akashi's role in Sri Lanka. She mentioned in a speech at the Foreign Correspondents' Club of Japan in Tokyo in December 2006 that Akashi was not a real negotiator in the peace process; he was rather 'a helper for peace'.[53] (See also Chapter 4 by V. Blechinger-Talcott and Chapter 6 by M. Söderberg in this volume.)

Looking at Japan's ODA disbursements to Sri Lanka, one can see that almost ten times more money was disbursed to projects concerning infrastructure and economic development than to peace building. In spite of Japan being the largest donor to Sri Lanka and having funded several grass-roots peace-building projects – ranging from community approach projects, humanitarian de-mining activities to water sector development projects, to name a few – none of them had the 'strategic factor' that could influence political decisions or could contribute to peace, nor was Japanese aid used for peace conditionalities.

Using Goodhand *et al.*'s three-track approach to visualize the Sri Lankan case, Norway played a big role in Track One diplomacy.[54] In spite of Akashi's appointment as a 'secondary facilitator', and Japan's aim to get a slice of Track One (or Track One-and-a-half) diplomacy, the Goodhand *et al.* framework and Sri Lanka study had absolutely no explicit mentioning of Japan.[55]

The co-chair position of the Donor Conference as well as the peace negotiations in Hakone in March 2003 and the Tokyo Conference on the Reconstruction and Development of Sri Lanka in June of the same year could be regarded as Track One or Track One-and-a-half. Nevertheless, Japan did not succeed in linking Track Three – development aid and humanitarian assistance – to the politically influenced Track One. Peace-related development aid was given to grass-roots projects, and although it created an important role for humanitarian assistance (but still has a marginal stake in the total ODA disbursements to Sri Lanka), it did not have a transformational effect on the political processes.

The above-presented three-track framework presumes that the different tracks of diplomacy would be interlinked and coherent. It would mean then that ODA peace conditionalities could influence the peace process and the Track One negotiations. Japan is still seen as unwilling to attach political or conflict-related conditions to its assistance, therefore its peace building-based ODA diplomacy might partly work on the humanitarian and the grass-roots level, but it would not work on a political basis.

It is widely regarded that Japan's goal in Sri Lanka in the 1990s was to gain access to natural resources and to get closer to the markets of India. Later, Japan also aimed to meet its goals related to the strategic value of ODA when dealing with Sri Lanka. These include the assistance for regional networks, the fight against terrorism, maritime safety, ensuring safe sea lanes and assurance of stable procurement for energy and resources.[56]

In spite of Japan's desire to diversify its oil supplies, Japan moved much later than others to make use of Sri Lanka's oil opportunities. Two other regional giants, China and India, had already been present and making efforts to utilize the promising oil reserves off the coast of Sri Lanka. Statistics also show that Sri Lanka has no economic significance for Japan. According to JETRO 2005 statistics, Sri Lanka accounted for only 0.06 per cent of Japan's exports and 0.03 per cent of its imports, although the country might provide a favourable opening to Indian and Pakistan via free trade agreements.

According to a MOFA document of September 2005, the goals of Japanese ODA in Sri Lanka 'contributed to the consolidation of democracy and political stability in the entire South Asian region'.[57] However, not much stability was present in the years following MOFA's assessment, and at the time of Abe's resignation in 2007, Sri Lanka was still practically in civil war. In 2009, although the Sri Lankan government inflicted critical damage on the LTTE and claimed victory by military means, the view is that only a mutually acceptable political settlement can put a real end to the violence.[58] Most likely, however, such an outcome would not change the perception of Japan's increased peace efforts during the Koizumi and Abe administrations in Sri Lanka. Even Yasushi Akashi mentioned during his visit to Sri Lanka in January 2009 that Japan's efforts to assist and facilitate the peace process had not borne fruit until then.[59] Furthermore, human rights groups criticized the Japanese government for a passive stance.[60]

Other opportunities to satisfy Japanese interests are also missed. Politically, South Asia, especially Sri Lanka, is regarded as a 'safe region' for Japan, where wartime memories do not exist any more. In addition, international players are not as prominent there as in the Middle East, Africa or in South East Asia, therefore the place and the conflict have a relatively 'lower profile' (compared with other major international conflicts). Japan made efforts to secure friends in the region, and it was demonstrated during Japan's bid for a seat on the UN Security Council in 2006 that the only Asian countries supporting Japan – India, Afghanistan, Bhutan and the Maldives – were all from South Asia, although Sri Lanka was not one of them.[61]

One of the biggest obstacles of translating the coherent policies into action was the existence of the vertical division system (*tatewari*) at the Japanese government agencies. This refers to the phenomenon of government agencies guarding their own territory and being reluctant to cooperate with each other when it comes to implementing policies. JICA and JBIC officials have several times mentioned that they are only aid officials and they should not be concerned with other issues, including national interests, as that is the role of the MOFA. Without the eradication of or tapering the wall set forth by the *tatewari*, the whole-of-government policies and the networks – formal and/or informal – across different agencies do not function and do not achieve the desired objectives.

The same applies to the interaction between the headquarters – in Tokyo – and the field offices (representations of JICA and other Japanese agencies in the donor recipient countries). It was discovered that the field offices rely too much on Tokyo's instructions, and they are not sensitive enough to the local realities.

The Sri Lankan case highlights the shortcomings of the application of Japan's relatively coherent foreign policy rhetoric, which includes the concept of peace and the tools of ODA to support building and consolidating peace. The shortcomings of this policy can be characterized by aid, which is not well linked to the peace process, as well as by inefficient aid leverage and incoherent approaches.

In spite of the fact that Japan became more conflict-sensitive in 2002 than it used to be before, it failed to make a political impact in Sri Lanka. The peace envoy's tools were limited, and Akashi was not the key negotiator in the process, but was generally considered only to 'supplement the Norwegian facilitator's efforts'.[62] Moreover, humanitarian and development assistance there was not supportive to the political process of peacemaking. Japan did feel that aid and limited political support could pull the so-called 'peace cart', but aid in Sri Lanka was not well linked to the traditional tools of diplomacy – which were also weak – and as a result, apart from the grass-roots level, Japan failed to show any significant, large-scale, peace-related achievement in Sri Lanka.

Nevertheless, one should not forget to mention the role of domestic Sri Lankan factors when talking about the failure of the peace process in Sri Lanka. Also, the international community always had a significant impact on domestic actors and wider structural conditions.

The significant contribution of the international donors could not manage to eradicate the roots of hostility and create political will for sustainable peace. Japan, the largest donor, had a big stake in this failure. In this case, mostly due to the lack of coherent and integrated action (and partly because of other, external factors), no clear gains emerged in spite of the potential of Sri Lanka to push forward the Japanese wish for diplomatic and peace building achievements supported by aid.

Conclusion

In this chapter we have endeavoured to explore Japan's peace and ODA policies, its tools and its application in the field. Japan has been seeking ways to exchange economic gains for political ones on the international scene in order to foster an increased and more visible political role. A new geopolitical situation in Asia – the rise of China and India – the US influence on Japan's foreign affairs, domestic and foreign stakeholders – especially under the Koizumi and Abe governments – contributed to move Japan towards a new type of somewhat more active foreign policy. Under Koizumi, this policy was complemented by centralized decision making, and the new foreign policy rhetoric included highlighting the importance of the visibility in the field and contributions to international operations by manpower – troops – and the de facto support of the American-led War on Terror. These developments were partly a result of 9/11 that led to the emergence of the rhetoric of a coherent and proactive Japanese diplomacy, which explicitly pledged to serve wide-ranging national interests. Peace building-based ODA also became one of the cornerstones of this policy, and it now shares many similarities with other countries' interpretations of whole-of-government approaches.

Although constitutional constraints prevented the emergence of an even wider scale of international cooperation, the concepts of human security and peace building did give a new opportunity for Japan's peace diplomacy. In spite of efforts to take a whole-of-government approach, Japan is not a leader in the world's peace processes. The country does not use ODA as an effective tool for political leverage, and Japan is reluctant to use aid with political or peace conditionalities. Following the relatively successful case of Cambodia (where aid was not truly linked to the peace process), there was an opportunity to transform Japan's participation into a success story. Sri Lanka seemed to be the instance where Japan's twenty-first-century coherent and centralized foreign policy initiatives could be observed in the field. Moreover, it could have been a place where Japan's national interests could have benefited, and the country could have shown the results of its new policies on both a grass-roots and a political level.

Action, however, did not bring the same degree of coherence as was observed in the policies' rhetoric. In spite of Japan's large aid contributions to Sri Lanka, its commitment to the conflict there, Japan failed to achieve significant gains on the political level and to eradicate the conflict. There is a gap between what is being said and what is being done. Moreover, aid does not effectively support the peace process, and Japan's national interests are not well satisfied by peace-diplomacy.

Japanese peace building-based ODA diplomacy is not necessarily a failure. The grass-roots-level contributions, the policies and the increasingly coherent rhetoric are good signs, but Japan could do much more, given the amount (in spite of its shrinking nature) it provides as aid. Active Japanese peace diplomacy could be an excellent opportunity to satisfy all stakeholders' interests. It could be linked to the public's expectations regarding Japan's foreign policy and to the image the international community has of Japan. It could serve for the benefit of the recipient countries and could improve lives; it could also fit into the transformation of the US–Japan Alliance, thereby linking peace diplomacy to national interests. In order to achieve this in a balanced way, however, Japan has to improve in implementation.

Notes

1 BBC World Service Poll, *Israel and Iran share most negative ratings in global poll*, 27 March 2007, www.worldpublicopinion.org/pipa/pdf/mar07/BBC_ViewsCountries_Mar07_pr.pdf (accessed 25 June 2007).

2 See the results of the MOFA opinion polls. In both surveys, an overwhelming number of respondents perceived Japan as 'peace country'. Ministry of Foreign Affairs (MOFA), *Japan Image among European Opinion Leaders*, Tokyo: MOFA, 25 June 2007a, www.mofa.go.jp/announce/announce/2007/6/1174186_828.html (accessed 16 October 2007) and Ministry of Foreign Affairs (MOFA), *2007 U.S. Image of Japan*, Tokyo: MOFA, 25 June 2007, www.mofa.go.jp/announce/announce/2007/6/1174181_828.html (accessed 16 October 2007).

3 Kantei, the Cabinet Office of Japan, *Survey on Diplomacy by the Cabinet Office of Japan*, Tokyo: Kantei, 11 December 2006, www.mansfieldfdn.org/polls/2006/poll-06-17.htm (accessed 20 May 2007). In the survey, 44 per cent responded 'Contributions to maintaining world peace such as cooperation toward peaceful resolutions of regional conflicts, disarmament, and non-proliferation' to the question 'Mainly, what roles do you think Japan should play in the international community?'

4 A number of East Asian countries, especially the two Koreas and China, see it somewhat differently. Those countries, while acknowledging Japan's leading position in a number of fields, question Japan's true intentions in the international political stage. Both South Korea and China have territorial disputes with Japan, and from time to time both claim that Japan has not yet fully accepted responsibility for its wartime past.

5 E. van Veen, 'Developing the security agenda: in the long run national security requires an enlarged development agenda', *Journal of Security Sector Management* 5 (1), 2007, www.ssronline.org/jofssm/issues/jofssm_0502_vanveen.pdf?CFID=324346&CFTOKEN=71164869 (accessed 22 October 2007).

6 B. Bot, Dutch Minister of Foreign Affairs, 'The Dutch Approach: Preserving the Trinity of Politics, Security and Development', speech delivered at the SID and NCDO Conference on Security and Development, the Hague, April 2006.

7 Department of the Prime Minister and Cabinet, *Annual Report of the Prime Minister, 2001–2002*, Canberra: Prime Minister of Australia, 2002, http://pmc.gov.au/annual_reports/2001-02/pdf/pmc_annual_report2001-02.pdf (accessed 19 October 2007).

8 Organization for Economic Cooperation and Development, Development Assistance Committee (OECD-DAC), *Whole of Government Approaches to Fragile States, DAC Guidelines and Reference Series*, Paris: OECD, 2006, p. 4.

9 S. Patrick and K. Brown, 'Greater than the sum of its parts? Assessing "whole of government" approaches to fragile states', *CGD Brief*, Washington DC: Center for Global Development, June 2007.

10 S. Patrick and K. Brown, *Greater than the Sum of its Parts? Assessing 'Whole of Government' Approaches to Fragile States*, New York: International Peace Academy, 2007.

11 D. Cammack, D. McLeod, A. Rocha Menocal and K. Christiansen, *Donors and the 'Fragile States' Agenda: A Survey of Current Thinking and Practice, Report submitted to the Japan International Cooperation Agency*, London: Poverty and Public Policy Group, 2006.

12 J. Goodhand, K. Bart, D. Fonseka, S. I. Keethaponcalan and S. Sardesai, *Aid, Conflict and Peace Building in Sri Lanka, 2000–2005*, Colombo: Asia Foundation, 2005.

13 J. Montville, 'Track Two diplomacy: the arrow and the olive branch: a case for Track Two diplomacy' in V. D. Volkan, J. Montville and D. A. Julius (eds) *The Psychodynamics of International Relations*, Vol. II, *Unofficial Diplomacy at Work*, Lexington, MA: Lexington Books, 1991, pp. 161–75.

14 Goodhand *et al.*, *Aid, Conflict and Peace Building in Sri Lanka*, p. 27.

15 O. Koike, M. Hori and H. Kabashima, 'The Japanese Government Reforms of 2001 and Policy Evaluation System: Efforts, Results and Limitations', paper presented at the Panel on 'Evaluation of Public Sector Reforms: Transaction Costs as the Ignored Dimension', International Conference of the International Political Science Association, Fukuoka, 11 July 2006.

16 *Japan Times*, 'State sets up ODA Strategy Panel', 29 April 2006, http://search.japantimes.co.jp/cgi-bin/nn20060429b3.html (accessed 20 May 2006).

17 As of 15 October 2007.

18 T. Aso, Minister of Foreign Affairs, 'ODA: Sympathy is not merely for Others' Sake', Tokyo: Japan National Press Club, 19 January 2006, www.mofa.go.jp/announce/fm/aso/speech0601-2.html (accessed 3 February 2006).

19 Ministry of Foreign Affairs, *Japan's Official Development Assistance White Paper, 2006*, Tokyo: MOFA, International Cooperation Bureau, 2007.

20 Ibid., p. 6.

21 Ministry of Foreign Affairs, *The Revision of Japan's Official Development Assistance Charter*, Tokyo: MOFA, 2003, www.mofa.go.jp/policy/oda/reform/revision0308.pdf, p. i (accessed 13 June 2005).

22 Ibid.

23 Japan International Cooperation Agency (JICA), *Research Study on Peace Building*, Tokyo: JICA, 2001, p. 1.
24 Ministry of Foreign Affairs, *Japan's Official Development Assistance White Paper, 2006*, 2007, p. 46.
25 Ministry of Defense (MOD), *Defence of Japan 2007*, Tokyo: MOD, 2007.
26 Ibid., p. 3.
27 J. Miller, 'Japan crosses the Rubicon?', *Asia-Pacific Security Studies* 1 (1), 2002, 1–5.
28 Ibid., 2.
29 Prime Minister Junichiro Koizumi, 'Japan and Australia toward a Creative Partnership', Sydney: Asia Society, 1 May 2002, www.mofa.go.jp/region/asia-paci/pmv0204/speech.html (accessed 2 March 2005).
30 JICA, *Peace-building: Towards Ensuring Human Security*, included the two key concepts of peace and nation building: human security and peace building.
31 Ibid., p. 6.
32 Ibid., p. 8.
33 P-E. Lam, 'Japan's human security role in Southeast Asia', *Contemporary Southeast Asia: A Journal of International and Strategic Affairs* 28 (1), 2006, 141–59.
34 A. Fukushima, *Human Security and Japanese Foreign Policy*, Seoul: Proceedings of the International Conference on Human Security in East Asia, 2003, 121–68.
35 Lam, 'Japan's human security role in Southeast Asia', p. 148.
36 Fukushima, *Human Security and Japanese Foreign Policy*, p. 139.
37 MOFA's home page lists at least 400 documents that connect human security with Japan's engagement in Iraq, and the same amount of sites refer to the Afghan involvement by human security.
38 Y. Kawaguchi, Minister of Foreign Affairs, *Human Security: Its Role in an Era of various Threats to the International Community*, Tokyo: International Symposium on Human Security, 2003, www.mofa.go.jp/policy/human_secu/sympo0302_fm.html (accessed 12 June 2007).
39 Ibid.
40 Ministry of Foreign Affairs, *Japan's Official Development Assistance: Accomplishment and Progress of Fifty Years*, Tokyo: MOFA, 2005, www.mofa.go.jp/policy/oda/cooperation/anniv50/pamphlet/index.html (accessed 16 June 2005).
41 Ministry of Foreign Affairs, *Japan's Efforts on Peace Building: Towards Consolidation of Peace and Nation Building*, Tokyo: MOFA, 2007, www.mofa.go.jp/policy/un/pko/effort0704.pdf (accessed 25 May 2007).
42 Ministry of Foreign Affairs, *Japan's Official Development Assistance White Paper, 2006*, 2007.
43 Ministry of Foreign Affairs, *Japan's Official Development Assistance: Accomplishment and Progress of Fifty Years*; N. Ram, 'Japan and Sri Lanka: interviews with Akashi Yasushi', *Frontline: India's National Magazine* 20 (9), 2003, www.hinduonnet.com/fline/fl2009/stories/20030509002404400.htm (accessed 26 August 2005); K. Nabeshima, 'Peacemaker for Sri Lanka', *Japan Times*, 21 April 2003.
44 Hisashi Nakamura (Ryukoku University), personal communication, 2 February 2006.
45 B. Flyvbjerg, 'Five misunderstandings about case-study research', *Qualitative Inquiry* 12 (2), 2006, 219–45.
46 Y. Takeda, 'Japan's role in the Cambodian peace process: diplomacy, manpower and finance', *Asian Survey* 38 (6), 1998, 553–68.
47 Ibid., 567.
48 R. Venugopal, 'The Global Dimensions of Conflict in Sri Lanka', Working Paper 99, Oxford: Queen Elizabeth House, 2003.
49 Ministry of Foreign Affairs, *Country Assistance to Sri Lanka*, Tokyo: MOFA, 2004, p. 9.
50 Ibid.
51 Goodhand *et al.*, *Aid, Conflict and Peace Building in Sri Lanka*, p. 77.

52 A large part of the Japan Bank for International Cooperation (JBIC) became part of Japan International Cooperation Agency (JICA) in October, 2008.
53 S. Ogata, *Q&A of Public Speech*, Tokyo: Foreign Correspondents' Club of Japan, December 2006.
54 Goodhand *et al.*, *Aid, Conflict and Peace Building in Sri Lanka*, p. 64.
55 Ibid., p. 27.
56 Ministry of Foreign Affairs, *Japan's Official Development Assistance White Paper, 2006*, 2007, p. 56.
57 Ministry of Foreign Affairs, *Outline of Japan's ODA to Sri Lanka*, Tokyo: MOFA, 2005.
58 D. Blair, 'Lasting peace is unlikely even if the Tamil Tigers are beaten', *Guardian*, 2 January 2009, www.telegraph.co.uk/news/worldnews/asia/srilanka/4077839/Lasting-peace-is-unlikely-even-if-the-Tamil-Tigers-are-beaten.html (accessed 3 January 2009); *Indian Express*, 'Fall of LTTE "capital" not end', 3 January 2009, www.indianexpress.com/news/fall-of-ltte-capital-not-end/405957/ (accessed 3 January 2009).
59 S. Jayasekera, 'No peace in Sri Lanka without a political solution: Akashi', *Daily Mirror*, 26 January 2009, www.dailymirror.lk/DM_BLOG/Sections/frmNewsDetailView.aspx?ARTID=38756 (accessed 30 January 2009).
60 The *Daily Mirror*, 'Rights groups urge Japan to change stance on Lanka', 27 May 2009 (accessed 1 June 2009).
61 C. Bajpee, 'Strategic interests pull Japan and India together', *Power and Interest News Report*, 16 February 2007, www.pinr.com/report.php?ac=view_report&report_id=618&language_id=1 (accessed 20 June 2007).
62 Y. Sato, 'Case study on peace-building in Sri Lanka', *Asia Breeze* 42, November 2004, 1–4; P.-E. Lam, 'Japan's peace-building diplomacy in Sri Lanka', *East Asia* 21 (2), 2004, 3–17.

8 The changing political economy of defence production

The rise of a military-industrial complex?

Christopher W. Hughes

Japan's security trajectory, militarization and the military-industrial complex

Japan's post-Cold War proactivity in international security – especially since 11 September and the participation of the Japan Self Defense Forces (JSDF) in supporting the US-led 'war on terror' in Afghanistan and Iraq – has reinvigorated the academic and policy debate on the trajectory and implications of Japan's re-emergence as a military power.

The current academic and policy debate is dominated by three discourses, with contributions from a fourth, more peripheral, discourse. The first discourse appropriated by specialists in International Relations from a variety of Realist, Constructivist, and Liberal perspectives, has focused on explaining the key drivers for change in Japanese security policy, with particular emphasis on the relative importance of domestic institutions and norms versus international structural.[1] The second discourse also found in International Relations has focused on the degrees of continuity or discontinuity in Japan's so-called 'grand strategy', with a split between those who see re-adherence with modifications to the 'Yoshida Doctrine', and those who see Japan prepared to embark on a more radical course in its international security role alongside the United States.[2]

The third discourse appropriated by Japanese and US policy makers but also with significant input from the academic community in both states, concentrates on the appropriateness of Japan's evolving international security role. This discourse tends to emphasize that Japan is becoming a 'normal' military power, undertaking 'international peace cooperation activities' commensurate, appropriate and proportionate with its status as a leading industrialized democracy, and, indeed, that it should seek to do yet more in supporting the US–Japan alliance, multinational security, and the United Nations (UN). In essence, this discourse argues that Japan's enhanced military stance is measured and responsible, and poses no concerns for the East Asia region or the international community.

Ranged against the mainstream academic and policy discourse, there is a fourth, if increasingly marginalized discourse, which explicitly employs the language of militarization to examine the trajectory and implications of Japan's security policy. This discourse, employing diverse insights from *inter alia*

Marxist and Critical Theory and Japanese Peace Research, argues that Japan's military proactivity is leading inexorably to the recrudescence of militarism under US tutelage, and that this process will lead Japan to turn against the United States and its East Asian neighbours.[3]

Although the militarization discourse, with some notable exceptions, has often been critiqued or dismissed by the mainstream in recent years as overstated or unscientific, the objective of this chapter is to develop and reapply the militarization discourse in the form of a framework to investigate the means by which it can assist in understanding the causes and ramifications of Japan's changing security policy.[4] For it is arguable that if the militarization framework is applied in sober social science terms, rather than viewed in knee-jerk reaction terms as implying an instant rewind to 1931–45, then it has much to offer in analysing Japan's contemporary security stance.

First, the militarization framework, as elaborated in more detail in the next section, offers a means to overcome the paradigmatic divide in understanding the key drivers of change in Japanese security policy.[5] The militarization framework is an inherently eclectic and multidisciplinary one, drawing on insights from Marxism, Liberalism, Constructivism and Realism, and from International Relations, International Political Economy, Economics and Sociology. Hence, whilst it may not offer a parsimonious explanation of change, it does help to combine the most powerful insights of various perspectives and enable a richer set of explanations that detail the full reality of Japan's security stance.

Second, the militarization framework presents a means to engage more effectively in the debate on the continuities and discontinuities of Japan's security stance. The militarization framework offers a set of objective historical baselines in order to contextualize and calibrate the degree to which any society has shifted its military stance. This should help in adjudicating between those who advocate the second discourse and see Japan holding to or diverging from the 'Yoshida Doctrine'.

Third, and interrelated to the second point, the militarization framework provides a tool of critical analysis to question the dominant orthodoxies and discourses of the policy mainstream. By employing the stark and uncomfortable language of militarization, analysts are forced to question and justify their own assumptions, and consider whether they are really 'calling a spade a spade' or are complicit in employing obfuscating language which hinders true understanding of political-military projects. Hence, placing militarization alongside the discourse of 'normalization' helps to interrogate more effectively its assumptions about the appropriateness of change in Japan, or whether it might actually be wise to question if Japan's remilitarization is a cause for concern.

This chapter applies the militarization discourse in the following ways. The next section offers a brief definition and explanation of militarization as an analytical framework across a range of features of security policy. This section then focuses in particular on the issue of the military-industrial complex and how this illustrates the dynamics and implications of militarization. The following section then explores the case study of Japan's defence production and the question of whether Japan is developing a domestic military-industrial complex. The section after it moves on to consider whether Japan is now fostering a transnational military complex in conjunction with the United States and other developed and developing states.

Japan's defence production – and the question of an emerging military-industrial complex – is chosen as the case study to test the militarization framework because it encapsulates and demonstrates well the key contributions of the framework for evaluating change in Japanese security policy. In regard to explaining the key drivers of security change in Japan, the military-industrial complex involves examination of both the domestic and international structural pressures driving security policy, and draws in Marxist, Liberal and Realist perspectives, and the related disciplines of IR and IPE.

The issue of the military-industrial complex is further important for measuring the continuities in Japan's grand strategy. This is because the degree of autonomy in Japanese defence production has often been seen as a barometer of Japanese strategic autonomy vis-à-vis the United States, and the rise of a transnational military complex tasks a re-examination of this autonomy.[6]

Finally, examination of defence production and the emergence of a military-industrial complex pose important questions for the discourse of 'normalization'. This is because in the post-war period one of the key features of Japanese demiltiarization is thought to have been the undercutting of collaboration between the military and industrial sectors. But if this collaboration is re-emerging, then it clearly poses questions once again about how far Japan's military stance is 'normal' or whether questions should be asked about the risks of the recrudescence in Japan of forms of militarism extant in the past or in other parts of the world.

The last section and conclusion of this chapter will then take stock of exactly how the militarization framework assists in analysing the current security trajectory of Japan. It concludes that there are indeed signs of an emerging Japanese military-industrial complex, embedded in the domestic political economy, but also most crucially an emerging transnational complex, driven in particular by the US–Japan alliance linkage. In turn, the conclusion argues that these developments do indeed demonstrate that the fourth discourse of militarization needs to be reintroduced more centrally to the study of Japanese security policy in order to achieve a multi-perspective, multidisciplinary approach which supersedes the current paradigmatic roadblock involving the three mainstream discourses, and which enables adjudication in favour of the views that see Japan as shifting away from the Yoshida Doctrine to closer integrated cooperation with the United States; and which demonstrates that the 'normalization' discourse needs much closer scrutiny in its claims that Japan's security stance is appropriate and unthreatening.

Militarization and military-industrial complexes

Militarism is a contested concept, but there is general agreement that it implies an undue preponderance, or excess, of military institutions and ideals over the civilian functions of societies and states. The consequence of states slipping into militarism is that they become predisposed to prioritize, or even to glorify, the malevolent usage of military force to settle international disputes.[7] Andrew

Bacevich offers a definition of US militarism, which is equally applicable to other societies, manifested in a 'romanticized view of soldiers, a tendency to see military power as the truest measure of national greatness, and outsized expectations regarding the efficacy of force'.[8]

Militarization as a process of moving toward militarism is thought to be manifested in a variety of institutional and ideological forms. Internal structural militarism for realists and Marxists tends to involve questions of the size of defence budgets and the military establishment.[9] Liberals, in contrast, tend to emphasize internal militarization not just the size of the military establishment per se, but the relative influence of the civilian and military establishments.[10] External structural militarism for Realists and Marxist is evidenced in the build-up of individual national military capabilities and doctrines for overseas deployments, and in overseas alliance relationships involving the provision of bases to hegemonic states or the integration of military forces for offensive power projection purposes.[11] Ideological militarism, or 'militarism of the mind', for Constructivists and Liberals is bound up with the erosion of normative constraints, both formal and informal, on the standing of the military in society, and on the procurement and use of certain forms of weaponry.[12]

The military-industrial complex is a key concept within the militarization framework. The Liberal and Marxist perspectives see a military-industrial complex emerging as a feature of internal structural militarization when a state's civilian leadership, including the bureaucracy and politicians, fail to exercise sufficient oversight over the military and industry. The risk is that military procurements and developments in military technology will be driven by the narrow commercial interests of the military and industry rather than for broader national defence interests.[13] It is thus important to monitor the size of the arms industry, its influence relative to civilian industry, and its democratic accountability.[14]

Similarly, a military-industrial complex is regarded as a feature of external structural militarism. Realists and Marxists view alliance relationships as promoting the creation of a transnational military-industrial complex, with the junior alliance partner finding it increasingly hard to keep in step with advances in military technology and to produce ever more expensive weapons systems, thus necessitating the economies of scale afforded by alliance co-production.[15] In turn, the demands for economies of scale in armaments production, especially under conditions of globalization and attempts to expand political influence through forging overseas military linkages, are likely to spur arms transfers, sales and military training to third countries – developed and developing – and thus a form of the external export of militarization.[16]

Japan's domestic military-industrial complex

Japan cannot be said to have possessed anything akin to a fully fledged military-industrial complex in the post-war period. The US-led Occupation in its initial stages, alongside its broader demilitarization and democratization reforms for Japan, emphasized the deconcentration and dissolution of the *zaibatsu* (industrial conglomerates), which were viewed as having colluded with the ultranationalists and military in pushing Japanese imperialism in the interests of their own defence production profits.[17] Japanese deconcentration as an element of demilitarization was allowed to wane with the 'reverse course' of the Occupation. Japan, following the outbreak of the Korean War and Supreme Command Allied Powers' (SCAP) lifting of the defence production ban in 1952, began to rebuild its defence production sector through its own rearmament and through procurement contracts for the US military.

Japan's policy makers preparing for the ending of the Occupation never lost sight of the importance of maintaining an indigenous defence production base for strengthening national autonomy and the overall economy. Nevertheless, Japan's post-war defence planners, even as they attempted to pursue wherever possible the build-up of indigenous defence production capabilities (*kokusanka*), rejected a policy of massive defence spending and the promotion of large-scale defence contractors. Instead, Japan, in line with domestic constraints on defence spending, would sustain its military technological base by re-embedding it within larger civilian and industrial conglomerates.[18] Japan's domestic defence production was subordinated to civilian developmental priorities, with the civilian sector drawing technological 'spin-off' from the military sector, and where necessary the smaller military sector deriving 'spin-on' technology from the civilian sector.[19]

Consequently, Japan's defence production sector in relation to overall national economic size has been moderate in scale, accounting for less than 1 per cent of total industrial production since the 1980s (see Table 8.1). Moreover, defence production has accounted for typically less than 1 per cent of total national production in most key industrial sectors, with shipbuilding and aircraft as exceptions, at between 10 per cent and 5 per cent and 80 per cent and 60 per cent respectively of national production (see Table 8.1).

Japanese defence production has been concentrated within a relatively small number of conglomerates focused predominantly on civilian production (see Table 8.2). Mitsubishi Heavy Industries (MHI) has remained the leading Japanese defence contractor in terms of sales and numbers of contracts, and the top twenty contractors have been dominated by another eight companies, namely Kawasaki Heavy Industries (KHI), Fuji Heavy Industries (FHI), Sumitomo, Toshiba, Ishikawajima Harima Heavy Industries (IHI), Mitsubishi Electric Company (MELCO), NEC, and Komatsu, with the presence of trading companies, such as Itochu and Sumitomo, involved in importing defence equipment. These companies dominate Japanese defence procurement, with over 70 per cent of total contracts. Nonetheless, defence tends to be a relatively small proportion of the overall business revenue of the largest companies (see Table 8.3). MHI, Japan's largest defence contractor, generally takes nearly a fifth of all defence contracts, but derived less than 10 per cent of its total revenue in 2006 from this sector. KHI, the second largest Japanese contractor, took around 9 per cent of its revenue from defence procurements in 2006. Fujitsu and IHI Marine United were the most heavily dependent on defence procurement at around 65 and 45 per cent respectively. For the others dependence was less significant, at around 3 per cent or lower.

Table 8.1 Japan's defence production by sector and as a share of total national industrial production, 1982–2004 (%)

Year	*Shipbuilding*	*Aircraft*	*Vehicles*	*Ammunition*	*Electrical*	*Oil*	*Coal*	*Textiles*	*Medical*	*Food*	*Others*	*Share of total*
1982	4.98	76.54	0.09	99.67	0.73	0.57	0.05	0.07	0.14	0.13	0.06	0.46
1983	4.40	77.10	0.10	99.80	0.92	0.69	0.02	0.08	0.13	0.13	0.06	0.50
1984	5.15	81.54	0.09	99.88	0.55	0.55	0.01	0.08	0.14	0.13	0.05	0.48
1985	4.82	83.73	0.06	83.44	0.56	0.67	0.01	0.07	0.12	0.12	0.06	0.51
1986	7.06	82.64	0.06	99.65	0.58	0.72	0.02	0.08	0.14	0.13	0.08	0.54
1987	8.26	79.56	0.09	99.93	0.67	0.68	0.03	0.09	0.13	0.13	0.08	0.58
1988	7.78	77.91	0.08	99.75	0.75	0.68	0.00	0.10	0.13	0.13	0.08	0.54
1989	7.16	74.68	0.07	99.62	0.65	0.64	0.00	0.11	0.12	0.13	0.08	0.54
1990	7.02	73.35	0.06	99.89	0.58	0.79	0.00	0.08	0.12	0.12	0.08	0.54
1991	7.09	73.46	0.06	99.92	0.50	0.77	0.00	0.12	0.12	0.11	0.01	0.57
1992	7.12	72.70	0.06	99.87	0.55	0.67	–	0.14	0.13	0.10	0.12	0.57
1993	6.26	72.07	0.06	99.88	0.56	0.67	–	0.16	0.13	0.10	0.11	0.58
1994	8.81	73.23	0.06	99.87	0.59	0.65	–	0.18	0.14	0.10	0.13	0.61
1995	9.51	75.32	0.08	99.69	0.63	0.64	–	0.20	0.13	0.10	0.13	0.61
1996	9.33	72.47	0.08	99.78	0.62	0.60	–	0.21	0.13	0.11	0.13	0.63
1997	7.93	60.22	0.07	99.76	0.57	0.52	–	0.23	0.13	0.10	0.13	0.57
1998	7.46	51.88	0.07	99.59	0.53	0.67	–	0.20	0.14	0.10	0.14	0.57
1999	10.00	54.50	0.08	99.19	0.56	0.63	–	0.26	0.12	0.10	0.16	0.62
2000	12.12	61.24	0.09	99.57	0.51	0.60	–	0.24	0.12	0.10	0.14	0.58
2001	9.55	54.66	0.09	99.69	0.64	0.64	–	0.33	0.11	0.10	0.18	0.65
2002	7.28	59.22	0.07	89.74	0.66	0.72	–	0.40	0.11	0.10	0.19	0.69
2003	6.89	59.58	0.08	87.31	0.64	0.64	–	0.43	0.12	0.11	0.21	0.66
2004	8.34	60.12	0.06	87.22	0.63	0.79	–	0.44	0.11	0.10	0.20	0.64

Source: Asagumo Shimbunsha, *Bōei Handobukku*, Tokyo: Asagumo Shimbunsha, various years.

Table 8.2 Japan's top twenty defence production companies, 1997–2006 (¥100 million)

1997					*1998*					*1999*				
Position	*Company*	*No. of contracts*	*Amount*	*% of annual procurements*	*Position*	*Company*	*No. of contracts*	*Amount*	*% of annual procurements*	*Position*	*Company*	*No. of contracts*	*Amount*	*% of annual procurements*
1	MHI	235	2,719	20.6	1	MHI	222	3,234	26.7	1	MHI	208	2,797	22.1
2	KHI	117	1,468	11.1	2	MELCO	188	1,030	8.3	2	KHI	97	1,322	10.5
3	MELCO	197	1,287	9.7	3	KHI	93	872	7.0	3	MELCO	200	1,121	8.9
4	NEC	306	746	5.6	4	IHI	78	644	5.2	4	Toshiba	116	538	4.3
5	IHI	82	662	5.0	5	NEC	207	446	3.6	5	IHI	72	535	4.2
6	Toshiba	130	486	3.7	6	Toshiba	127	377	3.0	6	NEC	293	426	3.4
7	Marine United	4	377	2.9	7	Komatsu	47	353	2.8	7	Komatsu	44	371	2.9
8	Komatsu	44	344	2.6	8	Mitsui Zosen	6	277	2.2	8	Hitachi	37	344	2.7
9	Nissan Motors	60	253	1.9	9	Nissan Motors	63	267	2.2	9	Nissan Motors	61	273	2.2
10	NEC Business Machines	220	252	1.9	10	Marine United	1	267	2.1	10	NEC Business Machines	233	255	2.0
11	Hitachi	70	238	1.8	11	NEC Business Machines	231	262	2.1	11	Marine United	1	247	2.0
12	Daikin Industries	67	179	1.4	12	Hitachi	53	219	1.8	12	Hitachi	55	218	1.7
13	FHI	49	171	1.3	13	Mitsubishi Corporation	19	157	1.3	13	Fujitsu	129	166	1.3
14	Oki Electric Industry	62	164	1.2	14	Oki Electric Industry	68	150	1.2	14	Yamada Corporation	39	160	1.3
15	Itochu Aviation	48	157	1.2	15	Daikin Industries	49	148	1.2	15	Daikin Industries	53	134	1.1
16	Shinmaywa Industries	9	148	1.1	16	Fujitsu	115	147	1.2	16	JSW	21	127	1.0
17	Kanematsu	12	130	1.0	17	Itochu Aviation	23	136	1.1	17	Itochu Aviation	32	120	1.0
18	NKK Steel	19	114	0.9	18	FHI	35	133	1.1	18	FHI	25	112	0.9
19	Fujitsu	137	112	0.8	19	JSW	16	130	1.0	19	Shinmaywa Industries	8	107	0.8
20	Isuzu Motors	62	100	0.8	20	Kanematsu	5	111	0.9	20	Oki Electric Industry	64	104	0.8
Total		1,930	10,106	76.6		Total	1,646	9,457	76.1		Total	1,788	9	75

2000					2001					2002				
Position	*Company*	*No. of contracts*	*Amount*	*% of annual procurements*	*Position*	*Company*	*No. of contracts*	*Amount*	*% of annual procurements*	*Position*	*Company*	*No. of contracts*	*Amount*	*% of annual procurements*
1	MHI	222	3,074	24.4	1	MHI	226	2,755	21.7	1	MHI	205	3,481	27.2
2	MELCO	205	1,208	9.6	2	KHI	114	1,213	9.6	2	KHI	102	1,102	8.6
3	KHI	112	987	7.8	3	MELCO	185	1,010	8	3	MELCO	178	735	5.7
4	IHI	72	540	4.3	4	NEC	328	577	4.5	4	IHI	48	527	4.1
5	NEC	336	465	3.7	5	IHI	45	545	4.3	5	Toshiba	123	498	3.9
6	Toshiba	128	430	3.4	6	Toshiba	126	452	3.6	6	NEC	312	485	3.8
7	Mitsui Zosen	5	363	2.9	7	Hitachi Zosen	33	398	3.1	7	Komatsu	43	357	2.8
8	Komatsu	47	354	2.8	8	Komatsu	55	372	2.9	8	Itochu	5	232	1.8
9	Shinmaywa Industries	11	323	2.6	9	IHI Aerospace	53	273	2.2	9	Shinmaywa Industries	13	229	1.8
10	NEC Business Machines	234	277	2.2	10	NEC Business Machines	179	256	2	10	Fujitsu	166	223	1.7
11	IHI Aerospace	46	261	2.1	11	Hitachi	78	251	2	11	FHI	38	216	1.7
12	Hitachi	78	183	1.5	12	Shinmaywa Industries	10	250	2	12	NEC Business Machines	164	187	1.5
13	Yamada Corporation	47	159	1.3	13	Marine United	2	250	2	13	Daikin Industries	57	179	1.4
14	FHI	42	149	1.2	14	FHI	28	180	1.4	14	IHI Aerospace	42	159	1.2
15	Daikin Industries	53	146	1.2	15	Fujitsu	144	160	1.3	15	Nippon Kokan	22	143	1.1
16	Fujitsu	143	146	1.2	16	Daikin Industries	57	160	1.3	16	Hitachi	69	142	1.1
17	Mitsubishi Corporation	23	144	1.1	17	JSW	19	120	1	17	Mitsubishi Corporation	17	109	0.8
18	JSW	18	143	1.1	18	Nippon Kokan	2	111	0.9	18	Isuzu Motors	61	94	0.7
19	Itochu Aviation	23	112	0.9	19	Isuzu Motors	62	109	0.9	19	Universal Shipbuilding Corporation	26	82	0.6
20	Oki Electric Industry	72	98	0.8	20	Oki Electric Industry	60	102	0.8	20	Itochu Aviation	33	81	0.6
	Total	1,917	9,563	75.9		Total	1,806	9,544	75.2		Total	1,724	9,261	72.4

continued

Table 8.2 continued

2003					2004					2005				
Position	*Company*	*No. of contracts*	*Amount*	*% of annual procurements*	*Position*	*Company*	*No. of contracts*	*Amount*	*% of annual procurements*	*Position*	*Company*	*No. of contracts*	*Amount*	*% of annual procurements*
1	MHI	213	2,817	22.1	1	MHI	164	2,706	20.7	1	MHI	192	2,417	17.6
2	KHI	97	1,588	12.5	2	KHI	97	1,429	10.9	2	KHI	83	1,297	9.4
3	MELCO	170	949	7.5	3	MELCO	169	1,032	7.9	3	MELCO	165	1,142	8.3
4	NEC	306	563	4.4	4	NEC	270	906	6.9	4	NEC	314	10,078	7.8
5	Toshiba	107	389	3.1	5	IHI	40	493	3.8	5	Toshiba	96	495	3.6
6	Komatsu	56	376	2.9	6	IHI Marine United	5	480	3.7	6	Universal Shipbuilding Corporation	27	397	2.9
7	IHI	39	361	2.8	7	Toshiba	74	415	3.2	7	Kawasaki Zosen	5	353	2.6
8	FHI	35	288	2.3	8	Komatsu	50	347	2.7	8	IHI	47	348	2.5
9	Kawasaki Zosen	4	257	2	9	FHI	36	240	1.8	9	Komatsu	45	338	2.5
10	Itochu	3	219	1.7	10	Itochu	2	228	1.7	10	Fujitsu	185	313	2.3
11	Fujitsu	164	210	12.6	11	Fujitsu	161	218	1.7	11	FHI	41	291	2.1
12	Hitachi	78	210	1.6	12	IHI Aerospace	35	157	1.2	12	Itochu	7	274	2.0
13	IHI Aerospace	38	169	1.3	13	Hitachi	76	145	1.1	13	Hitachi	88	210	1.5
14	Nippon Kokan	22	151	1.2	14	Nakagawa Bussan	135	142	1.1	14	Nakagawa Bussan	174	207	1.5
15	Daikin Industries	60	142	1.1	15	Daikin Industries	53	136	1.0	15	Nippon Oil	88	127	0.9
16	NEC Business Machines	131	130	1	16	Universal Shipbuilding Corporation	25	111	0.9	16	Daikin Industries	52	122	0.9
17	Mitsubishi Corporation	16	88	0.7	17	Nippon Oil	94	107	0.8	17	Cosmo Oil	103	121	0.9
18	Isuzu Motors	58	86	0.7	18	JSW	18	104	0.8	18	MCC	2	116	0.8
19	Oki Electric Industry	43	84	0.7	19	NEC Business Machines	84	101	0.8	19	Shinmaywa Industries	11	105	0.8
20	Sumitomo Trading	42	77	0.6	20	Cosmo Oil	118	94	0.7	20	IHI Aerospace	39	103	0.7
	Total	1,682	9,155	71.9		Total	1,706	9,590	73.4		Total	1,764	9,854	71.6

2006

Position	*Company*	*No. of contracts*	*Amount*	*% of annual procurements*	*Major procurement items in 2006*
1	MHI	190	2,776	21	SAM guided missile, Patriot; combat aircraft (F-2); submarines; new tank type; patrol helicopters (SH-60K); rescue helicopter (UH-60J); Type 90 tank; BMD interceptor guided missile
2	KHI	103	1,306	9.9	Next generation fixed-wing patrol aircraft (P-X); next generation fixed-wing transport aircraft (C-X); medium-range multi-purpose guided missile; Type 87 anti-tank missile; transport helicopter (CH-47JA); submarine electric generator
3	MELCO	166	1,177	8.9	Type 03 medium-range SAM; fixed-position warning radar system (J/FPS-5); Sea Sparrow missile (RIM-162); radar sets (AN/APG-63 (V) 1)
4	NEC	304	831	6.3	Divisional communication system; shipborne sonar system (OQQ-21); reception equipment (GFRR-4-C); sono-buoy (HQ-33C)
5	IHI Marine United	1.0	446	3.4	Destroyer helicopter (DDH)
6	Fujitsu	185	441	3.3	Ground command system; central command system
7	Toshiba	79	423	3.2	Type 81 short-range SAM (upgrade); Type 81 SAM
8	IHI	48	365	2.8	F110-IHI-129 turbofan engine; LM2500 gas turbine; next generation fixed-wing patrol aircraft (P-X); next generation fixed-wing transport aircraft (C-X); P-X engine
9	Komatsu	40	363	2.7	120 mm TKG-JM12A1 anti-tank grenade; 120 mm M-JM1 anti-tank grenade; light armoured vehicles
10	FHI	34	199	1.5	Combat helicopter (AH-64D); multi-purpose helicopter (UH-1J); primary trainer (T-5); primary trainer (T-7)
11	Hitachi	78	194	1.5	Satellite data reception equipment; mine detection equipment (ZQS-4); submarine launch control equipment (ZYQ-51)
12	Nakagawa Bussan	210	148	1.1	Light fuel oil, heavy fuel oil
13	Nippon Oil	106	143	1.1	Aircraft turbine fuel; light fuel oil
14	Daikin Industries	62	133	1.0	81 mm mortar and JM41A1 mortar projectiles; Type 00 120 mm tank gun practice ammunition; Type 00 105 mm tank gun practice ammunition
15	Cosmo Oil	95	131	1.0	Aircraft turbine fuel; light fuel oil
16	Showa Shell	95	120	0.9	Aircraft turbine fuel; light fuel oil
17	Oki Electric Industry	55	118	0.9	Submarine sonar system (ZQQ-7B); sono-buoy (HQS-13F), marine listening devices
18	IHI Aerospace	32	111	0.8	110 mm R and JM18 practice ammunition; multiple launch rocket system 298 mm M28A1; 110 mm R ammunition; JM12 anti-tank projectile
19	JSW	19	107	0.8	Type-99 self-propelled 155 mm howitzer
20	Kamei	395	92	0.7	Light fuel oil, heavy fuel oil

Source: Kankōkai Henshūbu, *Bōei Nenkan 2006*, Tokyo, Kankōkai Henshūbu, Tokyo, various years.

Table 8.3 Global top 100 defence companies, 2006 (top twenty and selected Japanese companies in bold) (USD million)

	Company	*Country (company's headquarters)*	*2005 rank*	*2006 defence revenue*	*2005 defence revenue*	*2006 total revenue*	*Revenue from defence (%)*
1	Lockheed Martin	US	1	36,090.0	34,225.0	39,620.0	91.0
2	Boeing	US	2	30,800.0	29,200.0	61,530.0	50.0
3	BAE Systems	UK	4	25,070.6	20,935.2	26,967.6	93.0
4	Northrop Grumman	US	3	23,649.0	23,332.0	30,148.0	78.4
5	Raytheon	US	5	19,500.0	18,200.0	20,291.0	96.1
6	General Dynamics	US	6	18,769.0	16,570.0	24,063.0	78.0
7	EADS	Netherlands	7	13,202.7	9,120.3	52,018.6	25.4
8	L-3 Communications	US	8	9,989.6	8,549.2	12,476.9	80.1
9	Finmeccanica	Italy	11	9,057.1	7,125.7	16,466.4	55.0
10	United Technologies	US	12	7,652.6	6,832.0	47,829.0	16.0
11	Thales	France	9	6,997.4	8,523.3	13,598.8	51.5
12	KBR	US	*n.r.*	6,400.0	*n.a.*	9,600.0	66.7
13	SAIC	US	13	5,800.0	5,400.0	8,300.0	69.9
14	General Electric	US	14	4,600.0	3,500.0	15,400.0	29.9
15	Honeywell	US	32	4,400.0	*n.a.*	31,600.0	13.9
16	Rolls-Royce	UK	17	4,062.3	3,293.6	14,007.8	29.0
17	ITT	US	18	3,659.3	3,220.0	7,807.9	46.9
18	DCNS	France	16	3,564.7	3,352.0	3,564.7	100.0
19	Computer Sciences Corp.	US	15	3,530.0	3,368.9	14,615.6	24.2
20	ATK	US	20	3,066.0	2,882.0	3,565.0	86.0
25	**Mitsubishi Heavy Industries**	Japan	23	2,354.4	2,055.9	26,024.9	9.0
43	**Kawasaki Heavy Industries**	Japan	43	1,107.7	1,103.2	12,201.4	9.1
47	**Mitsubishi Electric**	Japan	47	998.3	971.4	30,568.2	3.3
53	**NEC**	Japan	53	704.8	917.0	39,460.0	1.8
89	**IHI Marine United**	Japan	*n.r.*	378.3	*n.a.*	848.1	44.6
90	**Fujitsu**	Japan	*n.r.*	374.0	266.2	581.0	64.4
92	**Tōshiba**	Japan	88	358.8	421.1	53,801.0	0.7
96	**IHI**	Japan	100	310.0	296.0	10,466.0	3.0
98	**Komatsu**	Japan	*n.r.*	307.9	287.5	16,058.0	1.9

Source: Defencenews.com, http://defensenews.com/index.php?S=07top100.

Notes
n.r. not ranked; *n.a.* not available.

The statistics in Table 8.3 reveal that Japanese corporations as a whole played a relatively small role in total global defence revenues in 2006. Moreover, the percentage of their business derived from defence is relatively low. Only IHI Marine United (ranked 89) and Fujitsu (ranked 90) can be said to rank among the top global defence contractors in that they depend heavily on defence revenues and thereby share a business profile with such global defence corporations as Boeing (US, ranked 2) and Northrup Grumman (US, ranked 4), Finmeccanica (Italy, ranked 9) and Thales (France, ranked 11).

With only two major corporations mirroring the profiles of the world's top military corporations, it is fair to say that Japan does not have the classic features of a military-industry complex. However, it is certain that there has been consistent collusion over the years between the Japan Defense Agency (JDA) and the Japan Self Defense Forces (JSDF) and defence contractors. This has taken the form of: *amakudari* (literally 'descent from heaven'), the placing of retired bureaucrats and uniformed officers on the boards of companies; the influence of the LDP's *bōei zoku* (literally 'defence tribe') consisting of policy makers seeking to influence, if not broader policy on weapons acquisition, then at least the patronage to be dispensed to their constituencies through defence contracts; and a high degree of discretionary (non-competitive bidding) contract awards, at typically around 80 per cent of the total value of all contracts awarded (see Table 8.4).[20]

Recent evidence suggests that there has been an intensification of these practices, and that this has strengthened the characteristics of the military-industrial complex in the Japanese defence production sector. For instance, the former director-general and deputy director-general of the JDA's Central Procurement Office were arrested in September 1998 for allowing defence contractors to pad out (*mizumashi*) procurement contracts, obliging the JDA to abolish this office in January 2001 and split the functions of contracting and costing in an attempt to assure more rigorous checks on equipment procurement.[21] The JDA was again hit, though, by a scandal in January 2006, with the arrest of officials from the Defense Facilities Administration Agency (DFAA) for colluding with private construction and electronics firms for the securing of defence contracts. The DFAA was dissolved and its functions were absorbed into the Ministry of Defense (MOD) in September 2007.

The MOD since October 2007 became engulfed in its most significant procurement scandal to date, and involving former Administrative Vice-Minister Takemasa Moriya. Moriya is alleged by prosecutors to have received a total of around JPY 12 million in golf hospitality and cash bribes from Motonobu Miyazaki, a former employee of the Yamada Corporation and president of the Nihon Mirise Corporation trading companies, in order to influence MOD procurement decisions in favour of Miyazaki. Moriya has admitted to have used his influence within the MOD to steer it towards signing discretionary contracts with Nihon Mirise for the supply of General Electric engines for the Air Self Defense Force's C-X transport aircraft and for the MSDF's 19DD destroyer. In addition, Moriya received golf hospitality bribes from an Itochu subsidiary to secure a

Table 8.4 Method of procurement of contracts, 1993–2005

Financial year	*Amount*	*Competitive bidding*		*Limited competition*		*Non-competitive awards*		*Total No.*
		¥100 million	*%*	*¥100 million*	*%*	*¥100 million*	*%*	
1993	Number	957	9.85	4,954	51.00	3,803	39.15	9,714
	Value	95	0.69	1,899	13.84	11,724	85.46	13,718
1994	Number	1,287	12.38	5,205	50.06	3,905	37.56	10,397
	Value	138	1.02	1,759	12.99	11,640	85.99	13,536
1995	Number	1,581	14.56	5,248	48.32	4,032	37.12	10,861
	Value	209	1.57	2,004	15.00	11,141	83.43	13,353
1996	Number	2,058	19.98	4,645	45.10	3,595	34.90	10,298
	Value	356	2.62	1,588	11.72	11,611	85.66	13,555
1997	Number	2,771	28.04	3,659	37.03	3,450	34.92	9,880
	Value	493	3.73	1,430	10.83	11,277	85.43	13,200
1998	Number	3,247	33.80	3,223	34.50	3,046	31.70	9,616
	Value	565	4.60	1,146	9.20	10,720	86.20	12,431
1999	Number	5,297	51.74	2,124	20.75	2,817	27.52	10,238
	Value	953	7.54	1,580	12.50	10,106	79.97	12,639
2000	Number	5,872	60.77	912	9.44	2,879	29.86	9,663
	Value	1,063	8.44	1,604	12.74	9,928	78.82	12,595
2001	Number	6,021	61.43	847	8.64	2,934	29.93	9,802
	Value	1,000	7.88	1,495	11.78	10,192	80.33	12,687
2002	Number	5,432	61.12	674	7.58	2,782	31.30	8,888
	Value	973	7.61	1,324	10.35	10,495	82.04	12,792
2003	Number	5,045	59.22	681	7.99	2,793	3.28	8,519
	Value	893	7.01	770	6.05	11,069	86.94	12,732
2004	Number	4,586	56.30	678	8.30	2,878	35.30	8,142
	Value	840	6.40	1,242	9.50	10,979	84.10	13,062
2005	Number	4,839	56.00	676	7.80	3,127	36.1	8,642
	Value	1,099	8.00	901	6.60	11,738	85.4	13,738

Source: Kankōkai Henshūbu, *Bōei Nenkan*, Tokyo, Kankōkai Henshūbu, Tokyo, various years.

discretionary contract for the importation of two Eurocopter EC225LP helicopters for the Ground Self Defense Forces (GSDF).[22] At the same time, the scandal has threatened to involve the former JDA/MOD Ministers, Fukushiro Nukuga and Akio Kyuma, who were known to have associated with Miyazaki and are influential defence *zoku* figures.[23]

The Moriya scandal has fully exposed for the first time the degree of potential collusion between politicians, bureaucrats and elements of the defence industry, and the government is clearly concerned that it represents deepening structural corruption. The Ministry of Defense Reform Council (Bōeishō Kaikaku Kaigi) in the Prime Minister's Office revealed in 2008 that over the previous five years there had been around 500 cases of retired JSDF personnel requiring permission under the JSDF Law to take up positions with commercial enterprises, including close to 200 former officers of colonel/captain rank and above, and that the most popular destination for these personnel were companies involved in MOD procurement, with MHI, NEC and MELCO the top-ranking destinations.[24] The JDA was also forced in 2006 to reveal in the Diet that in 2004 there had been a total of 718 retired JSDF personnel working in firms with JDA contracts, again mostly concentrated in MHI affiliates.[25] The JDA/MOD is also believed to collude with defence contractors through the section-chief and above level exclusive 'Hinoki-kai' social network grouping.[26]

The MOD has attempted to curb this emerging domestic military-industrial complex through a series of internal ministerial and wider government reform panels dealing with the Central Procurement Office, DFAA, and now Moriya cases. In response to the Moriya scandal, the Ministry of Defense Reform Council and the MOD itself are looking once again to increase transparency in procurement procedures, and is seeking to monitor their pricing practices more carefully, although the Ministry remains reliant on trading companies for overseas procurements and is likely to do so into the foreseeable future.[27] However, as all the reform panels have concluded over the last decade, Japan faces a problem of essentially structural corruption due to the combination of a relatively young retirement age and delayed pensions by international standards of MOD bureaucrats and JSDF officers, and defence contractors seeking to offer re-employment in return for information on defence procurement.[28]

Hence Japan's defence production sector can be argued to be beginning to exhibit the features of a military-industrial complex in accordance with Japan's past history and the general literature on the militarization framework. Japan's defence sector displays signs of deep structural collusion between the bureaucracy, politicians, industry and the military. The degree of novelty of this collusion is hard to assess, given the difficulties, for instance, of obtaining the statistics for *amakudari* for the JDA/MOD.[29] Recent scandals may also have been magnified by enhanced media scrutiny. However, what appears to be strikingly new about Japan's emergent domestic military-industrial complex – and thus what has most perplexed the government in the wake of the Moriya scandal – is the concern that military-industrial–bureaucratic–political collusion has escalated to the extent that minor interest groups, not only as in the past extract a degree of patronage from defence contracts, but that they have threatened to take hold of the overall policy of defence procurement and direct it without reference to broader national security interests. Moreover, as seen below, even as Japan attempts to tackle domestic industrial militarization, its challenges are compounded by continuing pressure to integrate into a new transnational military-industrial complex.

Japan's emerging transnational military-industrial complex

Japan for much of the post-war period has been divorced from international military production. Japan's emphasis on maintaining indigenous production has been one factor making for a degree of autonomy and autarky in the defence sector (with the domestic procurement levels close to 90 per cent of total expenditure).[30] The other factor, of course, has been Japan's self-imposed bans in 1967 and 1976 on the export of weapons technology. Japan's arms export ban has been promoted by its government as one of the key totems of its relatively demilitarized stance. Indeed, one of the chief variables in the recent Global Peace Index responsible for placing Japan fifth globally in the rankings of the most peaceful nations was its restrained stance on arms exports.[31]

Japan did maintain a significant arms export sector until the imposition of the twin bans, and since then has continued to maintain significant foreign military sales (FMS) procurements from the United States, licensed production of key weapons systems from the United States, and has embarked on thirteen co-development projects with the United States since the 1980s, the most notable of which was the FS-X/F-2 fighter. Moreover, Japan has exported certain dual-use technologies with military applications, but it can state with conviction that since the 1960s it has not engaged in significant arms transfers to spur militarization in other regions.[32]

However, since the late 1990s Japan has been forced to reconsider its defence production policy and to begin to expand international collaborative linkages. Japanese defence industry is beset by the twin problems of limited demand in Japan itself, due to tight defence budgets, stagnant at a level of around JPY 5 trillion and just under 1 per cent of GNP, and the lack of access to co-development partners and economies of scale for increasingly expensive weapons systems, due to the ban on arms transfers. Japan has experienced some consolidation in its defence industry, especially in military shipbuilding (IHI and Sumitomo Heavy Industries moved their military shipbuilding activities into IHI Marine United; in September 2001 IHI, KHI and Mitsui Zosen formed a work share agreement; in October 2002 NKK and Hitachi integrated their military shipbuilding into Universal Shipbuilding; and in October 2002 KHI formed Kawasaki Zosen, a new subsidiary shipbuilding company).[33] But Japan by and large has found consolidation difficult due to its post-war model of embedding production capabilities within larger civilian conglomerates, which cannot easily be separated without damaging civilian production. Japan is now facing the situation of a number of larger firms but also especially crucial subcontracting small to medium enterprises (SME) exiting the defence industry altogether.[34] The Japanese government has sought to maintain an indigenous defence production base by initiating some new *kokusanka* projects, such as the P-X surveillance aircraft and C-X transport aircraft, and even plans for a prototype F-X (to replace the F-4J), the aim of which are to identify and continue to nurture 'strategic' and 'specialist' technologies and to preserve the potential for systems integration and building larger platforms. But despite these efforts, and a plethora of government and industrial advisory reports, the JDA concluded in 2005 that Japan's defence production base is 'seriously weakening'.[35]

Japan's creaking defence industry policy means that it has now little chance but to consider increasing the opportunities for international collaboration, unless it once again wants to risk technological isolation (*gijutsu-teki na sakoku*). Thus its policy makers and industrialists have fixed upon a partial or total lifting of the arms export ban as a key means to reverse the decline in the domestic defence production base.[36] In January 2004, in a speech at The Hague, Ishiba, in his first stint at the JDA/MOD, touched upon the need to lift the ban on exports to facilitate defence production with the United States and other countries. The Prime Minister's Office later stressed that the government was considering a further partial lifting solely with regard to the United States and ballistic missile defence (BMD). Nevertheless, Ishiba's remarks reflect strengthening opinion within the MOD and segments of domestic industry regarding the need to end the export bans. The LDP's Defense Policy Subcommittee in 2004 proposed that the total ban be lifted in favour of an export licensing scheme.[37] This call was repeated by the Keidanren's Defense Production Committee in July of the same year.[38] Shinzo Abe in 2004, as the then LDP Secretary General, advocated a return to the principles of the 1967 ban on arms exports to communist countries, countries under UN sanctions and states party to conflict, thereby clearing the way for high-tech weapons sales and co-production with other developed states.[39] The Prime Minister's Council on Security and Defense Capabilities (in the Araki Report) commented in 2004 that expanding technological military cooperation with states other than the United States should not be seen as Japan acting as a 'merchant of death'.[40]

Although momentum seemed to be growing for a wholesale revision of the arms export ban by the end of 2004, this was eventually halted by the intervention of the New Komei party.[41] However, the government did in part move to breach the ban on 10 December 2004 in order to facilitate co-development with the United States of BMD. The Chief Cabinet Secretary's statement stressed that BMD would not conflict with the arms export ban because the project was designed for the smooth functioning of the US–Japan alliance and Japan's own defence.

Japanese defence industry has inevitably looked to the United States as its prime international partner, perceiving the advantages of producing highly interoperable equipment for alliance cooperation, and the possibilities to access the United States' leading-edge technologies. For its part, the United States favours co-development in order to share costs and to access Japanese advanced manufacturing techniques and certain technologies. The main bilateral project is the upgrading of the Standard Missile (SM)-3 BLK-IIA interceptor missile for the Aegis BMD system, and which will eventually move into some form of co-production stage (either through wholesale exchange of technologies or the establishment of a joint plant in Japan or the United States) involving the deeper integration of US and Japanese industry. The 'second Armitage–Nye' report of 2007 advocated the lifting of all further restrictions on Japanese arms exports.[42]

Hence it may not be too far-fetched to consider the rise of a US–Japan transnational military-industrial complex. The Japanese and US defence industries have allied through the formation in 1996 of the US–Japan Industry Forum for Security Cooperation (IFSEC), chaired by MHI and Boeing and consisting of the DPC, the Japan Defense Industries Association and leading defence contractors in both countries (MHI, IHI, KHI, Shimadzu Corporation, Toshiba, IHI Aerospace, Komatsu, Daikin Industries, NEC, Hitatchi, Fujitsu, MELCO, Boeing, GenCorp Aerojet, GEC, Lockheed Martin, Northrop-Grumman, Raytheon, Science Applications International Cooperation, United Defense), and which has advocated increased bilateral defence production cooperation and the lifting of the arms export ban.[43]

The Moriya procurement scandal further demonstrated the strength of US–Japan political-military-industrial linkages. Naoki Akiyama, Executive Director of the Japan–US Center for Peace and Cultural Exchange (known as the Center), has been accused of accepting payments from Yamada Corporation in order to assist in influencing the MOD to employ the company as a sales agent for GE Engines for the C-X, and to act as the subcontractor for the disposal of poison gas shells abandoned by the imperial army in Fukuoka prefecture.[44] Motonobu Miyazaki, the prime figure involved in the bribery of Moriya, stated in Diet testimony in May 2008 that he had paid Akiyama JPY 100 million to deal with potential difficulties in the poison gas shell disposal from 'fishing interests and organized crime' in Fukuoka.[45] Miyazaki had been a member of the board of the Center until 2006, and the board, until the scandal broke in November 2007, was packed with prominent political, bureaucratic and industrial figures from both states. The Japanese side included the former JDA Director Generals/Ministers of Defense Tsutomu Kawara, Fumio Kyuma, Fukushiro Nukuga, Tokuichiro Tamazawa, Gen Nakatani, Shigeru Ishiba; former DFAA Director General Noboru Hoshuyama; former DPJ leader Seiji Maehara; former JDA Administrative Vice-Minister Ken Sato; former LDP Secretary General Tsutomu Takebe; and the Chairman of MHI, and senior representatives from MELCO, KHI, NEC, Hitachi, IHI, Toshiba, Itochu, Sumitomo, Marubeni and Yamada Corporation. Former Prime Minister Abe and former Prime Minister Fukuda are also reported to have been members of the board in the past.[46] On the US side, the prominent figures included former Secretary of Defense William Cohen, former US ambassador Michael Armacost, and former Pentagon adviser William J. Schneider.

The Center in turn is associated with the congressional National Security Research Group (NSRG) (Anzen Hoshō Giin Kyōgikai, also known in Japanese as Anzen Hoshō Kenkyūsho), with Akiyama serving as the Office director, and drawing on many of the same Japanese Diet members. The Center and NSRG, in conjunction with the Heritage Foundation, have been responsible for organizing the Japan–US Security Strategy Conference (Nichibei Anzenhoshō Senryaku Kaigi), which invites a number of other prominent figures to discuss a range of issues connected with the alliance, such as BMD technological cooperation. The meetings usually include speakers from industry in Japan and the United States, and feature presentations by Raytheon, Boeing, Lockheed Martin and Northrup-Grumman.[47]

At the same time that Japanese external remilitarization is gaining ground with enhanced US–Japan industrial linkages it is also challenging the arms export ban in other ways. The Chief Cabinet Secretary's statement of 2004 has now been interpreted by the MOD as providing grounds for investigation, on a case-by-case basis, with other countries into joint research and development of technologies to respond to terrorism and piracy.[48] Japan has already exported 'demilitarized' JCG patrol craft to Indonesia for anti-piracy activities, and begun new, if small-scale, international defence technological cooperation.[49] The MOD's Technical Research and Development Institute (TRDI) has despatched observers to Sweden's nuclear biological and chemical warfare research facilities, and used French facilities to calculate stealth technologies. Moreover, Japanese policy makers see future possibilities for international cooperation with non-US partners in technologies to clear land mines and lessen the threat from improvised explosive devices (IED), and have also shown some interest in the Eurofighter Typhoon as an option to replace the F-4J. Hence the indications are that as Japan's domestic defence industry predicament grows in terms of stagnant domestic budgets and rising unit prices for equipment, and thus limited domestic opportunities to maintain leading technologies, it will gradually seek to re-enter the international military co-development and export markets.

Japan's military-industrial complex and remilitarization

Examination of Japan's changing defence production sector confirms the validity of the identification of a rising military-industrial complex in Japan, and the utility of reapplying the militarization framework as a means to understand the significance of Japan's security trajectory. The use of the terminology of militarization as a fourth discourse enables us to engage more effectively with the first discourse regarding the key explanatory drivers for change in Japan's security policy. The military-industrial complex case study demonstrates that this key feature of Japanese security policy is driven by both internal domestic and external structural considerations. Japan's defence production collusion is the product of its domestic political economy power structures. In turn, the rise of transnational military-industrial interests is the outcome of changes in the global political economy, combined with Japan's strategic interests vis-à-vis the United States, other major powers and its own region. In this way, it can be seen that Realist, Liberal and Marxist perspectives, in combination with IR, IPE and Sociology, all offer significant analytical purchase in understanding Japanese security policy change, and many of the claims for parsimonious, monocausal explanations utilizing only one perspective are inadequate.

The militarization framework, moreover, contributes strongly to overcoming the roadblock in the second discourse concerned with the degree of change in Japan's security posture. If defence production is taken as a manifestation of long-term attempts by Japanese policy makers to maintain their autonomy and thereby sustain the grand strategy of the 'Yoshida Doctrine', then the evidence presented in this chapter indicates that Japan is certainly attempting in many ways to follow its post-war path. Japan's exploration of the globalization of its defence production sector is perhaps a bid to preserve its autonomy through selecting new international partners which can purvey essential technology: a traditional pattern of Japanese engagement with its external environment. However, the fact that Japan is increasingly been drawn into military-industrial linkages predominantly with the United States, and the revealed extent of the penetration of Japan's defence production sector by US interests, argues forcefully that Japan is gravitating more strongly towards dependence on the United States rather than attempting to maintain a higher degree of autonomy. Consequently, the rise of Japan's transnational military-industrial complex indicates that Japan is moving away, whether inadvertently or deliberately, from the 'Yoshida Doctrine' and moving more towards a new US–Japan alliance relationship which spells entrapment for Japan in US global strategy.[50]

Furthermore, the fourth discourse of militarization certainly provides a critical tool of analysis of the third discourse of 'normalization'. Contrary to the arguments of policy makers and academics which posit that Japan's security policy is undergoing appropriate and responsible change, the case of the military-industrial complex argues for less sanguine trends. Japan in allowing the forging of closer collusion between bureaucratic, political, military and industrial interests has clearly undermined civilian control of its military establishment, and thus indicates a repeat of historical precedents which must pose some concerns about the 'normal' path of Japanese security policy. Similarly, Japan's emergent transnational military-industrial complex has involved increasing de facto breaches of the anti-militaristic principles banning the exports of armaments, and thus a significant turning away from one of the key features of its demilitarized stance in the post-war period. It might yet be argued that Japan is only doing what is 'normal' for other major states in terms of the globalization of military production and searching out arms export markets, but it cannot be denied that this still constitutes in plain and objective language an escalation in Japan's remilitarization. The manner in which Japan is remilitarizing may also give grounds for concern over its normality – the transnational military-industrial complex driven in part by narrow US–Japan commercial interests allegedly involving corrupt practices.

Finally, the militarization framework offers one additional insight which argues for its necessity in the mainstream on the debate on Japanese security policy. The framework presents a range of objective indicators concerning the military-industrial complex, such as the size and structure of the defence industry, personnel linkages between different military-industrial interests and so forth. This is also true of other features of the militarization framework such as defence budgets and the size of the military establishment. Hence the framework offers a range of rich comparators which might be used to judge just how far Japan has militarized in terms of its own historical trajectory and in comparison to other developed states. This would further help to settle the argument in more objective fashion about just how far Japan has shifted in its post-war trajectory and just how 'normal' its trajectory really is.

Notes

1 For examples of arguments favouring structural determinants of Japan's security policy see K. A. Waltz, 'The emerging structure of international politics', *International Security* 18 (2), 1993, 44–79; C. Layne, 'The unipolar illusion revisited: why new great powers will rise', *International Security* 17 (4), 1993, 5–51; E. Heginbotham and R. J. Samuels, 'Mercantile Realism and Japanese foreign policy', *International Security* 22 (4), 1998, 171–203; T. Christensen, 'China, the US–Japan alliance, and the security dilemma in East Asia', *International Security* 23 (4), 1999, 49–80; C. Twomey, 'Japan, a circumscribed balancer', *Security Studies* 9 (4), 2000, 167–205; M. J. Green, *Japan's Reluctant Realism: Foreign Policy Challenges in an Era of Uncertain Power*, New York: Palgrave, 2001; P. Midford, 'The logic of reassurance and Japan's grand strategy', *Security Studies* 11 (3), 2002, 1–43; J. Lind, 'Pacifism or passing the buck? Testing theories of Japanese security policy', *International Security* 29 (1), 2004, 92–121. For more domestic and norms-oriented approaches see T. U. Berger, 'From sword to chrysanthemum: Japan's culture of antimilitarism', *International Security* 17 (4), 1993, 119–50; and P. J. Katzenstein and N. Okawara, 'Japan's national security: structures, norms, and policies', *International Security* 17 (4), 1993, 84–118.

2 Prime Minister Yoshida Shigeru, although he would not have recognized it as a 'doctrine' as such, established the basic Japanese diplomatic line for the post-war period (known in Japanese as the 'Yoshida Rōsen') during his tenure in office from 1949 to 1952. Yoshida concluded that Japan should concentrate on economic reconstruction and light rearmament in the post-war period, in order to avoid the damaging costs of attempting to restore Japan as a great military power, of antagonizing its neighbours, and of precipitating domestic controversies over defence. For Yoshida the mechanism for Japan to achieve these objectives was to align with the United States, and to accept de facto guarantees of military security in exchange for providing the United States with military bases in Japan to fight the Cold War. However, Yoshida was also aware of the risks of alignment with the United States, and that Japan should seek to maintain a certain distance from the United States in order to avoid being sucked into unwanted conflicts in East Asia. For views of Japan essentially maintaining the Yoshida Doctrine with modifications see M. M. Mochizuki, 'Change in Japan's grand strategy: why and how much?', Book Review Roundtable, *Asia Policy* 4, 2007, 191–6; R. J. Samuels, *Securing Japan: Tokyo's Grand Strategy and the Future of East Asia*, Ithaca, NY: Cornell University Press, 2007. For views arguing for divergence from the Yoshida Doctrine see Green, *Japan's Reluctant Realism*; C. W. Hughes, *Japan's Re-emergence as a 'Normal' Military Power*, Adelphi Paper, Oxford: Oxford University Press/IISS, 2004, pp. 368–9; K. B. Pyle, *Japan Rising: The Resurgence of Japanese Power and Purpose*, New York: Public Affairs Books, 2007.

3 K. Fujiwara, *Demokurashii no Teikoku: Amerika, Sensō, Gendai Sekai*, Tokyo: Iwanami Shinsho, 2002; A. DiFilippo, *The Challenges of the US–Japan Military Arrangement: Competing Security Transitions in a Changing International Environment*, Armonk, NY: M. E. Sharpe, 2002; J. Yamaguchi, *Sengo Seiji no Hōkai*, Tokyo: Iwanami Shoten, 2004; M. Tamamoto, 'Japan's politics of cultural shame', *Global*

Asia: Journal of the East Asia Foundation 2 (1), 2007, 14–20; R. Tanter, 'With eyes wide shut: Japan, Heisei militarization, and the Bush doctrine' in M. Gurtov and P. Van Ness (eds) *Confronting the Bush Doctrine: Critical Views from the Asia-Pacific*, London, Routledge, 2005, pp. 153–80; G. McCormack, 'Remilitarizing Japan', *New Left Review* 29, 2004, 29–44; G. McCormack, *Client State: Japan in the American Embrace*, London: Verso, 2007.

4 G. D. Hook, *Demilitarization and Remilitarization in Contemporary Japan*, London: Routledge, 1996.

5 For the debate on paradigmatic divides in Japanese security studies and the need to overcome it see P. J. Katzenstein and N. Okawara, 'Japan, Asian-Pacific security, and the case for analytical eclecticism', *International Security* 26 (3), 2001,153–85.

6 Accounts of Japanese defence production and the key role that it plays in ensuring national security autonomy are provided in R. J. Samuels, *Rich Nation, Strong Army: National Security and the Technological Transformation of Japan*, Ithaca, NY: Cornell University Press, 1994; M. J. Green, *Arming Japan: Defense Production, Alliance Politics, and the Postwar Search for Autonomy*, New York: Columbia University Press, 1995.

7 A. Vagts, *A History of Militarism*, Westport, CT: Greenwood Press, 1959; Kjell Skjelsbaek, 'Militarism, its dimensions and corollaries: an attempt at conceptual clarification', *Journal of Peace Research* 16 (3), 1979, 213–29; A. L. Ross, 'Dimensions of militarization in the Third World', *Armed Forces and Society* 13 (4), 1987, 561–78.

8 A. J. Bacevich, *The New American Militarism: How Americans are Seduced by War*, Oxford: Oxford, University Press, 2005, p. 2.

9 H. Hummel, 'Japan's military expenditures after the Cold War: the "Realism" of the peace dividend', *Australian Journal of International Affairs* 50 (2), 1996, 137–55.

10 H. D. Lasswell, 'The garrison state', *American Journal of Sociology* 46 (4), 1941, 455–68; S. P. Huntington, *The Soldier and the State: The Theory and Politics of Civil–Military Relations*, Cambridge, MA: Belknap Press, 1964; S. E. Finer, *The Man on Horseback: The Role of the Military in Politics*, 2nd edn, Boulder, CO: Westview Press, 1988; M. Janowitz, *The Professional Soldier: A Social and Political Portrait*, New York: Free Press, 1971; J. Snyder, 'Civil–military relations and the cult of the offensive, 1914 and 1984', *International Security* 9 (1), 1984, 108–46; M. C. Desch, 'Threat environments and military missions' in L. Diamond and Marc F. Plattner (eds) *Civil–Military Relations and Democracy*, Baltimore, MD: Johns Hopkins University Press, 1996; P. D. Feaver, 'The civil–military problematique: Huntington, Janowitz, and the question of civilian control', *Armed Forces and Society* 23 (2), 1996, 149–78.

11 N. Stargardt, *The German Idea of Militarism: Radical and Socialist Critics, 1866–1914*, Cambridge: Cambridge University Press, 1994; C. Johnson, *The Sorrows of Empire: Militarism, Secrecy and the End of the Republic*, London: Verso, 2004.

12 Finer, *The Man on Horseback.*

13 Skjelsbaek, 'Militarism', pp. 223–4; M. W. Doyle, *Ways of War and Peace*, New York: W. W. Norton, 1997, 241–6; R. Luxemburg, *The Accumulation of Capital*, London: Routledge & Kegan Paul, 1961, pp. 454–67; J. Schumpeter, *Sociology of Imperialism*, New York: Meridian, 1955; C. Wright Mills, *The Power Elite*, Oxford: Oxford University Press, 1956; J. Slater and T. Nardin, 'The concept of a military-industrial complex' in S. Rosen (ed.) *Testing the Theory of the Military-Industrial Complex*, Lexington, MA: Lexington Books, 1973, pp. 27–60; Finer, *The Man on Horseback*, pp. 41–9, V. R. Berghahn; *Militarism: The History of an International Debate, 1861–1979*; Leamington Spa: Berg Publishers, 1981; Skjelsbaek, 'Militarism', pp. 213–29 .

14 Ross, 'Dimensions of militarization', p. 565.

15 M. Kaldor, *The Baroque Arsenal*, London: André Deutsch, 1982, pp. 131–62.

16 J. F. Galloway, 'Multinational corporations and military-industrial linkages' in S. Rosen (ed.) *Testing the Theory of the Military-Industrial Complex*, Lexington, MA: Lexington Books, 1973, pp. 267–90; D. Smith, and R. Smith, *The Economics of Militarism*, London: Pluto Press, 1982, pp. 42–3; Skjelsbaek, 'Militarism', p. 225; R. A. Bitzinger, 'The globalization of the arms industry: the next proliferation challenge', *International Security* 19 (2), 170–98; K. Krause, *Arms and the State: Patterns of Military Production and Trade*, Cambridge: Cambridge University Press, 1992, pp. 12–18, 97–8.

17 I. Hatano, *Kindai Nihon no Gunsangaku Fukugōtai: Kaigun, Jūkōgyō*, Daigaku, Tokyo: Sōbunsha, 2005.

18 M. E. Chinworth, *Inside Japan's Defense: Technology, Economics and Strategy*, Washington, DC: Brassey's US, 1992, Samuels, *Rich Nation, Strong Army*.

19 Samuels, *Rich Nation, Strong Army*, pp. 154–97.

20 Chinworth, *Inside Japan's Defense*, pp. 21–6; Green, *Arming Japan*, p. 122; Masako Ikegami-Andersson, 'Arms procurement decision making: Japan' in Ravinder Pal Singh, *Arms Procurement Decision Making*, Vol. I, *China, India, Israel, Japan, South Korea and Thailand*, Oxford: Sipri/Oxford University Press, 1998, p. 168.

21 Bōeichōhen, *Bōei Hakusho 1999*, Tokyo: Ōkurashō Insatsukyoku, 1999, pp. 296–322.

22 *Asahi Shimbun*, 'Itōchū kogaisha mo Moriya hikoku o gorufu settai keijūnikai', www.asahi.com/special/071029/TKY200802180474.html (accessed 18 February 2008).

23 'Shikin ryūnyū "nai" Kyūma-shi seikai kanyo o hitei', *Asahi Shimbun*, 25 July 2008, p. 4.

24 Bōeishō, *Bōeishō Kaikaku Kaigi Dai4kai Setsumei Shiryō*, www.kantei.go.jp/jp/singi/bouei/dai4/pdf/siryou2.pdf (accessed 1 February 2008); Bōeishō, *Dai4kai Bōeishō Kaikaku Kaigi Sankō Shiryō*, www.kantei.go.jp/jp/singi/bouei/dai4/pdf/siryou2.pdf (accessed 1 February 2008).

25 *Shimbun Akahata*, 'Bōeichō amakudari ōi kigyō juchū mo mashi', 12 April 2006, p. 15; Shūkan Kinyōbihen, *Mitsubishi Jūkō no Seitai: Kokusaku Bōei Kigyō*, Tokyo: Kinyōbi, 2008, pp. 26–32.

26 *Shimbun Akahata*, 'Kokubōzoku no Giin Kyōgikai, Beigun jusangyō to hinpan ni kaigō', www.jcp.or.jp/akahta/aik07/2007-12-03/2007120301_02_0.html (accessed 3 December 2007).

27 Bōeishō Kaikaku Kaigi, *Hōkokushō Fuyōji no Bunseki to Kaikaku no Hōkōsei*, Tokyo, www.kantei.go.jp/jp/singi/bouei/dai11/pdf/siryou.pdf, pp. 36–40 (accessed 15 July 2008); Bōeishō Sōgō Shutoku Suishin Purojekkuto Chiimu, *Hōkokusho*, Tokyo, www.mod.go.jp/j/info/sougousyutoku/pdf/siryou/10_02.pdf (accessed March 2008).

28 Bōeichōhen, *Bōei Hakusho 2006*, Tokyo: Ōkurashō Insatsukyoku, 2006, pp. 276–80; G. Nakatani, *Daremo Kakenakatta Bōeishō no Shinjistu*, Tokyo: Gentōsha, 2008.

29 R. A. Colignon and Chikako Usui, *Amakudari: The Hidden Fabric of Japan's Economy*, Ithaca, NY: Cornell University Press, 2003, pp. 22–3.

30 Bōei Kankōkai Henshūbu, *Bōei Nenkan 2007*, Tokyo: Kankōkai Henshūbu, 2007, p. 329.

31 Global Peace Index, *Japan 2008: Global Peace Index*, www.visionofhumanity.org/gpi/results/japan/2008 (accessed 7 February 2009).

32 R. Drifte, *Arms Production in Japan: The Military Applications of Civilian Technology*, Boulder, CO: Westview Press, 1986, pp. 74–8; A. L. Oros, *Normalizing Japan: Politics, Identity, and the Evolution of Security Practice*, Stanford, CA: Stanford University Press, 2008, pp. 94–110.

33 Nihon Keizai Dantai Rengōkai Bōei Seisan Iinkai, 'Waga Kuni Bōei Sangyō no Genjō Nado ni Tsuite', p. 32, presentation provided by personal contact at Keidanren Defense Production Committee, 2007.

34 Asahi Shimbun Jieitai 50nen Shuzaiha, *Jieitai Shirarezaru Henyō*, Tokyo: Asahi Shimbunsha, 2005, pp. 268–70.

35 METI Bōei Sangyō Gijutsu Kiban Kenkyūkai, *Bōei Sangyō Gijutsu no Iji Ikusei ni Kansuru Kihon-teki Hōkō: Nijū Isseiki ni okeru Kiban no Kōchiku ni Mukete*, Tokyo,

November, 2000; Bōeichō, *Arata na Jidai no Sōbi Shutoku o Mezashite: Shin ni Hitsuyō na Bōei Seisan Gijutsu Kiban no Kakuritsu ni Mukete*, Tokyo: Bōeichō, 2005, p. 1; Bōei Kenkyūjo, *Waga Kuni no Bōei Gijutsu Kiban ga Sōbihin Shutoku ni oyabasu Kōka ni Kansuru Chōsa Kenkyū*, Tokyo, 2006.

36 J. Nishiyama, 'Buki yushutsu to anzen hoshō', *Kaigai Jijō* 56 (3), 2008, 20; J Nishiyama, 'Nihon no bōei to gijutsu kaihatsu' in S. Morimoto (ed.) *Kiro ni Tatsu Nihon no Anzen: Anzen Hoshō, Kiki Kanri Seisaku no Jissai to Tenbō*, Tokyo: Hokuseidō, 2008, p. 353.

37 Defense Policy Studies Subcommittee, National Defense Division, Policy Research Council, Liberal Democratic Party, *Recommendations on Japan's New Defence Policy: Toward a Safer and More Secure Japan in the World*, www.jimin.jp/jimin/main/seisaku.html (accessed 30 March 2003).

38 Nihon Keizai Dantai Rengōkai Bōei Seisan Iinkai, Teigen 'Kongo no Bōeiryoku Seibi no Arikata ni tsuite': Bōei Seisan Gijutsu Kiban no Kyōka ni Mukete, 2004, reported in Nihon Keizai Dantai Rengōkai Bōei Seisan Iinkai, Bōei Seisan Gijustu Kiban ni Tsuite: Kokunai Kiban no Jūjutsu to Kokusai Kyōryoku, Tokyo, September 2005, p. 6.

39 S. Abe, 'Kaiken de kōsenken mo mitomeru beki', *AERA*, 5 August 2004, p. 17.

40 Anzen Hoshō to Bōeiryokyu ni Kansuru Kondankai, *Anzen Hoshō to Bōeiryokyu ni Kansuru Kondankai ni Okeru Kore Made no Giron to Gaiyō*, 2004, p. 5, www.kantei.go.jp/jp/singi/ampobouei/dai7/7siryou1.pdf (accessed 7 February 2009).

41 *Asahi Shimbun*, 'Kenshō buki yushutsu sangensoku kanwa: kokubōzoku, zaikai ga kenin', 11 December 2004, p. 4.

42 R. L. Armitage and J. S. Nye, *The US–Japan Alliance: Getting Asia Right through 2020*, CSIS report, Washington, DC, February 2007, p. 27, www.csis.org/media/csis/pubs/070216_asia2020.pdf (accessed 7 February 2009).

43 Keidanren/IFSEC, Keidanren, *IFSEC Joint Report: Revised US–Japan Statement of Mutual Interests*, www.keidanren.or.jp/japanese/policy/2003/005e.html (accessed 21 January 2003).

44 *Asahi Shimbun*, 'Yamada Yōkō, Bōeizoku Dantai ni ichiokuen ka, kyōryokyhi shishutsu no bunsho', www.asahi.com/politics/update/1026/TKY200711300364.html (accessed 30 November 2007).

45 *Yomiuri Shimbun*, 'Shōnin kammon no Yamada Yōkō, Miyazaki motosenmu "Akiyama-shi gawa ni ichiokuen shishutsu"', www.yomiuri.co.jp/politics/news/20080522-OYT1T00426.htm (accessed 22 May 2008).

46 Shūkan Kinyōbi, *Mitsubishi Jūkō*, p. 18.

47 *Asahi Shimbun*, 'Kokubō ugomeku kane', 25 July 2008, p. 39.

48 Bōeishōhen, *Bōei Hakusho 2007*, Tokyo: Zaimushō Insatsukyoku, 2007, p. 388; Kankōkai Henshūbu, *Bōei Nenkan 2006*, Tokyo: Kankōkai Henshūbu, 2006, pp. 147–8.

49 Samuels, *Securing Japan*, p. 164.

50 Hughes, *Japan's Re-emergence as a 'Normal' Military Power*.

9 Stability and the status quo

Changing power structures in the optics industry

Patricia A. Nelson

Inter-organizational institutions are a significant feature of the fabric of Japan's political and economic system. There are over 13,400 *zaidan hōjin* (foundation corporations) and nearly 12,500 *shadan hōjin* (association corporations) as defined by Article 34 of the Civil Law of 1898.[1] Together, *zaidan* and *shadan hōjin* account for roughly one-tenth of Japan's public benefit corporations (*kōeki hōjin*). Until the passage of the NPO Law in 1998 that broadened the existing legal space for non-profits, they were said to be 'the nearest equivalent in Japan to a US-style not-for-profit organization'.[2]

Historically speaking, *zaidan hōjin* and *shadan hōjin* have played an important role in many areas of Japan's political and economic system as inter-organizational institutions that offer opportunities to build horizontal networks and create personal links between organizations such as corporations. Due to their connection with social, cultural, educational and promotional activities, however, their involvement with industries has often been overlooked.[3] Another reason they have been overlooked is the common presumption of evil intent; it is often assumed that when business people meet, their sole purpose is to collaborate and develop new ways to hoodwink the consumer. In the current financial crisis, bankers are being blamed for seeking to achieve short-term profits while lining their pockets. Evil intent by corporations seems not an unreasonable assumption. But we should remember that not all bankers are the same, nor are all institutions that bring business people together illegal. The fundamental lesson of the current crisis is the need for better controls on and regulation of the financial sector, and for this to be done, we need a deeper understanding of what has happened. The same is true for inter-organizational institutions. These institutions play a crucial role in Japan's economy but because they lurk under the radar we know relatively little about them. We need to understand them better to regulate against their negative nature and nurture them for the benefits they can provide.

There are a number of reasons why analyses of specific instances of change within institutions are useful. First, as already noted, historical analyses of institutions can highlight the breadth of responses that occur in coordinated economies such as Japan, from slow to rapid, depending on the degree of consensus that is required for change.[4] Second, they alert us to the important and continuing function of under-researched institutions in Japan (and elsewhere) and the public benefits that they can offer, e.g. stability – a necessary condition for the perception that business can and will prosper – and standards of legal and normative behaviour. Third, understanding the industry associations, for example, as they function over time within their political economic context offers an opportunity to monitor, regulate as necessary, and promote desirable behaviour rather than simply presuming the worst, i.e. collusion.[5] Fourth, because information transmission has always been important, institutions that assist with improving horizontal communication and information flows among vertically oriented organizations – for example, industry associations that provide horizontal connections among companies that often suffer from being isolated and self-contained like grain silos – can offer essential support for a vibrant economic, business and social environment.[6]

This chapter moves from general to specific, starting with the background of *zaidan hōjin*, which are a significant feature of Japan's business system. Then I examine the past and present roles of industry associations and discuss their power structures. To understand the variety and type of organizations that exist in the case of the optics industry, I analyse how it evolved over time, particularly the institutions operating within the industry and those operating in the overall political and economic system. I then discuss horizontal linkages in the industry and how power holders dealt with the problem of adjusting to a new status quo. This analysis helps explain how and why inter-organizational institutions are able to adjust to changing circumstances and specifically highlights the cumulative nature of events which pushed industry leaders in the direction of embracing reorganization while deftly holding on to key positions of power.

Background

Coordinated market economies such as Japan are known to have high levels of social capital; institutions are important elements of their political economy.[7] In Japan, there are many types of *zaidan hōjin* or inter-organizational institutions, e.g. cooperative associations, business groups, industry associations and intra-industry networks, which are often referred to as 'cartels' or organizations that are apt to engage in cartel-like behaviour. The suspicion of evil intent, in particular when business people meet to talk about issues that affect them all, originates with the neoclassical approach to economics. Indeed, Adam Smith wrote, 'People of the same trade seldom meet together, even for merriment and diversion, but the conversation ends in a conspiracy against the public or in some contrivance to raise prices.'[8]

In highly coordinated economies such as Japan, the organizational structures themselves become activated in the search for solutions to problems. Individual organizations embedded in coordinated contexts rely on inter-organizational structures to deal with the process of developing consensus. As noted above, inter-organizational structures can provide significant horizontal links between vertical silo-type organizations and facilitate communication that might be difficult or impossible without them. Thus it is expected that we find a variety of inter-organizational institutions in coordinated market economies and rather fewer in liberal market economies.[9] These inter-organizational institutions are frequently presumed to act as cartels.

A cartel is defined as: (1) 'a combination of independent commercial or industrial enterprises designed to limit competition to fix prices;' (2) 'an association of manufacturers or suppliers formed to maintain high prices and restrict competition'; or (3) 'an agreement among two or more firms in the same industry to co-operate in fixing prices and/or carving up the market and restricting the amount of output they produce'.[10] Taking those definitions together, the implication is that inter-organizational institutions, especially those operating in business, are engaged in conspiratorial and unlawful activities.

There are close linkages among the words 'cartel' and 'monopoly' (and its opposite, anti-monopoly) and 'trust' (and its opposite, anti-trust). They form part of our socially constructed reality, part of the accepted norms and values in our current business system, which has been dominated by the success of the liberal orthodoxy.[11] The liberal market economies are characterized by the neoclassical approach, laissez-faire and the invisible hand. In recent years, the perception of the success of liberal ideas over coordination has found expression in the view that the market is best because the latter is not timely enough and thus does not offer the solutions people require when they need them.[12] Solutions often come after a new consensus is formed and this can take much time, especially when compared with liberal market economies such as the United States.

I argue in this chapter that the purpose and structure of organizations, specifically *zaidan hōjin*, change over time and it behoves us to understand what they do, how they change and why. To achieve that aim, this chapter takes the case of the optics industry in Japan and analyses the process of change. Despite critiques to the contrary, Japanese optics manufacturers were prepared for the so-called 'disruptive' changes brought about by the rise of digital imaging.[13] The evidence is clear from a historical analysis of the industry that leading firms reorganized the inter-organizational institutions over time in response to changing business conditions. In order to carry through change, visionary leaders took the reins of power and propelled the industry's business associations forward. Here I use the notion of structural power which 'confers the power to decide how things shall be done, the power to shape frameworks [...] relate to people, or relate to corporate enterprises'.[14] The structure of an organization itself – in this case the industry association – can thereby convey power to those who hold leadership positions – in this case the heads of the leading firms – and due to this perception of power, likely assisted by financial assets as well as charisma, they were able to stimulate ideas of how they could bring about change. This is how the optics industry leaders brought about the clever reorganization of their industry association.

Adjustments to structural power can occur over a prolonged period of time, very rapidly or somewhere in between. Often those in power are not able to hold on to it when an institution undergoes a major change. This is because the structure itself conveyed power to them and once that structure is gone, so is their power. However, at various points along a continuum of slow to rapid responses, there are ways to adjust creatively to new conditions (whether they be affected by technical, political, social, global influences or a combination thereof) such that those who hold power adjust their expectations and transmit that to their organizations and succeed in retaining their positions of power in a reconstructed institution. That is the story of the optics industry presented in this chapter.

Non-profit organizations past and present

In the aftermath of World War II it was initially unclear to the Occupation forces if the *zaidan hōjin* had been active supporters of the military. Along with all other economic and business organizations, they were reviewed not only for their past roles but also for their expected future usefulness in post-war Japan. At first, the Scientific and Technical Division of the Economic and Scientific Section (ESS/ST) of the Occupation found that *zaidan hōjin* were administered under 'extremely loose and ill-defined laws', including liberal interpretations of patent rights, manufacturing privileges and tax exemptions.[15] Given the questionable legality of some of these practices and the perceived useful role that the *zaidan hōjin* could play in reorganizing Japan for business after the 'reverse course', the leaders of the Occupation drafted a law on 19 January 1949 'to assure that more meaningful controls were applied so the *zaidan hōjin* were in all cases operated in the public interest'.[16] The law was clearly intended to make it legal for post-war *zaidan hōjin* to, for example, receive government support for scientific research. In effect, they acted as non-profit organizations serving a vital role as inter-organizational institutions, between business and government.

In the wake of the January 1995 Kobe–Awajishima earthquake, the Law to Promote Specified Nonprofit Activities (NPO Law, 1998) was promulgated, expanding the designation of non-profit organizations to include those that had previously fallen into other categories – namely *zaidan hōjin* and *shadan hōjin* – or that had been operating without legal status altogether.[17] The catalyst for changing and expanding the legal designation of non-profit organizations (NPOs) and public interest corporations was the significant role that community groups had played in dealing with the Hanshin earthquake.[18] In short, the law created a new category, the NPO, which now sits alongside the older designations *zaidan hōjin* and *shadan hōjin*.[19] These NPOs continued to work for the benefit of each institution and its respective members as well as for society's benefit, just as before. What this means is that inter-organizational institutions working in the interests of businesses, governments and the public at large all are – and have been since 1949 – non-profit organizations.

Keidanren sits at the top of Japan's business organizations as a peak organization representing big business. Individual product associations (e.g. pencils, scarves and optics) are found at the other extreme. In between there are thousands of industry-specific associations that often take the role of umbrella organizations responsible for several products (e.g. exported textiles, measuring instruments and imaging products).[20]

From a broad perspective, including studies on the role of the state in Japan's economy, informal policy networks and the formulation of policy have been analysed from the 'top down'[21] as well as from the 'bottom up'.[22] Most analyses of Japan's industry associations concentrate on activities such as the exchange of information and public relations-type of activities, at times playing down the link that such organizations have had with industrial policy.[23] It is generally agreed that industry associations have their early origins in the pre-war industry control associations that collected information as well as managed and controlled the supply and demand of goods during the wartime economy.[24] A key function is acting as a channel through which information flows.

Competitive pressures in the 1950s and 1960s acted to change the role of industry associations from the control of resources (pre-war) to the promotion of technological change and innovation (post-war). Post-war promotion activities helped firms enter export markets in the United States and Europe. Especially in the early post-war years (and/or in the early years of an industry), they also provided members with opportunities to exchange vital information on technological advances and competitor intelligence. Industry associations were important for increasing 'the political bargaining power of each industry' because they provided critical 'points of access'.[25] These access points allowed influence to run in two directions, from bureaucrats to firms through, e.g., old boy networks and *amakudari* as well as from firms to bureaucrats through, e.g., consensus building and lobbying.[26]

In his path-breaking study Witt argued that 'intra-industry loops' transferred industry-specific information via informal, social loops among firms within an industry and non-firm organizations that include inter-organizational institutions.[27] In this logic, associations acted as intermediaries among firms as well as between the government and firms via loops of industry connections and personal networks. Utilizing networks and information loops, government officials communicated policy guidelines and business leaders communicated their concerns. They in effect helped their members share information via informal channels and facilitated the flow of information among chief executive officers as well as scientists. These networks – institutionalized and not – are one of the least researched yet pervasive aspects of the Japanese business system. Given the thousands of such institutions and networks in Japan, it is odd that so little is known about them.

Power in industry associations

In general, industry associations have one or two permanent staff members who are seconded (on rotation) from government, mainly from the Ministry of Economy Trade and Industry (METI).[28] Firms pay membership dues to the industry association and supply their own employees (seconded on rotation) for short stints at the association. The mix of government and firm employees is expected to contribute to achieving the objectives of the industry association, e.g. promoting exports, raising the industry's technological level and investigating new markets. These objectives, including promotion of exports, were used to maintain stability in the industry – if possible – and to prevent or limit intense rivalry that often emerged among the manufacturers. The goal was to encourage vibrant competition and that usually meant seeking to create a stable atmosphere with as many as five or six leading companies, if the industry could sustain it.[29]

In the early years of post-war economic recovery and rapid growth when firms could reap multiple benefits from cooperating with government initiatives, a great deal of power rested with bureaucrats who oversaw national economic and financial matters.[30] In those days, there was little or no need for coercion; firms generally understood that it was in their interest to comply with top-down policy decisions.[31] Industry associations were further linked with the bureaucracy through representatives who sat on government councils or *shingikai*,[32] a practice that began in 1964.[33] Bureaucrats, who rotated positions every few years and were encouraged to develop a total view of the economy and society, relied on the industry associations for specific information, e.g. product specifications, standards or details of specific skill sets. Industry associations acted as key resources of information for bureaucrats on the state of the industry as a whole and on emerging technologies and know-how.

Firms, and to a certain extent the industry associations, exercised influence over regulators because they held information that was necessary for bureaucrats to formulate industry policy. In short, firms held a certain degree of power to decide whether to cooperate or not in the implementation of policy directed toward them specifically and indirectly to the industry as a whole. Indeed, in rapidly changing, high-tech industries that became leaders in their specific product portfolio, power often rested with firms that could – if they so desired – sidestep guidance from bureaucrats.[34]

A case study of institutions in the optics industry

The Camera and Imaging Products Association (CIPA) represents a specific product area, namely imaging products, and is thus located at the bottom of a vertical hierarchy of industry associations. Immediately above the CIPA is the Japan Optical Industry Association (JOIA) an umbrella group for optic-related products. Above the JOIA is the Japan Machinery Federation, the umbrella organization for companies manufacturing precision machinery, then the Japan Electronic and Information Technology Association, and finally at the top, the Keidanren. Horizontally, the CIPA is connected with other umbrella organizations. Two other product-specific associations related to the CIPA are the Japan Photo-Sensitive Materials Manufacturers' Association (PSMA), whose membership includes all manufacturers of photographic film and paper,[35] and the Japan Optical Measuring Instruments Manufacturers' Association (JOMA), whose membership includes surveying instruments.[36] Membership overlapped since many optics manufacturers also specialized in optical measuring instruments and two of them produced photographic film.

The CIPA was established in 2002 as a reorganization of the Japan Camera Industry Association (JCIA) that was originally established in 1954.[37] The process of the transition from the long-standing status quo of the JCIA to the new CIPA is the focus of this case study. Figure 9.1 presents the membership of the JCIA and CIPA since 1952, indicating events in the history of the industry that help clarify what happened over the fifty-six-year period. The bubbles shown in Figure 9.1 are a selection of events that affected the membership and thereby the structure of power in the association, eventually leading to its recreation as the CIPA. In the early years, there was a substantial degree of industry compliance with government goals and policies, underlining the importance of top-down influence. By the late 1990s, competition in the industry had changed; the rise of digital imaging adjusted the status quo permanently and threatened to extinguish the industry association altogether. Instead of liquidating the institution, the leaders of the JCIA took action, expanding the membership of the association to make it a key player in the digital imaging industry.

In the early years of the JCIA, membership numbers fluctuated greatly (see Figure 9.1). As the institution settled into a status quo, member numbers became much more stable, although with a downward trend. In 2002, when the JCIA was dissolved and the CIPA established, member numbers jumped dramatically at first. After the initial transition period, the number of regular members returned to previous levels but the number of supporter members rose significantly. Supporter member status means that the firm is interested in what is happening in the industry association, but is not an active member. Since the CIPA is a broader industry association and product area than the JCIA was, the number of interested firms should be large. The total membership, regular and supporters, was fifty-seven in 2008, up from forty in 2002.

Figure 9.2 highlights the range of institutions that played important roles in the optics industry over time. Figures 9.1 and 9.2 portray the industry's history with slightly different emphases. In Figure 9.2 the focus is on the network aspect of the industry. It indicates the pre-war industry associations and early post-war groups prior to the official formation of the JCIA in 1954. It provides concrete details on the range of inter-organizational institutions, the intra-industry loops and networks that were in play in the optics industry.

The industry experienced its first burst of post-war international fame in 1952 when a *Life* magazine photo-journalist, David Douglas Duncan, replaced his broken Leica lens with a new Nikon lens (with a Leica mount).[38] Duncan was covering the Korean War at the time and could not obtain a new Leica lens easily. He was so impressed with the photographs taken with his Leica camera and Nikon lens combination that he published his views, saying that the Nikon lens was just as good, if not better, than the Leica lens. With such prominent praise, Nikon's reputation of dedication to high-quality products was secured among professional photographers.[39]

At about the same time, several export-oriented camera makers decided to explore sales and distribution possibilities in the US market, then the largest market in the world for cameras and photographic goods. Four of the top makers – Canon, Minolta, Nikon and Ricoh – had begun to distribute their products in the United States through local dealers, with varying degrees of success.[40] When Canon tried to set up its US distribution through Bell & Howell Company in

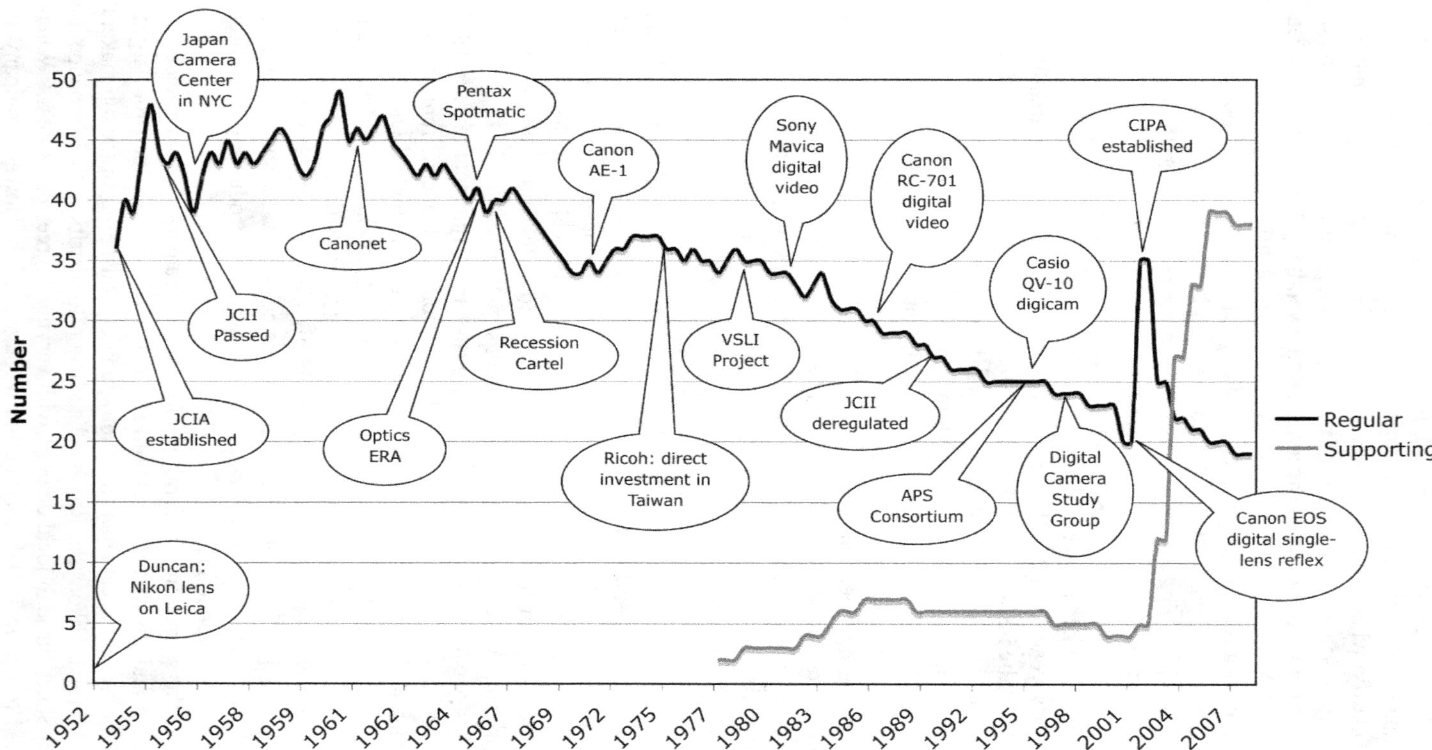

Figure 9.1 JCIA–CIPA membership, 1952–2008 (sources: JCIA, *Nihon kamera kōgyōshi*, Tokyo: JCIA, 1987, pp. 336–48; CIPA, *Camera Industry in Japan*, Tokyo: CIPA, 2004, p. 82; www.cipa.jp/english/annal/kaiin.html (accessed 2 June 2008, 10 February 2009); see text for additional sources).

1920s 1930s 1940s 1950s 1960s 1970s 1980s 1990s 2000s

35 mm Film — *Digital*

Optics innovations

- 1921 Leica's first 35 mm hand-held camera
- 1932 Leica Model II
- 1933 Contax Model I
- 1936 Hansa Canon 35 mm camera with Nikon lens
- 1951 Duncan uses Nikon lens with Leica camera
- 1951 Pentax single-lens reflex with return mirror
- 1961 Canon's Canonet and mass production
- 1964 Pentax Spotmatic
- 1971 Canon AE-1; com-ponent-ization
- 1981 Sony Mavica digital still video
- 1986 Canon RC-701 digital still video
- 1996 APS 24 mm hybrid
- 1996 Casio QV-10 compact digital
- 2001 EOS Kiss (Rebel) digital single-lens reflex

Industry-specific institutions

- 1920s-1945/49 Optical Industry Conference
- 1954-2002: Japan Camera Industry Assn (JCIA); 2002~ Camera and Imaging Products Assn (CIPA)
- 1955-1989: Japan Camera Inspection Institute (JCII); 1989~ Japan Camera Industry Institute
- 1952~ Japan Camera (and Photography) Shows; Photo Industry Expo
- 1956-1964: Japan Camera Center (New York); 1964~ JETRO Light Machinery Center
- 1963: London and Dusseldorf Camera Centres; 1964~ JETRO Light Machinery Centre
- 1966: Bangkok Camera Center; 1967 Okinawa Camera Center
- 1964-81: Optics Engineering Research Association (ERA)
- 1976-79: Very Large Scale Integration (VSLI) Project

Legal institutions

- 1937: Restrictions on production of civilian goods; 1939-45: wartime production only
- 1946-49: Conversion to 'peace industries'
- 1949~ Export promotion; export-led growth
- 1955~ Export Inspection Law; 1955-89: 'JCII passed' stickers
- 1965~ Industrial Design Law (to ensure original industrial designs)
- 1965-66: Recession Cartel

Figure 9.2 Innovations and institutions in the optics industry, 1920–2009 (sources: see text).

1952 the response was '"Made in Japan" means cheap and shoddy goods here.'[41] Not having much success, the companies gradually gave up trying to do it on their own, and in 1955 joined with the JCIA and JCII (see below) to establish the Japan Camera Information and Repair Center in New York City.[42]

To address the problem of the poor perception of Japanese goods overseas, the Japanese government legislated that all export items must be inspected for quality. In the camera industry this meant the establishment of a highly effective export quality gatekeeper, the Japan Camera Inspection and Testing Institute (JCII), established in 1955. With export inspection assuring quality, industry leaders decided that the JCIA, along with the JCII, should promote exports directly in the US market and provide repair services to Japanese cameras already sold to US servicemen stationed in Japan. The new Center could act as a convenient source of information while providing access to new products produced by all JCIA members whose cameras and lenses passed export inspection, confirmed by the use of an oval black-and-gold seal stating 'JCII passed'.[43]

In 1961 Canon shocked all camera manufacturers when it introduced the Canonet, the world's first mass-produced camera. In response, in the following year, and in accordance with the Engineering Research Association (ERA) Law (*kōkōgyō gijitsu kenkyū kumiai-hō*), an optics ERA (*kōgaku kōgyō gijutsu kenkyū kumiai*) was established, with 30 per cent of its budget from MITI (METI).[44] The optics ERA provided leadership in an industry characterized by many small firms to advance the research on lens technology being done by the firms themselves. Its specific objectives were: to improve lens calculation techniques that would raise lens quality; to introduce plastics and electronics into production; to use computers in manufacturing; and to achieve automatic exposure and automatic focusing technologies. In 1962 the optics ERA had forty-four members and by its end in 1981 thirty-six members. It had the longest duration, at nineteen years (the average in the 1960s was eleven and a half years and in the 1970s six years) and the most members (the average in the 1960s was seventeen members and in the 1970s twelve members).[45]

The Tokyo Olympics of 1964 saw the introduction of the Pentax Spotmatic, the most popular and best-selling SLR of that time. In preparation for the Olympics, where cameras (among other goods) could be sold to international visitors tax-free, all of the top manufacturers expanded production in anticipation of great demand. Expanded supply was satisfactory to meet demand during the Olympics, but once the Olympics ended, production capacity exceeded domestic demand, placing pressure on prices. Leading manufacturers also took advantage of a government measure allowing them to create a temporary recession cartel with the purpose of averting price gouging and preventing smaller companies from being run out of business.[46] The cartel proved most beneficial to the 'Big Five' firms – Nikon, Canon, Minolta, Olympus and Ricoh – that controlled over 50 per cent of the market and thus held structural power in the JCIA. Pentax felt the negative effects of the recession cartel keenly; their wildly popular Spotmatic camera suffered production restrictions during the cartel (1965–66) so that others could offload their excess cameras at reasonable prices.

Firms also began moving overseas in search of new markets. Ricoh became the first imaging firm to engage in foreign direct investment (FDI) in East Asia, setting up a facility in Taiwan in 1972.[47] The remaining Big Five firms followed thereafter, eventually expanding from small representative offices to large-scale manufacturing.

In 1971 Canon again challenged its competitors technologically with the introduction of the world's first computerized camera, the AE-1, which was far cheaper to manufacture than cameras with precision-machined parts, due to its component-based content. At this time, Canon began the practice of hiring professional athletes and other celebrities to advertise its products.

Later in that decade, Canon and Nikon and, to a lesser extent, Minolta became junior partners of the Very Large Scale Integration (VLSI) project (1976–79), a joint government–industry technology development project sponsored by MITI (METI).[48] The objectives of the project were to allow many firms with different areas of expertise to come together in a large-scale research effort that no single company could have been able to finance – or marshal all the technological capabilities needed – alone. Although essentially a project aimed at improving the international competitiveness of the electronics industry, the manufacture of integrated circuits required optics technology for the masking and printing functions. Nikon and Canon became world leaders in the manufacture of new industrial products, e.g. steppers and mask aligners, used in the manufacture of semiconductors.

The Sony Mavica introduced in 1981 was the first functioning prototype of a digital still movie camera.[49] Although the technology was not ready for commercial production, the innovation shook the industry, heralding the coming of a new filmless photographic camera. As with technological change, no one knew how slowly or quickly the change would occur. Five years later, in 1986, Canon introduced its first digital still video camera, the RC-701, developed out of the video department, not the camera department. Nearly a decade later, in 1995, Casio succeeded in producing an inexpensive compact digital still camera, the QV-10.

To prepare the consumer for the jump from the old standard, 35 mm photographic film, to the new digital photographic format (a 24 mm standard), industry leaders created a hybrid, the Advanced Photo System (APS) using 24 mm photographic film that allowed smaller, thinner compact cameras. The APS gained popularity with photographers in the United States and Europe, but was largely ignored in Japan. The APS Consortium, led by Kodak, comprised a combination of photographic film and optics manufacturers, namely Canon, Fujifilm, Minolta and Nikon. From the late 1990s, the market for digital cameras exploded as manufacturing capability improved, and, most important, as information storage capabilities developed large enough capacity to hold data-rich photographs.

For some time, it had been clear that Japanese camera, optical and precision measuring instrument manufacturers no longer required the export inspection services of the JCII. During the 1970s and 1980s, the JCII had become a world resource for industry standards-setting expertise. Responding to changes in the industry, the JCII was 'deregulated' in 1989 as part of fall-out from efforts to minimize direct government regulation or micro-management of industry.[50] The transition of the JCII to an industry information resource was relatively painless.

In the JCIA, the dramatic shift to digital imaging forced industry-leading firms to take action. In typical fashion, they first set up a study group in 1996 to focus on digital cameras. The study group eventually moved from the periphery to the centre of the JCIA as film-type camera sales plummeted and leading manufacturers moved decisively into the mass production of digital cameras in 2000 and 2001. On 30 June 2002 the JCIA was dissolved and re-established the next day as the CIPA.

The benefits of horizontal linkages

The general ethos among firms in Japan in the early post-war years was to export or die. As a result, the industry association members were keen to comply with government policy initiatives directed at export promotion. It is no coincidence that the leading firms of the JCIA, the 'Big Five', were also Japan's most successful exporters.[51] Information exchange was often in connection with technological issues and standards in the 1950s and 1960s, although this proved to be less true over time and as competition among the top firms grew in intensity. The effect was that many specific horizontal linkages fell away,[52] but the network of intra-industry loops was not so easily dissolved.

The creation and existence of the optics ERA substantiates clearly the importance of linkages and loops across silo-type organizations on technical issues pertaining directly to the development of the industry. The forty-four firms producing optics requested the creation of the ERA to help stimulate leadership in the industry.[53] The background of constant improvements in cameras, from the introduction of automatic exposure in the early 1960s to the incorporation of injection moulding in the camera bodies (and later in the interchangeable lenses) to the development of computerized components for single-lens reflex cameras in the 1970s (and later in compact cameras) paralleled technological changes that were taking place elsewhere in the economy, primarily pioneered by other firms (in e.g. process manufacturing and electronics). The appearance of new materials and new technologies in cameras – which in the early 1960s were thought to be simple, precision machinery products – underlines the impact of horizontal institutions that fostered communication.[54] Horizontal institutions such as the ERA linked up firms (which generally were organized silo-fashion in the economy) so they could share know-how regarding the direction of the industry's development through e.g. improving manufacturing processes and finding ways to build new, emerging technologies into existing products.

The VLSI project also underlines why horizontal linkages and loops were important, as optical engineering expertise was to be found only in the optics firms.[55] There were no other avenues of employment in the economy for rising stars in optical engineering except the leading optics firms. This was a key limitation of the VLSI project, as the electronics firms could not develop advanced integrated circuits without developing steppers and mask aligners, that is, industrial equipment required very precise optics technology. Since the electronics firms did not have the capability to develop the optical technology required for the project, optics industry leaders Nikon, Canon and, to a lesser extent, Minolta assisted with the VLSI project's goals. The cross-fertilization of technological goals among the firms was effective such that Nikon and Canon are now two of a total of three manufacturers of steppers, machines that are critical to the manufacture of integrated circuits.

The status quo and power

Throughout the forty-eight years of the JCIA, the Big Five firms took the top leadership positions in the industry association, rotating every few years. Executives from the Big Five always took the post of president, and the second-tier firms filled the vice-president positions. When Ricoh decided to pull out of the consumer side of the optics industry in the early 1970s, the leading firms decided to maintain the status quo of five, and allowed Pentax to replace Ricoh. Pentax, originally a specialist optics maker, had scored top points with innovations such as the instant return mirror for the single-lens reflex camera and the popular Spotmatic camera, allowing it to move into the top tier. As one of the Big Five, it became a strong leader in the JCIA, actively fulfilling its duties as president despite being a much smaller company than the other Big Five.

A decade later, in 1981, Sony smashed the tranquillity of the status quo when it introduced the Mavica, an innovative digital movie camera. Sony was *not* one of the JCIA Big Five firms; it was an electronics firm without its own in-house optics technology. Many of the initial innovations in digital cameras (both still and video) arose from video camera makers, both in the optics and electronics industries. Canon, for example, produced both film cameras in the camera division and video digital cameras in the video division.[56] This caused some confusion regarding brand names and brand image; it was not until 2000 that the camera and video divisions were able to develop synergies clearly visible in the unification of brand names for digital cameras (e.g. the Canon ELPH, called IXY in Japan, which began as an APS brand and later became the Digital ELPH/Digital IXY) and the rapid proliferation of Canon's digital camera offerings after 2000.[57] While the power of the electronics companies was strong, the optics companies were secure in the knowledge that history was repeating itself; only they had the technology and know-how to manufacture optics to the highest international standard. As digital camera sales grew in the early 2000s, firms began to ramp up for mass production, moving much of the low-technology manufacturing overseas to Asia.[58]

As the industry consolidated around digital imaging (which signalled the long, slow end of the photographic film era) the number of regular members in the JCIA began to fall off markedly (see Figure 9.1). Partly this was due to mergers and other changes as firms adjusted to the new technological race, some withdrawing and others experimenting with developing digital imaging products. Over the period 1952–2008 the curve indicates a slightly steeper downturn in regular membership numbers after the introduction of the Sony Mavica. At the same time the number of supporting members – originally international (i.e. non-Japanese) firms and later those in the electronics industry who participated in (among others) the digital camera study group – grew. When the CIPA was established, the regular membership peaked dramatically, thereafter returning to the trend while the number of supporting members rose rapidly.

After 2002 four of the original Big Five firms remained in power within the industry association – Canon, Nikon, Olympus and Pentax – with the addition of four new lead members – Casio, Matsushita, Sharp and Sony – from the electronics industry.[59] Leadership in optics and electronics, the two technological areas key to digital imaging, conferred power in the reformed industry association. Power was not determined by relative corporate size. In Figure 9.3, selected alliances and relationships between optics makers and electronics makers are indicated with the Big Eight in bold. With the merger of Minolta and Konica in 2003, followed by its decision in 2006 to license Minolta's 'alpha' single-lens reflex camera and optics technology to Sony, Konica-Minolta withdrew altogether. The arrows in Figure 9.3 indicate the direction of technology

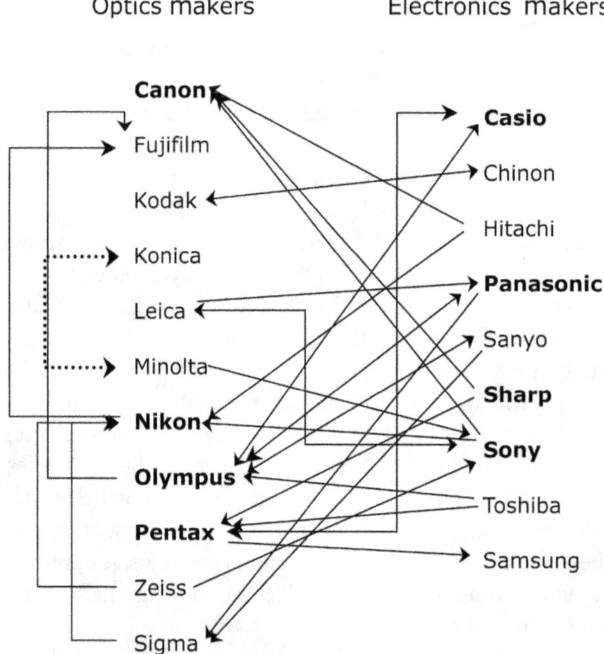

Figure 9.3 Selected alliances and relationships in digital imaging (sources: based on the author's research; also see the text for specific sources).

Notes

(1) Solid arrows indicate the direction of technology and/or supply relationships; (2) the companies in bold type are the Big Eight: four optics and four electronics; (3) Konica and Minolta merged in 2003, as indicated by the dotted line; (4) Sony licensed Minolta's 'alpha' series from 2006.

arrangements between the firms that supplied digital imaging electronics and those that supplied optics and image-processing technology. The relationships and alliances are highly complex and tend to be determined by the price and quality of individual end products. The acquisition by Hoya of Pentax is not reflected in these figures, as Pentax's technology is world-class, and Hoya is keeping the Pentax brand active for the present.[60]

This discussion highlighted the evolutionary changes that occurred in the industry association as it managed the technological change from film to digital. The evidence demonstrates that the industry association did not become powerless in response to the spectre of change. Rather, leaders in the association monitored developments in digital imaging as they emerged, even experimenting with the hybrid APS format. When the time came to make the JCIA defunct, industry leaders were able to embrace the situation and relatively rapidly dissolve the JCIA, replacing it with the CIPA. In so doing, leaders of the top firms kept their positions of power, becoming members of the Big Eight and splitting the responsibilities of running the CIPA between optics firms and electronics firms equally.

Conclusion: adapting to change

The JCIA–CIPA story provides an interesting case study of the process of change, showing how structural power, that is, power vested in the structure of the association, was exercised to allow firms to embrace change. It shows how adjustment occurs within coordinated economies when those in power choose to find creative solutions. Clearly, the leaders of the JCIA deliberated on how to bring about a successful transformation, and the process of change took time. Those in power in the JCIA were able to retain their positions and take control of the new industry association (the CIPA), sharing their power with leaders in the electronics industry.

Although it is not clear today, the CIPA may continue to evolve, becoming a new type of network without a physical 'bricks and mortar' location. It might be composed of optics manufacturers as well as others who have specific skill sets such as legal, logistical or financial skills that satisfy specific industry needs. The primary function of supplying industry information is likely to be augmented by lobbying, and as a global network it could take on lobby jobs that cross national borders. Similar types of inter-organizational institutions have developed into vast networks of individuals with interests in particular industries.[61] The Photo Imaging Expo (PIE) held in Tokyo every March has become a central focus of the CIPA, the lead organizer; PIE offers network-building opportunities to global industry players and could become the core of the future CIPA.[62]

In this chapter I focused on *zaidan hōjin*, institutions that are often seen as cartels. Inter-organizational institutions such as industry associations played a key role in horizontally linking companies – separate, vertical silo-type organizations – because they created and sustained intra-industry loops of communication among firms and non-firm organizations.[63] Horizontal networks supported a variety of functions, including transmitting the consensus opinion of firms in the industry to MITI (METI) when it suited their interests, e.g. forming the recession cartel and setting up the ERA. Lobbying also occurred through the Keidanren, especially in the early years when the survival of the firms was at greatest risk. Communication from the government also came through this channel, though in later years firms were less inclined to follow bureaucratic advice.

Coordinated market economies have many types of inter-organizational institutions, e.g. cooperative associations, business groups, industry associations and intra-industry networks. If we overlook the function and behaviour of such groups – groups that may or may not behave as cartels – we risk ignorance of institutions that play important roles, especially in coordinated economies. If these business groups, cooperative associations and the like do not offer beneficial service or play a helpful role in the sociopolitical economy, then it would be wise to know what they actually do. Highly competitive (and larger numbers of) businesses can coexist with positive regulation. Suspicion and fear need not be the drivers of regulation.

Communication across industries is beneficial to both society and business, therefore it is imperative to examine the institutions that support and surround industries and understand their historical trajectories. Taking into account the rich fabric of the political and economic system, I argue that studies of institutions that lie under the radar can intensify and deepen our understanding of the process of change.[64] The nature of these institutions and the assumption of their predatory nature – of businessmen who whenever they are in conversation seek to cheat the consumer – present an interesting research agenda, as we know so little about them. These institutions operate within the market in many instances for the public good. Keeping in mind that their primary objective is profit, businesses can and should be monitored and when necessary regulated. Undesirable, socially unacceptable and irresponsible behaviour can and should be understood and suppressed.

Acknowledgements

I would like to express my gratitude to Justine Bornstein for her extensive comments on an earlier version of this chapter, to Michael Witt and David Leheny for their insights, and to all the participants of the workshop on Japan's political economy in Stockholm June 2008 for their thought-provoking discussions, in particular Glenn Hook, Cornelia Storz and Marie Söderberg. All errors, omissions and oversights are my own.

Notes

1 See http://nonprofitjapan.home.igc.org/npo/npojp.html (accessed 2 February 2009); and T. Onishi, 'Current Conditions and Development Strategies of Philanthropy and Fundraising in Japan: A Comparative Study of the United States and Japan', Indiana University, no date, p. 7, www.afpnet.org/content_documents/onishi_fundraising_japan.pdf (accessed 2 February 2009).

2 B. C. Dees, *The Allied Occupation and Japan's Economic Miracle: Building the Foundations of Japanese Science and Technology, 1945–1952*, Richmond, UK: Japan Library/Curzon Press, 1997, p. 209. The Osaka Voluntary Action Center created in 2005 a comprehensive list of the English equivalents of various Japanese legal terms and types of organizations; their terms are used here.

3 R. A. Colingon and C. Usui, *Amakudari: The Hidden Fabric of Japan's Economy*, Ithaca, NY: Cornell University Press, 2003, p. 104.

4 Hall and Soskice characterize coordinate market economies, including much of Europe and Japan, as economies that have many levels of coordination among the players. A rather different type of economy is the liberal market one such as the United States, the United Kingdom and Australia, which is organized around the liberal, neoclassical model (see P. Hall and D. Soskice, eds, *Varieties of Capitalism*, Oxford: Oxford University Press, 2001). This chapter draws from the comparative capitalism and historical institutionalism literature. On the comparative capitalism debate see J. R. Hollingsworth and R. Boyer (eds) *Comparative Capitalisms*, Cambridge: Cambridge University Press, 1998; G. Redding, 'The thick description and comparison of societal systems of capitalism', *Journal of International Business Studies* 36, 2005, 123–55; S. K. Vogel, *Japan Remodeled: How Government and Industry are Reforming Japanese Capitalism*, Ithaca, NY: Cornell University Press, 2005; M. A. Witt, *Changing Japanese Capitalism: Societal Coordination and Institutional Adjustment*, Cambridge: Cambridge University Press, 2006; on the historical institutionalism perspective in socioeconomics see K. Thelen, *How Institutions Evolve: The Political Economy of Skills in Germany, Britain, the United States, and Japan*, Cambridge: Cambridge University Press, 2004; W. Streeck and K. A. Thelen (eds) *Beyond Continuity: Institutional Change in Advanced Political Economies*, Oxford: Oxford University Press, 2005; and S. Steinmo, K. Thelen and F. Longstreth (eds) *Structuring Politics: Historical Institutionalism and Comparative Analysis*, Cambridge: Cambridge University Press, 1992.

5 Industry associations are organizations in that they are collections of actors bound together for the achievement of specific goals, and their behaviour may be modified by rules, regulations and accepted practices and norms. Part of the challenge is to identify what is desirable; it is far easier to identify undesirable behaviour.

6 Isolated organizations that do not have well established links or communication with outsiders are called 'silos'. This is an allusion to grain silos that in order to function as grain storage containers are tall, enclosed and have few entrances and exits.

7 See Hall and Soskice, *Varieties of Capitalism*; Redding, 'The thick description and comparison of societal systems of capitalism'; G. Redding and M. A. Witt, *The Future of Chinese Capitalism*, Oxford: Oxford University Press, 2007; Witt, *Changing Japanese Capitalism*.

8 www.economist.com/research/economics/searchActionTerms.cfm?query=cartel; and U. Schaede, *Cooperative Capitalism: Self-regulation, Trade Associations and the Anti-Monopoly Law in Japan*, Oxford: Oxford University Press, 2000, p. 30.

9 It should be noted that such institutions often coordinate in a different fashion in liberal market economics.

10 See respectively www.merriam-webster.com/dictionary/cartel (accessed 1 June 2008); www.askoxford.com/concise_oed/cartel?view=uk (accessed 1 June 2008); and www.economist.com/research/economics/searchActionTerms.cfm?query=cartel (accessed 1 June 2008).

11 See Redding and Witt, *The Future of Chinese Capitalism*, 2007, p. 20; and P. L. Berger and T. Luckmann, *The Social Construction of Reality*, London: Penguin, 1966.

12 Hall and Soskice, *Varieties of Capitalism*; M. A. Witt and A. Y. Lewin, 'Outward foreign direct investment as escape response to home country institutional constraints', *Journal of International Business Studies* 38 (4), 2007, 579–94.

13 Christensen argues that disruptive innovations bring about rapid change for which industry players are unprepared. See, for example, C. M. Christensen and M. Overdorf, 'Meeting the challenge of disruptive change', *Harvard Business Review*, March–April 2000.

14 See S. Strange, *States and Markets*, 2nd edn, London: Pinter, 1984, p. 25. See also J. M. Stopford and S. Strange, *Rival States, Rival Firms: Competition for World Market Shares*, Cambridge: Cambridge University Press, 1991.

15 Dees, *The Allied Occupation and Japan's Economic Miracle*, p. 210. Bowen C. Dees was head of the ESS/ST.

16 Ibid., p. 211; see also S. Yonekura, 'The functions of industry associations' in T. Okazaki and M. Okuno Fujiwara (eds) *The Japanese Economic System and its Historical Origins*, Oxford: Oxford University Press, 1999, pp. 180–207.

17 R. Pekkanen, 'Japan's new politics: the case of the NPO law', *Journal of Japanese Studies* 26 (1), 2000, 111–48. For additional background about NPOs in Japan see also http://nonprofitjapan.home.igc.org/npo/npojp.html (accessed 2 February 2009) and Onishi, 'Current Conditions and Development Strategies of Philanthropy', no date, www.afpnet.org/content_documents/onishi_fundraising_japan.pdf (accessed 2 February 2009).

18 Since 1995 the Japan Association of Charitable Organizations (JACO), *kōeki hōjin kyōkai*, established in 1972, has investigated the best method for reforming Japan's PIC, including *zaidan hōjin*. In December 2005 the Cabinet decided to create a non-profit corporations (NPC) law to supersede the current PIC designation, to simplify the legal designation. JACO does not believe pure charities and foundations are one and the same and thus should not be lumped together. The legal status of non-profits is still under debate. See www.kohokyo.or.jp (accessed 1 June 2008) for details.

19 I would like to thank Akihiro Ogawa for pointing this out to me. The law also created new designations such as the Limited Liability Nonprofit Mutual Benefit Corporation, *yūgen sekinin chūkan hōjin*, a point that is germane to the case study in this chapter.

20 For further discussion of the structure of business organization in Japan see, for example, M. L. Gerlach, *Alliance Capitalism: The Social Organization of Japanese Business*, Berkeley, CA: University of California Press, 1992; N. Kikuchi, *Zaikai to wa nanika?* Tokyo: Heibonsha, 2005; G. Noble, *Collective Action in East Asia: How Ruling Parties Shape Industrial Policy*, Ithaca, NY: Cornell University Press, 1988; Schaede, *Cooperative Capitalism*, 2000.

21 See, for example, Colingon and Usui, *Amakudari*; C. Johnson, *MITI and the Japanese Miracle: The Growth of Industrial Policy, 1925–1975*, Stanford, CA: Stanford University Press, 1982; P. J. Katzenstein (ed.) *Between Power and Plenty: Foreign Economics Policies of Advanced Industrial States*, Madison, WI: University of Wisconsin Press, 1978; S. D. Krasner, *Defending the National Interest: Raw Materials Investments and U.S. Foreign Policy*, Princeton, NJ: Princeton University Press, 1978; D. I. Okimoto, *Between MITI and the Market: Japanese Industrial Policy for High Technology*, Stanford University Press, 1989.

22 See for example D. Friedman, *The Misunderstood Miracle: Industrial Development and Political Change in Japan*, Ithaca, NY: Cornell University Press, 1988; Noble, *Collective Action in East Asia*; R. Samuels, *The Business of the Japanese State: Energy Markets in Comparative and Historical Perspective*, Ithaca, NY: Cornell University Press, 1987; R. M. Uriu, *Troubled Industries: Confronting Economic Change in Japan*, Ithaca, NY: Cornell University Press, 1996; Yonekura, 'The functions of industry associations'.

23 H. Odagiri and A. Goto, *Technology and Industrial Development in Japan: Building Capabilities by Learning, Innovation and Public Policy*, Oxford: Clarendon Press, 1996; Yonekura, 'The functions of industry associations'.

24 B. Gao, *Economic Ideology and Japanese Industrial Policy: Developmentalism from 1931 to 1965*, Cambridge: Cambridge University Press, 1997; Odagiri and Goto,

Technology and Industrial Development; T. Okazaki and M. Okuno-Fujiwara, 'Japan's present-day economic system and its historical origins' in T. Okazaki and M. Okuno-Fujiwara (eds) *The Japanese Economic System and its Historical Origins*, Oxford: Oxford University Press, 1999, pp. 1–37; Schaede, *Cooperative Capitalism*; J. Teranishi, 'The main bank system' in T. Okazaki and M. Okuno Fujiwara (eds) *The Japanese Economic System and its Historical Origins*, Oxford: Oxford University Press, 1999, pp. 63–96; Witt, *Changing Japanese Capitalism*.

25 Uriu, *Troubled Industries*, p. 26.

26 *Amakudari*, or descent from heaven, is when bureaucrats retire and take a private-sector post usually linked with the work done at the Ministry. This is useful for the recipient for the network of contacts and potential influence held by the retired bureaucrat, and for the bureaucrat the benefit is in the additional income and general feeling of usefulness post-retirement.

27 Witt identifies three pure theoretical types of firm networks: Type I: horizontal networks (including horizontal keiretsu); Type II: vertical networks (including vertical keiretsu); and Type III: intra-industry networks. Witt, *Changing Japanese Capitalism*, 2006, pp. 95–101.

28 Many, though not all, industry associations are *zaidan hōjin*. The Ministry of International Trade and Industry (MITI) became the Ministry of Economy Trade and Industry (METI) in 2001.

29 The parallel objective was to avoid detrimental competition in which one company gained an upper hand, forcing many companies out of business due to a temporary situation that would pass (such as a temporary downturn in demand) but might leave the industry with an unbalanced structure (such as an oligopoly or one very large firm and a few small specialized ones).

30 Y. Kosai, 'The reconstruction period' in R. Komiya *et al.* (eds) *Industrial Policy of Japan*, London: Academic Press, 1988, pp. 25–48; Johnson, *MITI and the Japanese Miracle*.

31 Such top-down guidance often originated from MITI. Johnson argues that bureaucrats wielded a figurative 'sword' of power that made it difficult not to comply with MITI's guidance. Johnson, *MITI and the Japanese Miracle*, 1982.

32 Odagiri and Goto, *Technology and Industrial Development*.

33 J. Sigurdson, 'Industry and state partnership: the historical role of the engineering research associations in Japan', repr. *Industry and Innovation* 5 (2), 1998, 209–41 (originally published 1986).

34 In some cases, firms employed industry self-regulation through the industry association (see Schaede, *Cooperative Capitalism*, 2000). The emergence of the Euro-yen market in the early 1970s is another clear example of independence from bureaucratic control.

35 Photographic film is not the only type of photosensitive material; however, the decline of the silver halide film-type camera due to the rise of digital imaging has affected the association.

36 Other industry associations closely connected with the CIPA encompass products such as microscopes, binoculars, photographic lenses, business machines and watches.

37 The JCIA was a *zaidan hōjin*, and the CIPA is a Limited Liability Nonprofit Mutual Benefit Corporation, *yūgen sekinin chūkan hōjin*, a designation that came into being with the passage of the NPO law. The industry was originally called optics (*kōgaku*) in Japanese and camera (*kamera* in katakana) for the export market. There were several other early post-war associations established in part to support the government's goals of promoting exports of cameras, lenses and film. For additional background see P. A. Nelson, 'Putting Local Knowledge to Work in International Markets: The Valuable Role of the Impartial Third Party Negotiator', conference paper, Academy of International Business, 2007, available at www.ssrn.com.

38 For details see P. A. Nelson, 'The Effect of Innovation and Technological Change on Information Flows, Authority and Industry Associations in Japan', CIRJE Discussion Papers 2004-CF-301, Tokyo: Center for International Research on the Japanese Economy, University of Tokyo, 2004. Leica developed the world's first hand-held 35 mm camera in the early 1920s.
39 Canon devised a scheme immediately thereafter to encourage professional photographers to try their lenses and report on them.
40 JCIA, *Nihon Kamera Kōgyō Shi*, Tokyo: Japan Camera Industry Association, 1987, pp. 19–20; JCII, *Sekai no Nihon Kamera*, Tokyo: Japan Camera Inspection Institute, 1984, pp. 14–22.
41 *Japan Times*, 30 November 1961, as quoted in A. Miyabayashi, 'Japanese Camera Exports to the United States: A Case Study in Development and Competition', MBA thesis, City University of New York, June 1963, p. 115. Canon convinced Bell & Howell to become their US distributor from 1957. In 1973 Canon Sales took over all US distribution and by the following year had taken control of worldwide distribution. See Canon Inc., *The Canon Handbook*, Tokyo: Public Relations, Canon Inc., 1994.
42 For the first few months the Center operated out of the JETRO New York offices. Figure 9.2 shows that similar centres were opened in London, Düsseldorf, Bangkok and Okinawa.
43 JCII, *Sekai no Nihon Kamera*, 1984. Independent design was a problem, since all 35 mm cameras were modelled on the Leica and later the Contax (developed by Zeiss). To encourage new designs and ones that could not be called copies of German designs, the Design Law was enacted in 1965 and the Japan Machinery Design Centre (JMDC) was established. Thereafter design inspection was included in the JCII's activities and the 'Passed' sticker was adapted to include the JCII and JMDC names.
44 Sigurdson, 'Industry and state partnership'. The ERA law was enacted in 1961 by MITI to help small and medium enterprises in light and small machinery; however the *first* ERA was established in 1956 under MITI's Mechanical Engineering Laboratory.
45 In 1981 the defunct optics ERA was remade as the Japan Opto-Mechatronics Association.
46 Of all the cartels exempted from the Anti-monopoly Law over the 1955 to 1994 period, recession cartels were the least common; there was a peak in all cartels in the 1965–66 period, including recession cartels. Schaede, *Cooperative Capitalism*, p. 86.
47 See P. A. Nelson, 'Integrated production in East Asia: globalization without insulation?' in U. Schaede and W. W. Grimes (eds) *Japan's Managed Globalization: Adapting to the Twenty-first Century*, Armonk, NY: M. E. Sharpe, 2003, pp. 124–56.
48 M. Fransman, *The Market and Beyond: Information Technology in Japan*, Cambridge: Cambridge University Press, 1993.
49 Nelson, 'The effect of Innovation and Technological Change', 2004.
50 For an excellent discussion of how Japan has been remodelled see Vogel, *Japan Remodeled.*
51 Pentax replaced Ricoh when the latter pulled out of the industry in the late 1960s; Pentax became part of Hoya in April 2008.
52 Nelson, 'The Effect of Innovation and Technological Change', 2004.
53 Sigurdson, 'Industry and State Partnership'.
54 The product cycle thesis developed out of the experience of US firms up to the 1960s, suggested that countries moved out of relatively simple manufacturing as economies matured, letting countries with lower cost structures manufacture and sell to more advanced economies (see R. Vernon, 'International investment and international trade in the product cycle', *Quarterly Journal of Economics* 80, 1966, 190–207). It was thought that the more advanced economies would continuously move up the manufacturing chain into more complex goods; they would not bring technological complexity into 'simple' manufactured products because it was not believed that it could be done

or that it was desirable (see P. A. Nelson, 'Japanese high technology investment in East Asia: the case of the photography industry', *Pacific Focus* 14 (1), 1999, 159–83).

55 Fransman, *The Market and Beyond.*
56 Interviews with Canon, spring 2007.
57 E. Satoh *et al.*, 'Product Development Strategies and Price Dynamics: The Japanese Compact Digital Still Camera Industry, 1997–2005,' CPRC Discussion Papers CPDP-35-E, Competition Policy Research Center, Japan Fair Trade Commission, June 2008.
58 Nelson, 'Integrated production in East Asia'.
59 Pentax was by far the smallest of the Big Eight, yet due to the company's structural power in the JCIA it was able to remain in the top group in the CIPA.
60 Hoya's interest in Pentax was in the endoscope business, not the optics.
61 Global CONNECT and the San Diego Dialogue are two examples of such networks. See http://globalconnect.ucsd.edu and www.sandiegodialogue.org/initiatives.htm (accessed 2 February 2009).
62 See www.photoimagingexpo.com/info.html (accessed 9 February 2009).
63 Witt, *Changing Japanese Capitalism.*
64 Interestingly, they have been more thoroughly studied in Germany, Sweden, the United Kingdom and other parts of Europe.

10 Sources and processes of change

The case of the game software industry

Cornelia Storz

The Japanese innovation system appears to possess distinct weaknesses. In recent times, scholars have focused on the question of why Japan has been unable to establish new industries, as US firms did in the 1990s.[1] Japan's weaknesses seem to be especially obvious in the software and biotechnology industries, where Japanese firms are almost absent from the world market. In 2006 the Deutsche Bank declared that 'in Japan, incremental innovation is dominating at the expense of new future sectors',[2] and the OECD[3] stated in a policy brief that an 'upgrading [of] the national innovation system' is necessary. On the firm level, Collinson and Wilson[4] argued that path dependencies in innovation and human resource management caused inertia in Japanese organizations and impeded innovation beyond simple incremental improvements.

The reason for Japan's weakness is conventionally attributed to the mismatch of its innovation system to the needs of new industries. Namely, the system is said to offer incentives for 'catching up' with world leaders and diffusing knowledge within industries in Japan, but not for the creation of new industries. In particular, the rigidity of the Japanese labour market, insufficient inter-institutional knowledge flows, the closed nature of industrial organizations and the dominance of specific informal institutions, such as loyalty and diligence, have been identified as barriers.[5] The literature asserts that new industries need certain institutions and competences such as developed capital markets, open labour markets and a high specialization in new technologies, all of which Japan does not possess and will not be able to establish in the short term, given the path dependency of competence accumulation. This in turn will affect Japan's competitiveness.[6] Thus the literature maintains that the issue of undesired path dependencies is particularly true in its application to Japan.[7]

However, the weakness pointed out in Japan's most prominent 'failure', the software industry, must be juxtaposed with the fact that, in reality, Japan has a highly competitive game software industry.[8] In this subsector, Japanese firms such as Sony, Nintendo, Sega, Square Soft, Konami and Capcom belong to the most competitive worldwide.[9] These leading firms are not just minor players, as evidenced by the fact that Nintendo's turnover is about a seventh of Microsoft's, and about half of SAP's.[10] The success of the game software industry contradicts the literature mentioned above, indicating a specific weakness in the Japanese innovation system to establish new industries.

This chapter takes the success of the game software industry as a case study to examine and analyse the sources and processes of change within a national innovation system like Japan's. Recognizing the role of path dependency – a key concept in institutional economics which explains why a desirable institutional change does not take place even if it would lead to an increase in welfare for all people concerned – I go a step further in assessing how novelty does indeed emerge in a path-dependent system. As a central reason for the emergence of the game software sector in Japan, I isolate the property of plasticity – numerical and functional – of Japan's innovation system. Both numerical and functional plasticity result from the plasticity of its key configurations, namely institutions, competences and demand. By analysing the emergence of a new industry within the Japanese innovation system, I contribute to recent efforts to document how the resources for change and the emergence of new forms are in fact contained within systems themselves.

Understanding the inner processes and complexity of a rather new phenomenon calls for case study research that ultimately can be used for theory development. Accordingly, the research presented in this chapter is exploratory, qualitative, and based on case studies (see Appendix).

National innovation systems and sources of change

The focus of innovation systems research has been on the reasons for the relatively stable outcome of systems, in particular in the sense of specialization of technologies. There are different concepts of innovation systems, but they all share the interpretation that institutions, competences and demand are key configurations of innovation systems. More specifically, the design of institutions and inter-institutional interfaces, the specific accumulation of knowledge[11] and the domestic market and its quality of demand,[12] all influence the rate and direction of innovative activities, i.e. the way people relate to each other and how they exchange and use their knowledge.[13] Path dependency is an important explanation as to why, despite the ongoing global integration of production processes, the respective specializations and comparative strengths of nations still remain relatively stable.[14]

Increasing returns and positive feedback lead to stability in the system, but may at the same time induce a 'lock-in' into paths that become undesirable over the long term. Stability, which is basically a desirable state, may thus turn into rigidity. Applied to innovation systems, this means that there is certainly a chance that changes and adaptations that are necessary and desirable take place only to an insufficient degree.[15] The difficulty in escaping such an undesirable outcome explains why, for so many years, research has been interested in addressing the question of why and under which conditions lock-in takes place, as well as examining under which conditions and through which processes an unlocking can be expected.[16] The increasing concern with how change takes place is evident in different theoretical approaches, such as the concept of national innovation systems, approaches of the varieties of capitalism, and comparative institutional economics. The most conventionally proposed explanation is the argument that change is introduced externally, exemplified by North's well known phrase 'windows of opportunity'[17] or by what other authors refer to as exogenous shocks.[18]

Although these approaches are important, they fail to consider sufficiently internal factors that offer resources for forming and transforming the system and thus lead to change. In order to understand these internal processes of change, the concepts of national innovation systems are helpful. Quite early on, these concepts stressed that national innovation systems are not monolithic in nature but, rather, consist of different subsystems which often even contradict the logic of the national innovation system. Examples include regional and local innovation systems,[19] even if the degree of variety depends on the respective national governance system,[20] and sectoral systems and technological regimes, which can extend beyond national borders and add a further element of diversity and multiplicity.[21] Even if these sub- and metasystems are often not directly related to questions of change, these subsystems can be interpreted as offering optional sources for change.[22] Although it has not been much of a focus in the literature, the approach of identifying subsystems in given systems could also be enlarged to other kinds of systems, such as subsystems formed by small and medium enterprises.

Internal sources of change in innovation systems

In this chapter, I propose that plasticity is a concept ideally suited to explain how internally induced changes take place in systems. I choose the term 'plasticity' since it describes perfectly two important trends that characterize change.

First, although path dependence serves as a framework for the actors in the system, path dependence is in fact moulded and adapted by plasticity, through the reinterpretation of its given institutions and through the combination of dominant and peripheral institutions. In so doing, the concept of plasticity dissociates itself from Schumpeter's concept of 'creative destruction' as a pattern for change, an implicitly assumed concept which often dominates the literature on innovation management.[23]

Second, there is a further argument stemming from the discussion of 'related varieties', which states that subsectors of sectors each need different institutions, competences and demand.[24] The concept of plasticity follows the argument of 'related varieties', although differs in that actors also draw upon peripheral sources and create their own 'fitting' sectoral system. In the following, I will explain this concept more in depth.

I identify two sources of plasticity which allow dynamics and change in innovation systems: numerical and functional plasticity. *Numerical plasticity* results from the coexistence of different, often mutually incoherent configurations (institutions, competences and demand). In other words, the number of configurations related to the whole system indicates the property of numerical plasticity in a given system.

Amable[25] has categorized these elements into dominant[26] and peripheral institutions, each providing different incentives for behaviour, and has argued that institutions are there less to serve a certain function but more as a result of negotiations between the multitude of actors. When we enlarge Amable's concept of institutions more generally to configurations in an innovation system (institutions, competences and demand), this concept helps us in conceptualizing the possible variety and change in systems. Furthermore, as recognized in the literature on regional innovation systems, technological paths and sectoral innovation systems, a variety of peripheral systems may exist outside the dominant system and in fact may follow a different logic from the dominant system. An example for the Japanese case would be open labour markets (as an institution being 'outside' the dominant model), or competences in design (as competences which are not at the core of the Japanese innovation system).

The second source of change is the *functional plasticity* of an innovation system's configurations. Functional plasticity refers to the adaptability and mouldability of configurations to new ends, functions and purposes. For example, a new function may be ascribed to existing institutions, or conventional institutions may be enlarged to new functions by a combination with peripheral institutions. Since established configurations may be transferred to new ends, there is relatively high stability in the system while at the same time there is room for new operations. Thus, in order to create a 'fitting' surrounding for a new industry, innovative actors may create their own (sectoral) innovation system which combines and/or enlarges dominant and peripheral institutions, competences and demand. This is an ongoing process and becomes a further precondition for the emergence of new industries, which we, along with Augier and Teece,[27] call 'evolution with design'.

The Japanese game software sector

Game software products belong to a group of packaged software products, and it is only in this sub-category of the software sector that Japanese firms are internationally successful. This is remarkable and necessitates an explanation.

In terms of software in general, Japanese firms started exporting only in the mid-1990s, as up to that time, software firms had concentrated on the Japanese home market.[28] This is reflected in the trade balance of this period, where Japan showed high deficits in software products trade. However, there is one exception, namely in the trade in games. Whereas Japan shows deficits in the trade of basic, application and custom software, it shows a surplus in game software.[29] Although no official international data exist for this period, different sources confirm that, despite recent weaknesses, Japanese game software producers possess a strong position in the world market. Among the top ten game software publishers, five are Japanese (Sega, Nintendo, Sony, Square Enix and Konami). In the United States, thirteen of the fifty top-selling titles are Japanese, while, in contrast, almost no US software is sold in Japan. In 2005, 51.9 per cent of Japanese software was exported, 59.8 per cent of it to the United States, 36.3 per cent to Europe and 3.5 per cent to Asia.[30] Further, and remarkably, the International

Game Developers' Association (IGDA) awarded Japan a high share of awards in the categories of 'Lifetime Achievement' (three out of seven) and 'Visual Arts' (five out of seven) between 2001 and 2007.

Typically, a game's software becomes attractive to consumers for its variety and originality, even if it is true that hardware innovations are relevant to innovative game development.[31] Due to the mutual dependence of hardware (including SCE, Nintendo and recently Microsoft) and software producers, their relationship has been described as 'symbiotic'.[32] Game software is produced by so-called game software publishers. These publishers can, in the case of the largest firms, at the same time be hardware manufacturers, or specialized, independent software publishers which develop and produce game software on their own and sell their products to hardware makers. In addition, there are smaller software houses which due to restraints on their resources only develop the software and transfer production and marketing to the game software publishers. These smaller firms often operate solely in the domestic market, serving niches of a certain genre. SCE and Nintendo outsource the development of their game software at a rate of about 80 per cent and 20 per cent respectively (in numbers of items).

The Japanese innovation system: dominant configurations

The Japanese institutional setting induces the accumulation of certain competences and a distinct specialization, which I will outline below. This outline serves as a frame of reference for my consideration of the emergence of the game software subsector in Japan. I refer to two core institutional settings which are most central for specialization in innovation, namely the industrial organization and the labour market.[33]

Despite certain trends towards convergence, Japanese industrial organization is still characterized by long-term, quite exclusive transaction relations. In fact, at the level of first-tier suppliers, there is evidence of even greater intensification of interaction. Institutions which form the basis for long-term transactions and aim at knowledge exchange are dispatches of personnel between firms or the well known suppliers' associations. Further, and related to long-term transactions, is the institution of sponsored spin-offs. Sponsored spin-offs are a form of semi-private corporate venture capital, given by former employers as temporary investments in the start-ups founded by former employees. About 14 per cent of start-ups are sponsored by former employers, and this share is relatively stable.[34]

The labour market is characterized by a high degree of stability, and human capital is strongly bound to firms, as reflected in the length of employment, which is about double that in the United States.[35] Additionally, the exit options are lower, due to high opportunity costs. Nonaka and Takeuchi (1995), among others, have stressed that the J-firm possesses strengths in the use of implicit knowledge and in internal knowledge creation due to the structure of the Japanese labour market and the characteristics of the Japanese employment system. These institutions and competences belong to the conventionally perceived most 'dominant' innovation system which I call the 'J-system', in allusion to Aoki's 'J-firm',[36] and the concepts of national innovation systems discussed above.

This J-system has, as outlined above, been criticized for its inflexibility, and for its inability to give birth to new industries. Critics argue that in a radically changing technological environment these configurations are obsolete, and create a barrier to innovation. For example, the critics maintain that the industrial organization of Japanese firms is insufficiently open to new actors, stifling competition within and, in the case of software, between groups. The commitment to manufacturing means that competences beyond manufacturing are less acquired. This attitude is said to give rise to a common framing towards non-material technologies as being only 'add-ons' to manufactured hardware. The strength in systemic, integral technologies induces a weakness in modular design, which is characteristic of many new industries. By the same token, long-term employment hinders the mobility of human capital and thus the opening up of new industries. For instance, there is almost no researcher mobility between research organizations and firms, and academic entrepreneurship is almost non-existent.[37] This makes the creation of new industries difficult, since new industries are based on new knowledge stocks. These formal institutions are embedded in a socioeconomic system which stresses integration, group orientation and loyalty, but places no value on creativity and individuality.[38]

To sum up, the setting in which Japanese firms operate is seen as suitable for learning strategies which turn innovation into a continuous stream of high-quality, mass-produced, integral products. Relative comparative advantages (RCA), measured by share of exports/imports and the relative share of world trade (even if both indicators are not without controversy), indeed show that Japan has strong comparative advantages in those commodity groups which belong (except microelectronics) to medium to high-technology sectors and are characterized by integral product architectures and a pronounced necessity of coordination.[39]

However, it is argued that these very institutions also work as a barrier to the creation of new, more innovative industries. In fact, Japan's low international competitiveness in new industries came as quite a shock and led to serious discussion about the adaptability of the Japanese innovation system. In a broad consensus, both within and outside Japan, the necessity of reform was recognized.[40] The common explanation for the problem was that Japan's specific institutional settings and accumulated competences were inappropriate to new technological needs.[41] However, as we will see later, these same dominant configurations in fact play an important role in the emergence of the game software sector, in that they were combined, enlarged and transferred to new ends and uses.

A second glance: the Japanese innovation system through numerical plasticity

Hitherto, I have described the 'dominant' characteristics of the Japanese innovation system. Dominance refers to those characteristics in which Japan 'differs' from other countries, as, for example, the general preference for long-term transactions or long-term employment. At the same time, however, particularly differentiated research on Japan has stressed that, besides the dominant logic, there are in fact other institutional settings, competences and innovative demand, such as more open labour markets among small and medium enterprise firms, or more open transaction patterns in sectors outside the three dominant export-oriented sectors (transport, electronics and machinery). I will now turn to these conventionally neglected peripheral configurations.

Indeed, a second glance at Japan's innovation system reveals far more resources of variety. The discussion in the following section is based on thirty-two interviews (see Appendix) that were conducted to shed more light on the subject. In this section I will show how Japanese publishers introduced peripheral configurations into the game software industry, and why these peripheral configurations contributed to the successful emergence of the industry.

First, among game software publishers we find an industrial organization pattern which differs in its logic from the strategic investment pattern in the automobile, electronics and (partially) machinery industries. Specifically, game software publishers have refrained from investing in their cooperation partners. This holds true not only for SCE and Nintendo, which have refrained from investing in their main cooperating partners, but also for independent game software publishers (such as Square Enix or Bandai Namco) who also do not invest in their cooperating partners. This kind of industrial organization stands in sharp contrast to the more hierarchical organization in the core industries.[42] Even if it is difficult to quantify the degree of institutional change, it does appear that a very pronounced change took place in the industrial organization.

Second, even though game software publishers retained traditional practices in the labour market as well as in human resource management (HRM) practices, this institutional setting was also changed to an astonishing extent (see the next section). As previously stated, although internal labour markets are a core of the 'J-system', among small and medium enterprises (SMEs) one finds quite open and fluid labour markets as well as a variety of different HRM practices[43] such as performance-based incentives and career systems, which are flexibly implemented. This, however, does not imply that the dominant system does not also have its own highly competitive incentive mechanisms.

Taking a closer look at SMEs, it is remarkable that SMEs play a much more important role in the economy than they do in most other OECD countries. In fact, SMEs represent 99.2 per cent of all firms (most of them being spin-offs from other SMEs), and 79.9 per cent of all employees.[44] This pattern has held true since Japan's post-war era. From the 1960s until the end of the 1980s, the number of SME entries has by far exceeded the exits.[45] The shifting of resources to new sectors has been the norm in post-war Japan. This fact of mobility is hidden by the dominant notion of a lack of entrepreneurship in Japan, and is expressed in international rankings.[46] Indeed, the dynamic has slowed down in recent years, but this took place, first, in face of an above-average level of activity of SMEs and, secondly, in face of exits of less productive, mainly tiny firms without successors.[47] This pattern has been transferred to the new game sector, where, at least until 2000, the sector was very dynamic, characterized by numerous market entries by spin-offs, mainly out of SMEs.

The large presence of SMEs reflects a high level of entrepreneurship and indicates that the conventionally identified norms of group orientation, social harmony and collectivity have always coexisted with individualism.[48] All surveys of start-ups show that the central motivations to found a business are: to realize one's own dream, to try out one's own potential and to be independent.[49] It is only a slight exaggeration to take these entrepreneurs as a representative class of Japanese society who, being sceptical about traditional norms, have always looked for options outside the conventional employment system. Since the labour market among SMEs is relatively open, the opportunity costs for company founders are quite low. The change in society's values, which is heavily stressed in recent literature on Japanese society, seems to be overstated in the light of these strong roots of individualism.[50]

Recently the dynamism in starting-up a firm in the game software sector has decreased, but the 1990s exhibited a very vibrant environment. In Tokyo there are some 200–300 game software developers, all of which were founded during the last twenty years, and of these about 70 per cent have a paid-up capital of less than JPY 50 million. Thus, according to the Japanese industry classification, they belong to the class of small and medium-size enterprises. Most of the current developers were founded isochronously with the launch of new hardware of Nintendo, Sony or (earlier) Sega in the 1980s (notably Famicom Mega Drive) and in the 1990s (e.g. PlayStation, Sega Saturn 1994 and Super Famicon).[51] These high entry rates can partially be explained by high profits. Baba and Shibuya[52] found that, among the top fifty firms by turnover, the majority were small and medium-size firms. The stagnation of the domestic market, partially due to the appearance of second-hand game software shops, currently acts as a break on entrepreneurial dynamism. According to my own survey, though, most actors in the Japanese game software sector – be they publishers, developers or smaller suppliers – were confident about the future development of the sector, and expected an overall positive business outlook. One reason is that new platforms by new consoles (including Nintendo's Wii and Sony's PlayStation 3), and especially mobile telephones, offer new opportunities for game software firms. It can be assumed that the former dynamism was facilitated by the open industrial organization, which made entry quite easy and at the same time allowed leading firms to draw upon a pool of talents.

Furthermore, the labour market also witnessed new HRM practices. Again, as we know from the literature, SMEs often experiment with new forms of management,[53] for example the creation of new career lines or the active inclusion of mid-career workers. We also observe this in the game software industry, where, for instance, the recruitment process is comparatively open. A quite typical approach is to recruit part-timers who, if evaluated as being talented enough for the firm, are employed as contract workers, and ultimately even as regular employees. A further example is that quite commonly certain sub-grades of the ranking system are bypassed. This is discussed in more detail below.

The above discussion centred on the numerical plasticity of institutions. I would now like to turn to the numerical plasticity of competences and demand. The most central competence which existed at the periphery of Japan's innovation system is *manga*, a competence actually developed in numerous peripheral institutional settings, including the *manga* drawing clubs. The drawing of *manga* is a competence developed over many decades, with some authors even arguing that the Japanese woodblock prints of the nineteenth century are its direct forerunners. But even if this is not the case, *manga* is a blossoming industry in Japan and has developed into an important internationally successful one[54] that has attracted numerous sketch artists, painters and authors. In terms of game software, Japanese firms could draw on a pool of talented people who could either be employed directly as employees or who themselves could establish start-ups and/or become suppliers of certain parts of the game software. It is also not astonishing that, due to the rich tradition of *manga* drawing, Japanese firms have been recognized by the International Game Developers' Association (IGDA) by awarding them the most accolades in categories related to competences in visual arts.

The strength of Japanese firms in visual arts has directly contributed to the popularity of games, since the characters and the visualization of a story are the central criteria in the consumers' buying decision. They constitute the atmosphere and fascination of the whole game. From the game software publisher's strategic point of view, the characters, together with the scenario and the overall concept of the game, are therefore the most important strategic decision to be undertaken prior to designing a new game. Thus *manga* design competences, which were almost meaningless to the core industries, became important sources for the production of games. They are 'new' competences, but what made them relevant for the game industry was their combination with existing competences in consumer electronics and related competences in marketing and distribution. This I will discuss in more detail below.

Japan's domestic demand played an important role in the emergence of the game software industry too, in quantitative as well as in qualitative terms. Until 2001 the game market was considerably larger than the comparable market in the United States.[55] The quality of demand was also due to the *otaku*, i.e. enthusiastic Japanese players, who, although not socially accepted, presented a large and innovative demand, leading to the development of increasingly sophisticated games. In fact, Japanese games are famous for an extraordinary balance between the single parts of the game (including the graphics, music and story) and the high quality and brightness of graphics. The game software industry was thus not simply an export-driven industry but, rather, grew and developed through the important role played by local demand.

The Japanese innovation system: functional plasticity of its dominant configurations

Functional plasticity refers to the mouldability and adaptability of key configurations in a system. Applied to the Japanese case, it refers to the mouldability and adaptability of the dominant institutions and competences of the Japanese innovation system. In this section, we will show that the previously outlined 'rigid in nature' characterization of Japanese innovation system is not accurate and that the system's configurations were in fact adapted and combined, due to their property of functional plasticity, to create innovation.

In terms of industrial organization, I have outlined above the new characteristics in the industrial organization of Japanese game software firms, namely the abandonment of strategic investments. At the same time, however, dominant institutions were transferred to the game software sector and adapted to its new needs. Still, transactions retained their long-term focus, at least those with strategically relevant publishers. This, however, was different for suppliers delivering technically less demanding elements. Yet the long-term cooperation with strategically relevant partners as well as the arm's-length transactions with strategically less relevant partners resemble dominant strategies. Also some institutions have been transferred, and subsequently adapted, such as the institution of sponsored spin-offs, where the incubator provides capital, technical support, as well as services, such as legal advice and intellectual property rights counselling.

For game publishers, there are several incentives to function as a sponsor. First of all, start-ups are under intense pressure to get their products ready for the market. Sponsoring them fosters 'economies of speed'. Since this advantage may be undermined if the founder behaves opportunistically by pursuing opposing goals to that of the incubator, sponsoring is an instrument that can be employed to secure congruence between the sponsoring and the sponsored firms' strategies, as well as to help create a favourable basis for coordination. This includes creating an atmosphere in which former employees are not unduly discouraged if they are interested in becoming entrepreneurs. Instead of dissuasion, the former in-house career is supplemented by an external career in the new start-up.

Finally, outsourcing certain competences is one way to concentrate on one's own core competences.[56] Providing start-up capital for the seed phase is not new in the Japanese context, what is new is its target, which is directed to an entirely new sector. Even if the dynamism in supporting spin-offs has slowed down in recent years, about half of the interviewed publishers reported that they have 'repeatedly supported spin-offs', and, depending on the interviewed firm, they supported anywhere between three to twenty spin-offs. Japanese actors thus moulded and adapted an established configuration of the dominant system and combined it with peripheral configurations. These newly created institutions may better serve the interests of the actors, since they increase the flexibility of the firm, a necessary component, given the volatility of the game market, and at the same time guarantee coordination and dense information flows.

The labour market and related HRM practices are further core institutions of the J-system. Here again, Japanese actors not only introduce new institutions, as outlined above, but – perhaps even stronger than in the industrial organization institution (this is difficult to quantify) – they adhere to established practices. Most astonishing is that Japanese game software publishers continue to hold fast to the traditional institution of long-term employment, even for the creative staff, including programmers and testers. This fundamentally contradicts the logic of heterogeneity and quick competence destruction as a necessary requirement for creative developments, as found – at least in an ideal-type form – in the United States.[57] Thus, whereas on the one hand more openness and flexibility enter the system through a more open recruitment phase, on the other hand, the institution of long-term employment for core functions is retained and transferred to new ends, namely to the production of game software.

Furthermore, most interviewees argued that seniority as a basic framework is retained. For instance, 'high-potential' employees can progress over one or two sub-ranks but still cannot gain key positions in the early phases of their employment. Additionally, some firms experimented with the introduction of individual performance-based pay but realized that this did not have the desired effect, as, contrary to the intent, the system led to the demotivation of those not being rewarded. Obviously, due to the increasing complexity of modern games, it is the development team and not the ingenious individual alone who comes to the fore.

The notion of adapted and moulded, but nevertheless stable, institutions at the core is a dilemma: is the central role of conventional institutions a result of self-enforcing path dependences, or is it intentionally and strategically retained by the actors? My interviews suggest that Japanese game software firms intentionally retain the above-mentioned institutions in HRM and the industrial organization (e.g. long-term employment, sponsoring spin-offs) in order to facilitate cross-functional knowledge integration in teams. This does not mean that the problem of knowledge integration is resolved, but that the Japanese system may offer appropriate institutions for reducing the problem of knowledge integration. The background for this strategic decision may be that the production process of games is characterized by a high degree of heterogeneity of knowledge stocks, which contrasts with product development in manufacturing in that not only programmers, sometimes engineers, marketing and management (in the form of producers), but also creative disciplines such as design or music, become core members of a team.

Due to the expected more effective innovative outcome of heterogeneous teams (compared with homogeneous teams), cross-functional teams are increasingly spreading throughout organizations.[58] However, the problem of how to integrate different knowledge stocks of different functions remains basically unsolved.[59] It may be – but this can only be a research proposition – that the traditional, established institutions which helped ease coordination in the system also facilitate coordination in heterogeneous development teams. An indication for the affirmation of this research proposition is that Japan in fact shows an above-average strength in interdisciplinary publications.[60] At the same time, Nonaka and Takeuchi[61] have convincingly argued that knowledge integration in Japanese firms is eased by institutions such as long-term employment and job rotation, since the members of a firm develop a common cognitive frame and assimilate their different knowledge paths.

Besides dominant institutions, dominant competences also show a functional plasticity. Most obvious is that Japanese firms possess unique competences in consumer electronics and microelectronics. This opens up far-reaching possibilities for the design of game software, since, due to high memory capacity and speed, Japanese game software makers can produce highly attractive games in the areas of graphics and graphic controlling. The close attention that Japanese firms pay to the design of game characters as well as to low error rates is highly valued by the games community. This last aspect may be related to the traditional 'commitment to manufacturing'[62] which has been transferred to the game software sector. Most interview partners stressed – for the layperson perhaps unexpectedly – how much game production processes and traditional manufacturing processes are resembling each other. A quite separate source of competences is marketing competences, which were advantageous to the leading game software publishers SCE and Nintendo, since their existing networks for music and toy products presented them with marketing channels in foreign markets.

Discussion and conclusion

Research on innovation systems has contributed to an understanding of how stable patterns of technological specialization in different nations can be explained. Actual resources and processes of change, however, are still insufficiently understood. In contrast to the business software sector, where Japanese firms are almost absent on the world market, Japanese game software firms have gained a leading role on the world market. Why is this the case? In this chapter I proposed the simple concept of plasticity in order to gain a better understanding of change in innovation systems.

In terms of *numerical plasticity*, it was Japan's competences in the periphery, especially the competence of *manga* design, which was central to the success of Japanese game firms. But this success was possible only through combination with Japan's dominant competences in the electronics industry. At the same time, the emergence of the game software sector was enabled through *functional plasticity* of the key configurations in the Japanese innovation system. They were adapted to new needs by combining them with peripheral institutions, by enlarging them to new functions, or simply by transferring them to the new goal of game software production. This mouldability of sources is of central importance, and describes a process in which entrepreneurial actors create their own subsectoral innovation systems. In other words, there were two factors that favoured the emergence of the industry. First, the emergence of game software was favoured by certain competences that existing institutions could offer, such as technical competences in the electronics and entertainment sector, and organizational competences in the coordination of complex knowledge stocks. Second, in order to develop the subsector in a sustainable way, a specific innovation system was created.

We thus see that, on the one hand, new elements are introduced, including, a more open recruitment process, the abandonment of investment in cooperating partners and the more intensive inclusion of irregular and mid-term career workers. These new elements allow firms more flexibility as well as the incorporation of new knowledge stocks on the one hand, and on the other allow firms to retain institutions of the J-system, perhaps as a means to ease internal coordination. Numerical and functional plasticity thereby allow a combination of established and approved institutions with the inclusion of entirely new elements.

As a result, Japanese game software publishers work within different configurations than their competitors in other countries, for example, the United States or France. They have created their own system by utilizing the numerical plasticity and functional plasticity that exist within the Japanese innovation system.

The case of Japan's game software leadership raises the important question: to what degree are the commonly expressed views on the design of innovation systems valid? For innovation policy, it can be concluded that change need not be externally introduced, but can be internally induced as well. Furthermore, coherence within a national innovation system may not be desirable politically, since it may in fact reduce the possible sources of change. Innovation policy is well advised to maintain variety in the system in order to create the preconditions for inducing change through conversion. Needless to say, determining the exact degree of variety is difficult to prescribe as a general standard and needs to be assessed on a case-by-case basis.

At this stage, the questions posed here can merely be an indication of possible further research. What we can conclude, however, is that the innovation system approach, upon which this chapter draws, has a fruitful life ahead of it. We can also confidently state that the concept of plasticity is useful in helping us gain a better understanding of the sources and processes of change in innovation systems.

Appendix

A total of thirty-two interviews were conducted during May and June 2006. Interviewees included game software firms, firms in related sectors, education institutions related to game software, sector analysts, business associations, venture capitalists and key persons in Ministries, public institutions and research institutes. All interviews were carried out in Japan except for one telephone interview with one American leading publisher and one interview with one Japanese digital music firm, both of which were carried out from Germany.

Acknowledgements

Thanks go to Marie Söderberg and Patricia A. Nelson for their helpful comments. I would also like to extend my gratitude to my interview partners, in Japan, in the game software industry, and many others in related organizations, for their support. Finally, my thanks go to the Japan Institute of Labour, Policy and Training (JILPT) and to the Japan Society for the Promotion of Science (JSPS), both of whose generous support enabled this research in Japan.

Notes

1 Y. Baba, S. Takai and Y. Mizuta, 'The Japanese software industry: the "hub structure" approach', *Research Policy* 24 (3), 1995, 473–86; M. Hemmert, 'Japanese science and technology policy in transition: from catch-up orientation to front-runner orientation' in C. Storz (ed.) *Small Firms and Innovation Policy in Japan*, Routledge Contemporary Japan series, New York: RoutledgeCurzon, 2005, pp. 33–55.
2 Deutsche Bank, *Japan 2020. Ein steiniger Weg*, Deutsche Bank Research, 18 September 2006.
3 OECD, *OECD Information Technology Outlook (Information and Communications Technology)*, Paris: OECD Publishing, 2006.
4 S. Collinson and D. Wilson, 'Inertia in Japanese organizations: knowledge management routines and failure to innovate', *Organization Studies* 9 (27), 2006, 1359–88.
5 M. Anchordoguy, *Reprogramming Japan*, Ithaca, NY: Cornell University Press, 2005; C. Edquist, 'Systems of innovation' in *The Oxford Handbook of Innovation*, Oxford: Oxford University Press, 2005, pp. 181–208; J. M. Ratliff, 'The persistence of national differences in a globalizing world: the Japanese struggle for competitiveness in advanced information technologies', *Journal of Socio-economics* 33, 2004, 71–88.
6 F. Kitagawa, 'Regionalisation of innovation policies: the case of Japan', *European Planning Studies* 13 (4), 2005, 607–18; M. J. Lynskey, 'Transformative technology and institutional transformation: coevolution of biotechnology venture firms and the institutional framework in Japan', *Research Policy* 35 (9), 2006, 1389–422; C. Mueller and T. Fujiwara, 'The entrepreneurial environment for biotech start-ups in Germany and Japan', *International Journal of Biotechnology* 5 (1), 2003, 76–94.
7 M. Anchordoguy, 'Japan's software industry: a failure of institutions', *Research Policy* 29 (3), 2000, 391–408; T. Cottrell, 'Standards and the Arrested Development of Japan's Microcomputer Software Industry' in *The International Computer Software Industry*, Oxford: Oxford University Press, 1996, pp. 131–64; A. Goto, 'Japan's national innovation system: current status and problems', *Oxford Review of Economic Policy* 16 (2), 2000, 103–13.
8 There are several patterns of definition and classification of software (C. Storz and S. Strambach, 'Pfadabhängigkeit und Pfadplastizität von Innovationssystemen. Die deutsche und japanische Softwareindustrie', VJH 2/2008, DIW Berlin, 2008, 142–61.). Software in this paper is classified according to the end product (e.g. games, operating systems, office automation, science and technology, telecommunications and defence). When I refer to the game software industry, I restrict myself to video games, which are game software connected with hardware such as consoles, television sets or personal computers. In international usage the term 'video games' is accepted, whereas in Japan video games are called 'household games'. See Computer Entertainment Supplier's Association (CESA), *2006 CESA Games White Paper*, Tokyo, 2006, p. 53.
9 Compare the firms' Websites, and see J. Johns, 'Video Games Production Networks: Value Capture, Power Relations and Embeddedness', Global Production Networks Working Paper 10, September 2004.
10 The turnover of Microsoft was USD 32,187 million, that of SAP USD 8,467 million and that of Nintendo USD 4,695 million in 2003. See US Software 2007 (Markteinstieg USA), available at www.markteinstiegusa.de/SoftwareIndu-strie.10.0.html (accessed 14 November 2007).
11 B. T. Asheim and A. Isaksen, 'Regional innovation systems: the integration of local 'sticky' and global 'ubiquitous' knowledge', *Journal of Technology Transfer* 27 (1), January 2002, 77–86.
12 B-A. Lundvall, B. Johnson, E. Andersen and B. Dalum, 'National systems of production, innovation and competence building', *Research Policy* 31, 2002, 213–31; F. Malerba, 'Innovation and the evolution of industries', *Journal of Evolutionary Economics* 16 (3), 2006, 3–23.

13 B. Johnson, 'Institutional learning' in *National Innovation Systems: Towards a Theory of Innovation and interactive learning*, London: Pinter, 1992.

14 C. Edquist, *Systems of Innovation: Technologies, Institutions and Organisations*, London: Pinter, 1997; B-A. Lundvall, *National Systems of Innovation*, London and New York: Pinter, 1992; B-A. Lundvall and P. Maskell, 'Nation state and economic development: from national system of production to national systems of knowledge creation and learning' in G. L. Clark (ed.) *The Oxford Handbook of Economic Geography*, Oxford: Oxford University Press, 2000, pp. 353–72; F. Malerba, 'Innovation and the evolution of industries', *Journal of Evolutionary Economics* 16 (3), 2006, 3–23; R. R. Nelson and N. Rosenberg, 'Technical innovation and national systems' in R. R. Nelson (ed.) *National Systems of Innovation: A Comparative Study*, Oxford: Oxford University Press, 1993, pp. 3–21; D. C. North, *The Contribution of the New Institutional Economics to an Understanding of the Transition Problem*, United Nations University/World Institute for Development Economics Research, UNU-WIDER Annual Lectures 1, Helsinki, 1997.

15 G. Grabher, 'The weakness of strong ties: the lock-in of regional development in the Ruhr area' in G. Grabher (ed.) *The Embedded Firm: On the Socio-economics of Industrial Networks*, London: Routledge, 1993, pp. 255–77; F. Naschold *et al.*, *Ökonomische Leistungsfähigkeit und institutionelle Innovation*, WZB Jahrbuch, Berlin, 1997; D. Soskice, 'Divergent production regimes: coordinated and uncoordinated market economies in the 1980s and 1990s' in H. Kitschelt, P. Lange and G. Marks (eds) *Continuity and Change in Contemporary Capitalism*, Cambridge: Cambridge University Press, 1999, pp. 101–63.

16 H-J. Kujath, 'Knowledge-intensive services as a key sector for processes of regional economic innovation: leapfrogging and path dependency', in G. Fuchs and P. Shapira (eds), *Rethinking Regional Innovation and Change: Path Dependency or Regional Breakthrough*, New York: Springer, 2004.

17 D. C. North, *The Contribution of the New Institutional Economics to an Understanding of the Transition Problem*, United Nations University/World Institute for Development Economics Research, UNU-WIDER Annual Lectures 1, Helsinki, 1997.

18 G. Berk and M. Schneiberg, 'Varieties in capitalism, varieties of associations. collaborative learning in American industry, 1900–1925', *Politics and Society* 1, 2005, 44–86.

19 P. Cooke, 'Regional innovation systems, clusters and the knowledge economy', *Industrial and Corporate Change* 10, 2001, 945–74; G. Grabher, 'Switching ties, recombining teams: avoiding lock-in through project organisation?' in G. Fuchs and P. Shapira (eds) *Rethinking Regional Innovation and Change: Path Dependency or Regional Breakthrough*, New York: Springer, 2004; U. Staber, 'Entrepreneurship as a source of path dependency' in G. Fuchs and P. Shapira (eds) *Rethinking Regional Innovation and Change: Path Dependency or Regional Breakthrough*, New York: Springer, 2004.

20 S. Abe, 'Regional innovation systems in the less favoured region of Japan: the case of Tohoku', in P. N. Cooke, M. Heidenreich and H-J. Braczyk, *Regional Innovation Systems: The Role of Governance in a Globalized World*, 2nd edn, London: UCL Press, 2004.

21 S. Breschi and F. Malerba, 'Sectoral innovation systems' in C. Edquist, *Systems of Innovation: Technologies, Institutions and Organisations*, London: Pinter, 1997; M. Heidenreich, 'Conclusion: the dilemmas of regional innovation systems' in P. N. Cooke, M. Heidenreich and H-J. Braczyk, *Regional Innovation Systems: The Role of Governance in a Globalized World*, 2nd edn, London: UCL Press, 2004, pp. 363–90; B-A. Lundvall, B. Johnson, E. Andersen and B. Dalum, 'National systems of production, innovation and competence building', *Research Policy* 31, 2002, 213–31; F. Malerba and L. Orsenigo, 'Technological regimes and sectoral patterns of innovative activity', *Industrial and Corporate Change* 6 (1), 1997, 83–117; P. Maskell and A.

Malmberg, 'Localised learning and industrial competitiveness', *Journal of Economics* 23 (2), 1999, 167–86.

22 F. Malerba and S. Torrisi, 'The Software Sectoral Innovation System and the Role of National Systems', paper presented at the international workshop on 'Path Dependency and Path Plasticity: Innovation Processes in the Software Sector', JDZB, 28 January 2008.

23 K. Jakee and H. Spong, 'Uncertainty, institutional structure and the entrepreneurial process' in J. S. Metcalfe and U. Cantner (eds) *Change, Transformation and Development*, Heidelberg: Physica, 2003, pp. 125–44.

24 S. Casper, M. Lehrer and D. Soskice, 'Can high-technology industries prosper in Germany? Institutional frameworks and the evolution of the German software and biotechnology industries', *Industry and Innovation* 6 (1), 1999, 5–24.

25 B. Amable, *The Diversity of Modern Capitalism*, Oxford: Oxford University Press, 2004.

26 Since 'dominance' is a relative indicator (related to other national innovation systems), the share of peripheral configurations in relation to dominant configurations may be quite high.

27 M. Augier and D. J. Teece, 'Strategy as evolution with design: the foundations of dynamic capabilities and the role of managers in the economic system', *Organization Studies* 8–9, 2008, 1187–209.

28 M. Cusumano and C. Kemerer, 'A quantitative analysis of U.S. and Japanese practices and performance in software development', *Management Science* 36 (11), 1990, 1384–406.

29 OECD, *The Software Sector: A Statistical Profile for Selected OECD Countries*, 1998, pp. 31–2.

30 Own calculations based on: Computer Entertainment Supplier's Association (CESA), *2006 CESA Games White Paper*, Tokyo, 2006: 83, 102; compare also: Digital Contents Association Japan (DCAJ), *Dejitaru Kontentsu Hakusho*, Tokyo, 2007; *Famitsū Gēmu Hakusho* (Famitsu Games Handbook), Tokyo, 2006; C. Storz, 'Innovation, institutions and entrepreneurs: the case of 'Cool Japan', *Asia Pacific Business Review*, special issue 'Innovation in Japan', July 2008.

31 Until the appearance of the console XBox in 2001, consoles were produced almost solely by the Japanese firms Nintendo and Sony Computer Entertainment (SCE). As of 2004, Nintendo had a total shipment of about 325 million; Sony of about 160 million, and XBox of about 10 million. See Eurotechnology, *Japan's Game Industry*, Eurotechnology Japan, 2005.

32 J. Johns, 'Video Games Production Networks: Value Capture, Power Relations and Embeddedness', Global Production Networks Working Paper 10, 2004, p. 30.

33 M. Aoki, G. Jackson and H. Miyajima (eds) *Corporate Governance in Japan: Institutional Change and Organizational Diversity*, Oxford: Oxford University Press, 2008; K. B. Clark and T. Fujimoto, *Product Development Performance: Strategy, Organization, and Management in the World Auto Industry*, Boston. MA: Harvard Business School Press, 1991; E. Mansfield, 'Industrial R&D in Japan and the United States', *American Economic Review* 78 (2), 1998, 223–8.

34 C. Storz and S. Frick, 'Sponsored spin-offs in Japan: Anregungen für die deutsche Mittelstandspolitik?', *List-Forum* 25 (3), 1999, 310–27.

35 International Labour Organization, 'A stable workplace? A mobile work force? What is best for increasing productivity?' *World Employment Report 2004–2005*, Geneva: International Labour Office, 2004.

36 The J-firm is an idealized type of horizontal information structure with several institutions as e.g. diffuse job description, personnel dispatchment, specific incentive mechanisms, etc., which facilitate horizontal knowledge integration (contrasting with vertical structures and specialization in the United States), compare M. Aoki, 'Toward an economic model of the Japanese firm', *Journal of Economic Literature* 28, 1990,

1–27. Even if – to my knowledge – not explicitly, Nonaka and Takeuchi (1995) have elaborated this argument related to knowledge management, arguing that the distinct institutional settings in Japanese firms facilitate knowledge integration, compare I. Nonaka and H. Takeuchi, *The Knowledge Creating Company*, Oxford: Oxford University Press, 1995.

37 Global Entrepreneurship Monitor (GEM) 2005, Executive Report, 2006.

38 M. Anchordoguy, 'Japan's software industry: a failure of institutions', *Research Policy* 29 (3), 2000, 391–408; M. Anchordoguy, *Reprogramming Japan*, Ithaca, NY: Cornell University Press, 2005. M. Rebick, *The Japanese Employment System: Adapting to a New Economic Environment*, Oxford: Oxford University Press, 2005.

39 D. Schumacher *et al.*, *Marktergebnisse bei forschungsintensiven Waren und wissensintensiven Dienstleistungen. Außenhandel, Produktion und Beschäftigung*, Studien zum deutschen Innovationssystem 18, Berlin and Hanover: BMBF, 2003.

40 Y. Baba, S. Takai and Y. Mizuta, 'The Japanese software industry: the "hub structure" approach', *Research Policy* 24 (3), 1995, 473–86; Deutsche Bank, *Japan 2020 – ein steiniger Weg*, Deutsche Bank Research, 18 September 2006; M. Hemmert, 'Japanese science and technology policy in transition: from catch-up orientation to front-runner orientation' in C. Storz (ed.) *Small Firms and Innovation Policy in Japan*, Routledge Contemporary Japan series, New York: RoutledgeCurzon 2005, pp. 33–55; *The Hitotsubashi Business Review* 53 (3), 2005; R. Kishida and L. H. Lynn, 'Restructuring the Japanese national biotechnology innovation system' in C. Storz (ed.) *Small Firms and Innovation Policy in Japan*, Routledge Contemporary Japan series, New York: RoutledgeCurzon, 2005, pp. 111–36; OECD, *OECD Information Technology Outlook (Information and Communications Technology)*, Paris: OECD Publishing, 2006.

41 M. Aoki, 'The Japanese firm may be becoming too rigid for information-sharing in the digital age', Glocom Platform from Japan, August 2000, available at www.glocom.org/opinions/essays/200008_aoki_info_sharing/index.html (accessed 14 November 2007); T. Cottrell, 'Standards and the arrested development of Japan's microcomputer software industry', *International Computer Software Industry*, Oxford: Oxford University Press, 1996, pp. 131–64; A. Goto, 'Japan's national innovation system: current status and problems', *Oxford Review of Economic Policy* 16 (2), 2000, 103–13.

42 J. Shintaku *et al.*, *Gēmu sangyō no keizai bunseki*, Toyko: Toyo Keizai Shinposha, 2004, p. 21.

43 K. Ariga, G. Brunello and Y. Ohkusa, *Internal Labor Markets in Japan*, Cambridge: Cambridge University Press, 2000.

44 Chūshō kigyōchō (CKC), *Chūshō Kigyō Hakusho*, Tokyo, 2005.

45 KKKS, *Kokumin Kinyū Kōko Sōgō Kenkyūsho: Shinki kaigyō hakusho (White Book on Start-ups)*, Tokyo, 1996.

46 GEM, Global Entrepreneurship Monitor 2005, Executive Report, 2006.

47 Chūshō kigyōchō (CKC), *Chūshō Kigyō Hakusho*, Tokyo, 2007.

48 K. Ibata-Arens, *Innovation and Entrepreneurship in Japan: Politics, Organizations and High Technology Firms*, New York: Cambridge University Press, 2005.

49 CKC (Chūshō kigyōchō), *Chūshō Kigyō Hakusho*, Tokyo, 2005.

50 Storz, 'Innovation, Institutions and Entrepreneurs'.

51 Y. Baba and M. Shibuya, 'Tōkyō gēmu sofuto kurasutā', *Kenkyū Gijutsu Keikaku* 14 (4), 1999, 266–78.

52 Y. Baba and M. Shibuya, 'Tokyo gēmu sofuto kurasutā', *Kenkyū Gijutsu Keikaku* 14 (4), 1999, 268.

53 C. Storz, *Der mittelständische Unternehmer in Japan*, Schriftenreihe zur Ostasienwirtschaft 7, Baden-Baden: Nomos-Verlag, 1997.

54 Shuppan Kagaku Kenykūsho (SKKS), *Komikkusu shijō 2002*, Shuppan Geppo, February 2002, 4–11.

55 Ministry of the Economy, Trade and Industry, *Gēmu Sangyō Senryaku: Gēmu Sangyō no hatten to miraizō*, Tokyo: METI, 2006, available at www.meti.go.jp/press/20060824005/game-houkokusho-set.pdf (accessed 14 June 2007).
56 Storz and Frick, 'Sponsored spin-offs in Japan'.
57 S. L. Brown and K. M. Eisenhardt, 'Product development: past research, present findings and future directions', *Academy of Management Review* 20 (2), 1995, 343–78; K. Eisenhardt and C. Schoonhoven, 'Organizational growth: linking founding team, strategy, environment and growth among U.S. semiconductor ventures, 1978–1988', *Administrative Science Quarterly* 35, 1990, 504–29.
58 D. R. Denison, S. I. Hart and J. A. Kahn, 'From chimneys to cross-functional teams: developing and validating a diagnostic model', *Academy of Management Journal* 39 (4), 1996, 1005–23.
59 P. P. Saviotti, 'Considerations about the production and utilization of knowledge', *Journal of Institutional and Theoretical Economics* 160 (1), 2004, 100–21; A. Willem, H. Scarbrough and M. Buelens, *Impact of Coherent versus Multiple Identities on Knowledge Integration*, Working Paper series 2007/28, Vlerick, Leuven and Gent: Vlerick Leuven Gent Management School, 2007.
60 Institute for Systems and Innovation Research (ISI), *New Challenges for Germany in the Innovation Competition*, Frauenhofer Final Report, August 2008.
61 I. Nonaka and H. Takeuchi, *The Knowledge Creating Company*, Oxford: Oxford University Press, 1995.
62 M. Sako and S. Helper, 'Determinants of trust in supplier relations: evidence from the automotive industry in Japan and the United States', *Journal of Economics Behavior and Organization* 34, 1998, 387–417.

11 Conclusion

Perspectives on change

Marie Söderberg and Patricia A. Nelson

Japan is once again in a period of transition, and in accordance with the past, we know that the process of change is both dynamic and continuous.[1] As the chapters in this book have shown, there is a certain amount of alternation between rapid and gradual steps including periods of falling back into old patterns before taking new steps forward again. Further, change has been afoot for some time in various ways and at several levels. Notably, the processes of change have not always been obvious for several reasons. One is that change can occur unexpectedly and it can be a process in which immediate results may not be clear. Thus, although change may be taking place, its progress can be uneven, with some areas changing more quickly than others. A second reason that many of the cases in this book have not been obvious is that change in Japan has for the most part taken place in the shadow of other developments such as the rapid economic growth of countries in Asia and the emergence of an economically stronger and much more outward-oriented China than in the past.

In this book, we gathered a number of cases in which change is the central theme. Given the variety of disciplines and subject matters included in the book, it is nearly impossible to create a neat, short list of the specific drivers of change. Further, generalizing about the key drivers of change, given the range of responses to change in the cases, is not a productive exercise. Perceptions of change vary considerably, depending on the topic and the aspect of dynamism being analysed.

Nonetheless, as discussed in the introduction, we identified four levels of drivers of change – individual, local, regional and global – and noted that pressure for change can come from both outside Japan as well as from the inside. We can blend these two analytical constructs into a four-by-two matrix, shown in Figure 11.1. It encapsulates the interaction among the drivers of change at the four levels and two types of pressure. As we discuss below, all of the spaces in the matrix are not filled by each case. For example, a case might highlight a global level while the analysis focuses on the regional level with local and even individual implications. The matrix offers a useful visual and allows the possibility for each case to occupy several sections.

Pressures for change can be generated from both within and outside; at times the two drivers of change interact and result in a process of change that generates responses at various levels. It should be noted that there is not always a clear

	Individual	Local	Regional	Global
Pressure from within Japan				
Pressure from outside Japan				

Figure 11.1 Matrix: drivers of change.

delineation between the drivers of change on global, regional, local or individual levels. We do not want to focus on the direction of change, for example using arrows to indicate that change moves from individual to local to regional to global levels. Our focus is on the interaction of the drivers, noting that the processes are a complex web of action and reaction. In this sense it is not possible to identify precisely when a change process began, but it is possible to identify the dynamism in the process of change.

Each contributor focused on one case of change that may involve several levels as well as pressure that drives change from inside and/or outside Japan. Inevitably some cases fall more decidedly into certain areas in the matrix than others. We could, for example, have a case indicating pressure from inside and outside combined with regional and local levels with global implications (such as the case of the military-industrial complex by Christopher Hughes), and pressure from the inside affecting the individual, local and regional levels with implications for the global level (such as in the case of the development of political leaders by Verena Blechinger-Talcott). Pressures from outside Japan include the global War against Terrorism and the North Korean nuclear threat, and the two could be combined in the form of pressure for enhanced security cooperation between the United States and Japan as well as increased cooperation in missile defence as described in the stage-setting chapter written by Paul Midford.

Case-crossing drivers of change are many as Japanese politics and economics have become increasingly integrated with the rest of the world. Globalization and its effects are driving change in most countries throughout the world, and, while not unique to Japan, technological development, improved communication and access to information are other global, regional and even local drivers of change. The security situation has been changing considerably in recent years and with the increased threat of terrorism on a worldwide basis, it has also driven change. From Japan, we see the response in the form of a much more active nation. On a regional level, the shifting power balance in East Asia with an economically stronger and politically much more outward-oriented China is a driver for change. Another example is the combination of pressure from within Japan and outside Japan that drove the process of upgrading the Self Defense Agency to the Ministry of Defense.

John Swenson-Wright raised in his chapter some of the challenges in the security area and singled out key sources of tension on a regional level such as a nuclear North Korea, territorial disputes, competition over access to energy sources and non-traditional security threats including terrorism. These sources of tension are regional drivers of change, and Japan's perception of them as pressure from outside Japan or as pressure from inside Japan has implications for how Japan responds at various levels.

One of the most prominent local drivers of change in Japan is a more vocal public opinion. This is having implications for processes of change in Japanese policy and creating pressure inside Japan for change. Paul Midford discusses this point in his chapter. The LDP–Komei loss of the majority in the Upper House election in 2007 was a clear sign to leaders that the LDP will have to listen to public opinion if they want to stay in power. Other drivers of change on the local level are demographic changes, such as the aging of the population, changing industry structures and growing economic inequalities in the current phase of downturn in the economy. Verena Blechinger-Talcott shows how change in basic structures, such as the election system, has led to a change in what kind of leaders are likely to be elected as well as what kind of issues will be pushed on a global, regional or local level. Here drivers of change come from inside Japan as the pressure mounts to affect change regarding the expectations of what constitutes good political leadership.

At the individual level, Junichiro Koizumi is a good example of the fact that leadership matters in processes of change inside Japan. His popularity combined with his political style made a number of changes possible, such as the passing of the Special Anti-Terrorism Measures law and the dispatch of an SDF flotilla to provide fuel and other supplies to US Navy ships operating in the Indian Ocean. On a local level, his core reform agenda targeted the privatization of the postal service, a move that was intrinsically linked to his strategy to revive his party through a forcible shake-up. Even if most observers in hindsight claim that Koizumi failed in achieving his broader objective, to revitalize Japan's politically and economically, the changes he introduced to LDP decision-making institutions and processes are sustainable and have significantly affected the inner workings of the party.

Another driver of change at the individual level is the goal of many Japanese people to learn throughout their lives, according to Akihiro Ogawa. As lifelong learning is promoted through various means and social movements such as the culture volunteers emerge, it becomes possible for people at the grass-roots level to empower themselves and challenge conventional norms and practices where bureaucratic rationality often dominates. The individual that participates in various NGOs that, for example, work with Japanese foreign aid are also driving process of change in the way Japanese ODA is handled (chapters by Marie Söderberg and Norbert Palanovics).

We can further deepen our discussion of drivers of change by adding a framework of 'adaptation' and 'emergence'. We note two broad patterns of change: adaptation of old patterns to new circumstances and emergence of new patterns in response to new needs. In the context of the matrix in Figure 11.1, this means that once we identify the pressure (inside and/or outside) and the levels (individual, local, regional, global), then we consider if the change is adaptive (part of an evolutionary process) or emergent (a very new, radical change that may be unexpected).

The first and most common driver to change is adaption to new conditions and circumstances. Japan's diplomatic and security posture has constantly been adapting to a changing environment, as several chapters – especially those by John Swenson-Wright, Marie Söderberg, Norbert Palanovics, Christopher Hughes and Patricia Nelson – show. The role of ODA in Japan's international diplomacy toolbox is a clear example of adaptation to the changing needs of Japan and Japan's changing position in the international arena. Starting off as war reparations, ODA has gone through several stages. First, it was a tool for export promotion of Japanese goods and services in developing countries, then for securing natural resources from resource-rich countries and, most recently, improvements to the environment and peace-building initiatives. Similarly, the companies that supply the military sector have adapted over time to the changing needs of the market, and, as Hughes argues, in recent years this has meant expansion of the military sector. Nelson in her chapter on the business organizations in the optics industry shows how structural power, that is, power vested in the structure of an association, can be exercised to embrace change, transform the organization and adapt to new conditions. Japanese companies have for a long time been adapting to increased cost competition in manufacturing by moving production abroad.

As the second theme, we identified emergence of new patterns in response to new needs. Paul Midford, Akihiro Ogawa, Verena Blechinger-Talcott and Cornelia Storz provide examples. Midford's chapter alerts us to the influence of public opinion on the behaviour of Japanese politicians. As public opinion changes, new policies are likely to emerge. After the loss of the majority by the LDP–Komei coalition in the election of 2007 the Prime Minister stopped focusing on the constitutional reform and an expansion of Japan's overseas security role and instead turned to bread-and-butter issues such as growing economic inequality in Japan. Ogawa touches on training and learning from the angle of lifelong learning via volunteering, an emerging trend in Japanese society as a whole. Through this activity, it becomes possible for the people at the grass-roots level to challenge existing systems and, according to Ogawa, new patterns of civil society will emerge. Blechinger-Talcott sees a new type of political leader being groomed as a direct result of changes to the election system. There is a shift from the old politicians that were good at mediating inside the party to a new type of politicians that are well trained, highly professional and with a strong orientation towards grass-roots activities and cross-party policy consultation. Storz shows how innovation emerged in the very successful game software industry within the Japanese innovation system.

Some chapters demonstrate that adaptation and emergence can be intertwined. Specifically the chapters by Christopher Hughes, Marie Söderberg and Norbert Palanovics exemplify this intertwining of adaptation and emergence in the processes of change. Hughes's chapter clarifies why companies that manufacture military goods have been expanding and how there now appears to be an emergence of a military-industrial complex. Söderberg and Palanovics present different angles on the ODA issue and argue that Japanese ODA has been adapting to the general trend in other countries with a higher degree of securitarization of aid and a greater emphasis on peace building. From this a number of new initiatives have emerged such as Japan seeking leadership through assisting in the peace process in Sri Lanka, chairing the newly established Peace Building Commission at the UN or putting up a new programme of joint education for peace building of Japanese and other Asians at Hiroshima University.

In all our case studies we found ongoing processes of considerable change. The driving forces, as well as the extent, of change varied with the issues researched as well as the method used. This brings to mind the old Indian story of the men that touched an elephant in the dark. Each of them touched a different part of the animal and when they in the end tried to conclude what it was they were in total disagreement. In the case studies collected in this book we all see our bits and pieces of change but not the full picture. It is not certain if anyone can ever see the whole picture of change. What we can agree on, however, is that the process of change is constantly ongoing.

Looking back in history both to the Meiji Restoration as well as the period directly after World War II, we have learnt that Japan is most capable of changing. The changes that took place at these times were complex and difficult. Things rarely went smoothly, there were significant periods of trial and error and it often took several decades before changes became well established. Only when we look back on history from the vantage point of the present (or indeed for some the future) might we get an impression that there was coordination and cohesion and that there may have been a 'grand plan'. Often decision making on all levels was undertaken on a very pragmatic day-to-day basis. This does not seem too far off from the present situation. Again the Japanese decision makers or the general public do not have a grand strategy for how Japan's should change but rather act pragmatically on a day-to-day basis.

In any analysis of change – and the processes that bring it about – there are stories of great, immediate successes mixed with initially positive stories that are followed by retrenchment and adaptation creating new strategies that eventually have the potential to succeed. What we have seen are definite changes, although the norm has been gradual rather than radical change. The economic crisis of 2008/09 has, however, spurred a number of unprecedented changes, including stimulus packages of a hitherto unseen size of 3 per cent of Japan's GDP. This raises the question of whether it is only the tip of the iceberg we have seen so far when it comes to processes of change in Japan.

Note

1 K. Thelen and S. Steinmo, 'Historical institutionalism in comparative perspective' in S. Steinmo, K. Thelen and F. Longstreth (eds) *Structuring Politics: Historical Institutionalism in Comparative Analysis*, Cambridge Studies in Comparative Politics, Cambridge: Cambridge University Press, 1992, p. 17.

Index

Note: Page numbers in *italics* denote tables, those in **bold** denote figures or illustrations.

For Product Safety Concerns and Information please contact our EU representative GPSR@taylorandfrancis.com
Taylor & Francis Verlag GmbH, Kaufingerstraße 24, 80331 München, Germany

www.ingramcontent.com/pod-product-compliance
Lightning Source LLC
Chambersburg PA
CBHW050426280326
41932CB00013BA/2007

* 9 7 8 0 4 1 5 6 9 0 1 2 6 *